# What the OCLC Online Union Catalog Means to Me

## A Collection of Essays

**OCLC Online Computer Library Center, Inc.**
**6565 Frantz Road**
**Dublin, Ohio   43017-3395**

OCLC Online Computer Library Center, Inc.
6565 Frantz Road   Dublin, Ohio  43017-3395

1-614-764-6000
FAX 1-614-764-6096

March 18, 1997

Dear Colleague:

I am pleased to present to you and your library staff this copy of *What the OCLC Online Union Catalog Means to Me.*

Published in honor the of the 25th anniversary of WorldCat, the OCLC Online Union Catalog, this collection of essays from 340 librarians in 13 countries is a testament to the power of library cooperation.  It is also a tribute to the librarians in OCLC member libraries like yours who have helped to create this incomparable resource for library users around the world.

Thank you for your participation as a cataloging member of OCLC. We at OCLC look forward to continuing to earn your support and trust as we pursue our public purposes of furthering access to the world's information and reducing information costs.

Sincerely,

K. Wayne Smith
President and Chief Executive Officer

KWS/skk
Enclosure

# Contents

# Preface

August 26, 1996 marked the 25th anniversary of the OCLC Online Union Catalog. As part of a year-long tribute to this remarkable resource, OCLC and the U.S. regional networks sponsored an essay contest. We invited librarians and library users to write essays of 500 words or less on the topic, "What the OCLC Online Union Catalog Means to Me." We offered a grand prize of $1,000 and four prizes of $500 each.

The contest attracted entries from 340 librarians in 13 countries. These authors used the OCLC bibliographic database in libraries of all types and sizes, including one that measured 12 by 18 feet. If I could make one observation about these essays, it is that the Online Union Catalog is more than just a bibliographic database to these writers—it is a way of life.

Since the Online Union Catalog began operation in 1971, libraries and OCLC have built it into the world's foremost bibliographic database. At this writing, it contained more than 36 million records and 660 million location listings for materials that span over 4,000 years of recorded knowledge. Today, it is the most frequently consulted database in higher education.

Clearly, the Online Union Catalog is the most valuable asset that the OCLC membership has, and one of the most valuable assets the library community has. It is a unique cooperative venture, and it works. It saves libraries money. It gets materials out on the shelves faster. It increases the availability of information for all of its participating libraries. It is an incomparable information resource for researchers and scholars. It is a commons worth defending and nurturing. And it is a legacy for all of us to be very proud of.

On the occasion of the Silver Anniversary of the OCLC Online Union Catalog, I would like to thank OCLC member libraries, regional networks, and international distributors for their commitment to furthering access to the world's information and reducing information costs. Most of all, I would like to thank the thousands of anonymous catalogers and librarians who, keystroke by keystroke, record by record, have created one of the wonders of the library world. Because of your individual efforts, scholarship and research will never be the same. These essays are a tribute to what you have accomplished.

*K. Wayne Smith*

**K. Wayne Smith**
President and Chief Executive Officer
OCLC
December 15, 1996

# Grand Prize Winner

**George E. Bishop**
Ovid-Elsie Area Schools
Elsie, MI

In 1991 our small rural school library was included in an LSCA Grant project giving us our first access to OCLC through Group Access Capability. During the first year of this grant there was significant learning about the Union Catalog. We received excellent support and training from Michigan Library Consortium, our OCLC regional network. We added our holdings through RETROCON, and we did some sampling of the ILL subsystem in order to get our feet wet. After the first year I had learned the power of the OCLC database and was ready to extol its capabilities.

On the first teacher day of the fall of 1992 at the district staff meeting, I announced to over 100 teachers and administrators that our school library would supply "all books for any student, teacher, administrator or community member." There was disbelief. Teachers whispered their skepticism during the meeting. Within two weeks, one elementary teacher requested 17 monographs from a bibliography on euthanasia. Our library, using OCLC ILL, supplied ALL the materials she requested. Later I discovered it was a test to see if the library could do what I had promised. We passed the test! The library soon became a credible source for all information. I was not prepared for the domino effect that was ahead.

After gaining the respect of both faculty and students, the library has literally become the center of learning of the school. School improvement teams do extensive research, students use OCLC WorldCat for papers, students get plans for woodshop projects, and graduates now come back to do work for college. Teachers now use our school library to do graduate-level research for college classes they are taking. The attitudes are positive, and our mission of supplying everything for everyone is being achieved. Our OCLC ILL statistics are very high, and so is our level of patron satisfaction.

The most memorable change that has occurred has been in the funding area. Due to the increased visibility and performance of the library and the commitment to providing "everything for everyone," our book budget has been increased from $4,000 to almost $16,000 in only four years. All other budget areas have significantly increased as well. The single factor that started this snowball effect is our access to the OCLC Online Catalog. I now understand that the smaller the library, the more essential it is to have access to the OCLC Online Union Catalog containing the world's recorded knowledge. It is an integral part of the access and learning equation. The OCLC Online Union Catalog has made the single most significant contribution to our small rural school library beyond any book, database, program or person. Through OCLC our library mission has become achievable. Our library and its patrons will never be the same.

# Prize Winner

**Donald O. Case**
University of Kentucky
Lexington, KY

Herbert George Wells had mixed success as a prophet. In futuristic works written between 1895 and 1938, H. G. Wells correctly predicted, among other developments, the use of airplanes, tanks and atomic weapons in warfare, the growing emancipation of women, the growth of suburbs, and the start of the Second World War in Poland. Of course, Wells forecast many events that have not come to pass, such as the disappearance of warfare, nation states, and large cities.

One of Wells' visions was of a comprehensive World Encyclopedia that he also called a "World Brain."* In his 1938 description of the Encyclopedia, Wells depicted a global compendium of articles, indices and bibliographies that would serve as a central clearinghouse of information for the world's people. The purpose of the Encyclopedia was to capture, synthesize and condense, on a continuing basis, our evolving knowledge of the universe.

In 1971, more than a century after his birth, Wells' World Brain became reality with the initiation of the Ohio College Library Center (later to become the OCLC Online Union Catalog) and the establishment of computer networks to exchange information. By the 1980s the stem of Wells' World Brain was in place, eventually to include documentation of 4,000 years of recorded knowledge.

As a scholar, the utility and importance of the OCLC Online Union Catalog is evident. Twenty-five years ago, when OCLC started, I was a college freshman. At that time a literature search meant leafing through thousands of cards in oaken drawers; my search was only as good as my school's catalog and my own patience.

Now, through the member catalogs of OCLC, I can locate the description and location of almost any publication of potential importance to me. Studying the history of technology, as I do, it is vital that I be able to locate and verify information about older works. I can, for instance, not only locate copies and descriptions of Wells' prophetic books but also film and recorded sound versions of them, as well as editions in hundreds of languages. To be able to do this from my home or office, using an OCLC member's system, is a great leap forward for scholarship; and it has been accomplished within the space of one generation of scholars. That's why I think of the Online Union Catalog as my personal version of Wells' Encyclopedia.

Of course, the OCLC Online Union Catalog is not the World Brain of H. G. Wells; OCLC's Catalog does not contain the variety of encyclopedic entries that were described by Wells; but then neither is there the extent of agreement on the nature of "truth" that he imagined possible. The efforts of OCLC are the closest we have yet come to realizing Well's prophetic vision of a repository for global knowledge.

---

*Wells, H. G. 1938. World Brain. Garden City, NY: Doubleday.

# Prize Winner

**Patricia L. Hassan**
Johnson County Library
Shawnee Mission, KS

 Very proudly I tell you that I have helped to build an international knowledge base—I and many other ordinary catalogers the world over, during the last 25 years. From the largest scholarly institutions to the tiniest public libraries, this grassroots participation in creating the OCLC Online Union Catalog has resulted in an international infrastructure which many ordinary citizens may take for granted—or may be unaware of. But when a medium-size library in America's prairie heartland furnishes materials to the University of Moscow in Russia or the State Library of Berlin, Germany—as a routine function and without fanfare—isn't that a status quo which speaks eloquently of the power of dedicated technology strategy partnered with vision?

The OCLC Online Union Catalog has endowed new power to libraries—and to local library users. It's as if this capability transforms all libraries into "satellites of Alexandria," realizing the rebirth of a long-lost dream of capturing all the knowledge in the world. The ancients who mourned the burning of the Great Library of Alexandria would even recognize many of the works cited in the OCLC Online Union Catalog, since its holdings span 4,000 years of recorded knowledge. The most important part of its name is "Union," because its worth expands and contracts with the gain or loss of any one of the thousands of participating libraries. Rather than being limited to use by scholars, however, the OCLC Online Union Catalog benefits anyone—potentially, anyone at all—who needs information, any information at all, in any format.

Born of necessity, innovation and ingenuity, the OCLC Online Union Catalog has catalyzed a new era of exchange of information among libraries—and a shift in the average person's perception of what is possible in obtaining information, never mind whether that person knows the name of this tool. Its promise—and that fulfillment—fostered new expectations and assumptions and standards about library service. Because the Catalog is such a dynamic, rich resource serving as a foundation for many uses, it has actually become a piece of knowledge in itself. And instead of being "information archives," libraries have become "information access points."

Its impact has been to help launch the global Information Age—in that the scope of information is beyond borders—and cooperation in creating and obtaining that information is a daily, routine affair. We begin to feel that little is beyond our grasp—and to act as if that were true. Wherever technology now takes us and whatever the future holds, the OCLC Online Union Catalog cannot fail to be a cornerstone of the imagination and experience that fuels invention.

Catalogers created this groundbreaking tool, I among them; but as a library user, I am also its legatee.

# Prize Winner

**Jeanette C. Smith**
New Mexico State University
Las Cruces, NM

Furthering access to the world's information.

The Berlin Wall is coming down! An all-encompassing joy filled me on November 9, 1989, as I watched the images on TV. The next day I and my Government Documents staff put up a library display on German reunification. Little did I know that just a few short years later I would be visiting former East Germany to work on a research project. Nor did I realize the instrumental role that OCLC would play during every stage of this project.

Planned as a women's history project, my historiography of sources on a sixteenth century woman, Katharina von Bora, Martin Luther's wife, would have been impossible to complete without the combination of uncensored correspondence, unrestricted travel, and subject access to the world's largest bibliographic database.

I knew that there was more material on Katie von Bora than most people realized, but I was stunned to recover more than 100 catalog records from my FirstSearch subject search on OCLC WorldCat. No amount of time searching individual library electronic or card catalogs could have provided this solid base of information. I had very good luck receiving many materials through OCLC interlibrary loan. In addition, the OCLC Online Union Catalog locations for each record were helpful in planning my travels to see rare book materials unavailable through interlibrary loan.

Upon my return from travels to libraries in the U.S., my database on Katie had grown to more than 200 books and articles, thanks to painstaking tracing of references in books, indices, and bibliographies as far back as the sixteenth century. Despite my efforts, many of these references were still incomplete, and it was time for intensive verification. Again, OCLC came to the rescue as I searched the Online Union Catalog by the traditional author, title, and author/title keys as well as by the PRISM commands. I also used OCLC to verify the language of some titles.

A research trip to Berlin, Lutherstadt Wittenberg, and Leipzig in former East Germany was the highlight of my project. I visited many libraries, interviewed scholars, and walked in Katie's footsteps in many of the towns connected with her life. In Berlin as I looked at the remains of the Berlin Wall, I re-experienced my emotions of 1989. My joy was for mankind, for the breaking down of barriers that divide us. I realized that my project would have remained a dream just a few years earlier. Two factors alone, German reunification and the ability to do a subject search on the OCLC WorldCat, made it a feasible undertaking.

Not only are mankind's physical, political, and economic barriers coming down, but new bridges for international communication and scholarship are being built. Multiply my individual experience by thousands of libraries and millions of researchers, and it is clear that OCLC has truly revolutionized access to the world's information. These are exciting times for us as librarians and as library users. *Danke schoen*, and thank you, OCLC, for helping us to expand our world!

# Prize Winner

**Daofu Zhang**
Shandong University of Technology
Jinan Shandong, China

Having gone through a journey of 25 years, OCLC has grown up to a brilliant young man in his prime, following his beautiful childhood and smart juvenile years.

OCLC is now taking on a prosperous look. It is a milestone in the field of library information, and also a significant mark of man's entering into the information society. It collects the wisdom of the modern human and has created miracles one after another, shining with radiance and splendor all along.

OCLC has brought happy news to billions of people. As one of its users, it means a kind of noble enjoyment to me.

OCLC is a gold key which enables me to open easily the gate to all human knowledge and to explore freely the world's treasure-house of civilization.

OCLC is a telescope which helps me realize the old dream of "a thousand-li eye and a tailwind ear" described in classical Chinese novels. While simply sitting at home, OCLC makes it possible for me to look up tens of thousands of introductory passages and whole articles in libraries far away and listen to beautiful music played a long way off.

Using OCLC is faster than riding in a rocket. With it, I am able to travel around the world at the speed of light within a wide span of 4,000 years. OCLC reaches every corner of the world and greatly shortens the distances. It makes the globe magically small and turns a thousand years into an instant by providing the access to any information at the snap of the fingers.

OCLC is to me something like an international pass with which I can "visit" several thousand libraries in more than 100 countries without having to go through the complicated procedures for a passport abroad.

OCLC is a qualified secretary, a good companion and a friend. Whenever I meet with difficult problems in my teaching and research and need to refer to some materials, OCLC is always there to provide me with the best help, making me feel the warmth and encouragement of a relation.

OCLC has become a member of my family. We can no longer do without it. We all love it. I would like to wish the 25-year-old "young man" to be brighter and braver in facing the coming new century!

# Additional Entries

**Karling Clymer Abernathy**
Park County Library System
Cody, WY

The OCLC Online Union Catalog means access for the 24,000 residents of our rural county to the marvel of information represented by OCLC's 35 million bibliographic records. We serve a town of 9,000, with two branches that also make interlibrary loan requests for their towns of 6,000 and 400. If there is a wonder in libraries, it is that the residents of Meeteetse, Wyoming, can request materials from anywhere in the OCLC domain.

Cataloging from OCLC-member libraries benefits our patrons by providing quality records which accurately describe materials in our catalogs. As a public library, we provide both fiction and non-fiction materials for preschoolers through senior citizens. Subject information, as well as authors and titles, is extremely important to our patrons. OCLC bibliographic records, as, for instance, those records enhanced through the Fiction Project, offer expanded possibilities for our library users, whether they are searching for Sherlock Holmes or Computer art, the Boxcar Children or Grasshoppers.

We have recently added interactive-multimedia CD-ROMs to our collections through a generous gift and some purchases. The cataloging supplied by OCLC has allowed us to supply these materials to our patrons—specifically children—much more quickly than non-automated cataloging. One of our branches is slowly building a Spanish collection; the records we require for those materials, both adult and juvenile, are in OCLC. Again, this permits us to bring books for a distinctive audience to these readers rapidly and accurately.

A business in our town uses information from scientific journals; the immediacy of the turnaround for journal requests has greatly improved our service to this business. As more businesses move to our region to escape a frenetic lifestyle, they utilize our services to keep abreast of current information. As information professionals, our believability has risen as we find materials for patrons quickly. Reciprocally, our materials, some of which are unique to this area, are of benefit to patrons in other libraries who can borrow from us.

More and more, we recognize that we cannot provide in our town, county, state, all the information that knowledge-hungry library users want and need. However, through OCLC, we have increased the potential for finding essential data for our citizens. OCLC offers speed, quality, and access to the library patrons of Park County, Wyoming; we can find what they require!

**Carol Alberts**
Siouxland Libraries
Sioux Falls, SD

I hadn't a clue who "MARC" was that early fall day in 1977 when I sat in my first OCLC workshop. "What have I gotten into?" I wondered while frantically taking notes about "tags" (you're it?), "indicators" (like phenolphthalein?), "fixed fields" (as opposed to broken?), and "subfield delimiters" (what a weird symbol).

At first our interlibrary loan assistant and I shared a terminal with several other libraries. We marveled at the speed—300 baud, then 1200! Figuring out the most precise search key challenged me. Every time I received a "message not clear" response, I thought how nice it would be if people had an LCD embedded in their foreheads that would flash that when they didn't understand me.

Once the cataloger reviewed the printouts of my searches, I went back to edit and produce the records. A few days later the catalog cards from OCLC arrived—sorted, alphabetized, and ready to file—a vast improvement over LC cards. The downside was that I developed carpal tunnel syndrome from dropping cards filed above the rod by library assistants.

The library board raised the book budget and allocated money for our own terminal. OCLC card boxes became longer. Work room shelves sagged from books with OCLC labels ready to be processed. We hired volunteers to process books. (They're still at it, bless them!)

Though we seemed to be sowing seeds without knowing what we would harvest, we began weeding collections and bar-coding books for a systematic "retrospective conversion" (which is not as charismatic as it sounds). I hung a sign over the area being hoed—"WEED IT AND REAP"—hoping the book sale mountain would surpass the stacks of books to be bar-coded.

In the 80s the lingo became "turnkey integrated automated systems" so when our circulation blew holes in the roof, our director sent out an RFP—or was it an SOS? By now, I was editing the OCLC printouts and supervising the work of several part-time OCLC input operators. A crew of temps flipped cross-eyed through our shelf list to do retro big time and our cataloger moved on to greener fields. I interrogated vendor reps to be sure their system could create holdings records from data inadvertently recorded in 590 fields on our OCLC archival tapes.

Shortly after installing the local system, our new two-headed leader (system administrator/technical processing) turned most of the cataloging over to me and saw to it that I was reclassified as a librarian. Thus I became cataloger in name as well as function on late 1987.

CAT CD450, EPIC, FirstSearch, PRISM, PASSPORT, Format Integration. The pace of change catapults us toward the millennium. New digital access methods ignite the forests of obsolete catalog cards around the planet. Now we get fancy "ergonomic" keyboards to prevent carpal tunnel symptoms. If only someone would deliver the books to my door, I could work right at home!

That's what OCLC means to me: an ever-changing career at the cutting edge of technology. All because I sat in on an OCLC workshop.

———————————— ℳ ————————————

**Farooq Ali**
East Central University
Ada, OK

The OCLC Online Union Catalog is a marvel and wonder the global information world has come to know. Budgetary constraints and shrinking resources, thwart the growth of library collections. As the OCLC Online Union Catalog is the world's largest database of bibliographic information of recorded knowledge, it presents unparalleled and unprecedented opportunities to the global community of library users. Built by the collaboration of libraries around the world, it contains more than 35 million records and grows by 2 million records a year. The information in it spans 4,000 years of recorded knowledge in 370 languages. It connects the user to more than 23,000 libraries in 63 countries. Under its light, user access to worldwide information is no more an elusive goal of the library community. Easy access to key international collections is fast becoming more and more a reality. If any one has been searching for an easy way to the world's information, try the OCLC Online Union Catalog.

Electronic publishing and dissemination technologies are presently shifting the emphasis from what a library *owns* to what the library user can *access*. Libraries are at a crossroads and in crisis because of a massive swing to online resources that limit the access to print media services. Under the dazzling light of the technological innovations, librarians are blinded. They find it hard to know the strengths and weaknesses of their library collections. Unbalanced library collections do not give opportunity for choices which is the essence of freedom of speech and expression. The OCLC Online Union Catalog is a beacon light. Under its light, the user turns from darkness to light. It provides choices to its users to enable them to balance their viewpoints and make informed decisions.

The OCLC Online Union Catalog implements cooperation of all participating libraries in network settings for interlibrary loan services. Interlibrary loan services supplement to library holdings and give access to materials whether a particular library owns them or not. Online public catalogs provide locations for materials owned by libraries, and also act as gateways to other resources. Under the light of the OCLC Union Catalog, the gap between the information-poor and information-rich is closed. Inside the library or beyond its walls, what a boon is the catalog for library users!

The OCLC Online Union Catalog is available as WorldCat on the FirstSearch, and also has Internet access. Under the light of OCLC Online Union Catalog, scholarship grows to its noblest forms and scholars are not left to grope in darkness and doubt. To know the OCLC Online Union Catalog is to love it. It not only helps the researchers live to their full intellectual capacity, but also to live more research lives by making use of it. So yes, thanks to its unique one-source library resource sharing catalog, searching the OCLC Online Union Catalog means saving a wearisome search among many library catalogs. It is now the most frequently consulted database in higher education. The day seems not far off when the OCLC Online Union Catalog will replace the online public access catalogs of libraries because of a variety of access points it offers and the diversity of the materials it reflects.

**Althea Aschmann**
Emporia State University
Emporia, KS

Thinking about the past twenty-five years gives me the sense of being there from the beginning, because I watched OCLC grow from an experimental venture. (I helped test some of the early MARC formats, when I was a student at Kent State).

I can remember when there were two lines of fixed fields, and the entire amount of documentation needed for inputting a record into the OCLC Online Union Catalog fit into a skinny little notebook.

OCLC was originally conceived as a fast way to generate catalog cards, and to allow libraries access to each other's holdings through the creation of an online union catalog. This allowed catalogers to benefit from each others' work and stop duplication of efforts. The libraries I worked in were busy producing and filing cards. With the arrival of integrated local library systems and the PRISM export function, online catalogs became a reality, and OCLC became much more than an automated card generator. Many libraries, including my own, went through the rites of passage of letting card catalogs go and dumping shelf lists. I was certainly very happy to give up the simultaneous maintenance of card and online catalogs.

I am proud of the many original bibliographic records I created. I left my mark on the OCLC Online Union Catalog under various symbols: KSU, CLE, BHA, even a few from LNX. It astounds me that so little original cataloging is needed today, because of the millions of records in the OCLC database. The ideal of shared cataloging that I and others dreamed about in the 1970s has become a reality. Libraries collaborate with each other worldwide in generating catalog copy. Sometimes I worry that there is diminished opportunity for new catalogers to hone their skills, but as an administrator, I am thrilled with the increased productivity that results from shared cataloging.

I felt genuine excitement when the EPIC service came out—everyone I know hoped to be able to search the OCLC database by subject. It was a leap when I realized that I couldn't justify the expense of EPIC for my department, and that OCLC was no longer within the exclusive domain of Technical Services. It would have to be shared with Public Services, because EPIC was really a reference tool. Then along came FirstSearch—I remember putting it out for the public in 1993, so that everyone in our community could have access to the OCLC database, and benefit from Interlibrary Loan's increased capacity. This for me symbolizes the current trend of forming partnerships between departments within libraries.

My professional development parallels the growth of OCLC, along with the proliferation of information access and technological development in our time. It gives me great joy to be living that history.

## Berenice C. Astengo
University of South Florida (Tampa)
Gainesville, FL

It's a jungle out there! Thick with trees with high branches and low branches, long and short branches, and all these branches are covered with hundreds and thousands of leaves. Also, there are underbrush, vines and various and sundry other obstacles to obstruct clear view. You really can't see the jungle for the trees, or the leaves for the jungle. That's what it is like in the world of books. Hundreds of thousands of books published every year and billions of books in print, residing in different and distant libraries all over the country. Who knows where or how to locate these books? Thanks to the OCLC Online Union Catalog, clearing through these vast jungles is a less daunting task for librarians and researchers.

As a reference library assistant for many years, I have learned the value of the OCLC Online Union Catalog resource. Many of our most active library users are professors, researchers, retired academics, and students who rely heavily on Interlibrary Loan services to find information not available in the local public libraries. One patron, Gitana Du Bois, was very anxious to get a hold of a book on Spanish folk dances from Andalucia. She remembered that she had used a book on this specific subject as a graduate student at UCLA; she even remembered the title! She felt that the book was crucial for research for a class she was teaching on Spanish Folk Dances. She submitted an ILL request, and through our local network connection to the OCLC Online Union Catalog through SOLINET, the book was found and delivered to the patron in time to teach her class.

Most universities only offer ILL services to graduate students and professors and refer other users to the public library. The OCLC Online Union Catalog service then becomes an important public relations tool for public libraries demonstrating high quality service to the general public. Finding an obscure book for a patron can often seem like an amazing feat (which it is!) and patrons are usually very appreciative. When the next election comes around hopefully that patron will remember that amazing ILL feat and will vote for the tax initiative to support libraries.

With budgets, rising costs and reducing expenditures being at the forefront of the minds of all administrators, libraries can no longer afford to buy so many specialized books. Increasingly libraries are moving towards more specialized collections. By narrowing collections, libraries don't buy so many books on diverse subjects, but build up their specialty collections. For those libraries that contribute catalogued records, there is the additional savings of staff time and money in downloading catalogued records from the OCLC Online Union Catalog. With this trend, the value of the Catalog will continue to increase as libraries move towards borrowing from other libraries rather than purchasing particular books for their own collections and downloading rather than original cataloging.

As a tax payer, the OCLC Online Union Catalog services mean more efficient use of library money along with high quality service. As a student, it means access to specialized books that I'm not able to obtain through my local library or bookstore. As a librarian, the OCLC Online Union Catalog means better quality service to patrons with the most efficient use of resources available to us and a great Public Relations tool to show patrons how amazing and organized libraries are so that I can keep a job that I love.

**Patty Ayala**
Castle Rock Public Library
Castle Rock, WA

On being rural...

As I stare across the circulation desk at the stillness of the closed library and try to form an opinion of what the OCLC means to me, I notice the state of the building. The brown, tan and rust colors of the carpet merge into strange unwelcome patterns. The lime green walls with their water stains cry out to be covered, while the unstable "coffee" table tells its own story of depredation. And so I stray from my original topic and begin to think on how we will be able to give this building some sense of dignity or at least of decency.

This building... once it was a grocery store.

Many of my patrons knew the owners of the grocery store. My patrons are proud of their heritages, many of which are so intricately woven into the rich tapestry of this small, rural community. These patrons have told me stories about the store. As well, they have narrated the histories of this community and of this library—*this* library of which they are so proud. Many of them helped to move the books into this building; many of them have been coming to this library longer than I have been alive. How to give decency to this building—once a grocery store, but now home to nearly 16,000 books, five magazine subscriptions, one daily newspaper and one weekly.

"No..." I pick up the telephone and answer politely. "We have no information on Jewish customs or history. Try another library."

"No..." I pick up the telephone and answer. "We have no biography of Martin Luther King. Try the school library."

"No..." I answer, "No libros en Español."

"No... no computer."

So, what is wrong with this building? I know it needs some paint, some new carpet... yes, even new furniture. Some of the newer patrons of the library have begun to notice the state of the building. One young woman asked if she could perhaps help us fundraise to expand the building and make room for a better children's section. A mother, with her blind child, would like to know if we can access the holdings of the state library for the blind. A young man who works at the post office is interested in helping me get a computer, "to access all kinds of information on all kinds of databases for all kinds of people," he says.

About this time, I notice the two large, white buckets that catch the steady stream of drips flowing from the ceiling. I notice that although they have served their purpose (the sound of another loud drip tells me so), they are completely blocking access to the card catalogue. At once, I feel angry and sad and frustrated and ignorant and helpless and guilty.

In the next moment, I prepare to write my essay on what the OCLC means to me—right now, sitting in this closed and desolate space. And this time I am sure of what I will write.

**Martha Ann Bace**
Southern Arkansas University
Magnolia, AR

Try, if you can, to imagine the world without the OCLC Online Union Catalog. Heavens! What a nightmare! I've been cataloging materials using the Online Union Catalog since 1979 when I graduated from library school, and I can't imagine the library world without it. When asked by other cataloging source vendors to change from OCLC to their product, I don't even think twice. Why on earth should I replace my access to the world's largest bibliographic database with something less comprehensive? The OCLC Online Union Catalog rarely fails me whether I'm cataloging an item or helping the Interlibrary Loan Librarian find an obscure title. I mean, where else can you find a bibliographic entry for the *Arkansas Woodchopper Square Dance Calls* (with music and instructions) or what libraries have copies of *The Cynfeirdd*? I believe.

**Jane Bambrick**
William Paterson College
Wayne, NJ

My journey with OCLC...

Years ago someone described OCLC to me as a clumsy, monstrous octopus lacking the capability to organize or disseminate information in any efficient or effective manner. Of course, expectations for the then Ohio Catalog Library Consortium were limited. Few, including myself, ever imagined that OCLC would become the sophisticated online system that it is today. I began my career as a cataloger twenty-five years ago in a world of the *National Union Catalog*, electric erasers, and typewriters with special features for catalog cards. When our library joined in 1977, OCLC had already revolutionized the world of technical services. We soon tried the OCLC acquisitions system and later became part of the ILL system. When I transferred to the reference department, OCLC soon followed. It was the beginning of a beautiful friendship. Now an OCLC terminal graces our reference desk, as in thousands of other libraries dedicated to quality service. Rarely does a day go by when a reference librarian does not interface with OCLC, and access now on Sunday does not go unappreciated.

I see OCLC as a reflection of people: those who contribute to it, those who use it, those who benefit from it, and, of course, the database producers. Thousands of catalogers and technical service staff have contributed data that describe books, media and other material that constitute the database. Other librarians channel this information to library patrons through reference queries and interlibrary loans, as well as by accessing FirstSearch and EPIC, both outgrowths or "children" of OCLC. The programmers, regional representatives and training staff insure that new software enhancements are understood by all participating members.

I have found OCLC has increased the quality of reference service which we offer to our users. When a frantic student has procrastinated and his assignment requires books which are checked out, we can quickly refer him to neighboring libraries which have the titles he needs. For those who can't wait for articles through interlibrary loan, we can immediately refer them to those libraries which not only subscribe to the journals but identify those with the exact issues needed. I once encountered a man who had been searching for a year for a particular arrangement of a Jerome Kern record; I located it for him in seconds. On a return trip from the airport one day, I chatted with the driver and mentioned I was a librarian. He told me he had been unsuccessfully searching for videotapes on table tennis, and asked if I could help. I sent him a printout of the OCLC records with the holdings list. Over the years, I have used OCLC to assist hundred of patrons who range from teenagers to scholars. They all marvel at the capabilities of OCLC, and are not hesitant to express their appreciation to me for my assistance. Of course, I find their gratitude both personally and professionally revealing.

13

PRISM software has increased our ability to solve the never-ending mysteries of incomplete bibliographic citations. Patrons often recollect the title, author or date of a publication incorrectly. The PRISM fields give us more options to retrieve the full record in a most expeditious manner. The capability of searching by subject can bring up records for even the most unusual topics. And of course, with FirstSearch, end-users can search OCLC themselves via WorldCat, which brings millions of records to patrons with easy-to-follow directions for limiting searches by date, language, and publication type.

Although some RLIN users may snub OCLC as a database for pedestrian needs, *au contraire*. My personal research on medieval codices demonstrates that one can clearly locate materials for specialized research needs. I am studying illuminated manuscripts of the middle ages, and through PRISM software I located numerous records for original *Books of Hours*, as well as vellum and parchment pages from other medieval works. The MARC record provided me with the basic description, which helped me determine which libraries to visit during my last sabbatical leave. RLIN patricians might want to reflect on how OCLC did so much and made it look so easy!

The "clumsy cephalopod" has been transformed during the past twenty-five years. It is now a sophisticated bibliographic database whose "octamerous parts" permeate the majority of libraries in the United States and research libraries throughout the world. It is a refined, constantly updated system which meets the needs of our technological age. No doubt, OCLC will continue to thrive in the next millennium with capabilities now unimaginable!

## Norma L. Bartholomew
Fairfax County Government
Fairfax, VA

During the past twenty-five years, the OCLC—which started out as a simple cataloging consortium for libraries—has developed into a major provider of information related to products and services in the areas of resource sharing, reference, and electronic publishing. From time to time, the OCLC has been described as an information research center; a marketing agency; an information and database holder; a supplier, distributor, and creator; a national network; and a membership organization. However, the computerized library center is more widely employed in the capacity of a cataloging network with a database that contains more than 35 million records and more than 560 million location listings. It is also shared worldwide, by over 10,400 participating member institutions, including public, special, government, and academic libraries.

The OCLC Online Union Catalog—which was created as a result of the sharing of the data contained in the cataloging database—is part of the (easy to use) reference system that is available in most libraries. The database includes products and services, based on cooperative catalog and resource sharing on a large central computer system, and is utilized by OCLC-member libraries in 63 foreign countries. Today, the OCLC Online Union Catalog is the world's foremost database of bibliographic and holding information.

The online system of cataloging and resource sharing was developed to facilitate the end-user, in his/her search of the database for bibliographic information without the help or assistance of the librarian. The OCLC Online Union Catalog provides access to an enormous amount of information from established indexes, and is currently available in 36 foreign languages. The proficiency with which the end-user is able to access bibliographic information has afforded libraries, which have been maligned lately, to once again establish themselves as the primary provider of reference materials.

The records included in the Online Union Catalog appear in the form of books, serials, audiovisual media, maps, archives/manuscripts, sound recordings, (music) scores, and computer files; and encompasses an estimated 4,000 years of recorded information, dating back from 2000 B.C. to the present.

As a student of library and information science, I have been able to utilize FirstSearch, an online reference service of OCLC that was designed for library users to move easily through the process of online searches in a few simple steps, without training or online search experience. The FirstSearch service offers some 60 databases, including the OCLC Online Union Catalog (WorldCat). The service can be used to find books, articles, theses, films, computer software, and other types of material on any subject. The service is updated daily, and the information obtained is the most current that is available anywhere. Searches can be conducted in 5 topic areas: business and government, conferences and proceedings, education and medicine, general and reference, and a list of all databases; and the service has a coverage in excess of 30 million records, on any type of material cataloged by OCLC member libraries, including manuscripts written as early as the 11th century.

Accessing the OCLC Online Union Catalog is like having the world's information at your fingertips, because it affords the end-user access to information from around the world. Based upon my limited experience with the Online Union Catalog, I would say that it is user-friendly and requires no special training; it requires a lesser number of searches to research current events than the number required by DIALOG; it has reduced the amount of time required to search card catalogs or numerous bibliographies; and its most important feature is that searches conducted via the Online Union Catalog always seem to produce results.

**Patricia G. Beam**
Pittsburgh Theological Seminary
Pittsburgh, PA

While most searches in the OCLC Online Union Catalog are made from the user to the Catalog, a search that changed my life was just the opposite.

August 1971. Ohio colleges join Ohio University in the biggest library adventure ever attempted. The Online system is not well protected from the ineptness of beginners in its early days and interruptions in service occur without warning. One afternoon after several of these down times a cataloging assistant at Heidelberg College receives an irate call from OCLC operations—"Mrs. Jacobs, whatever you're doing, stop doing it!" A calmer caller later explains that a 505 field with corrections was too long and causing the problem.

June 1973. OCLC decides to increase exposure by hosting a demo booth at ALA, Las Vegas. Heidelberg College Librarian, Richard Owen, suggests his Cataloging Assistant Pat Jacobs go to explain system use. She joins Kaye Gapen, OSU Cataloger and Manager of Que, and Steve Beam, OCLC Operations Manager. Steve is charged with organizing the booth and keeping it up and running over two thousand miles from headquarters. The glimmering magic of Las Vegas acts as a catalyst causing Operations Manager and Cataloging Assistant to fall head over heels in love. They have a good laugh when they realize they had "met" before when Mr. Beam had searched the online users and found the person responsible for shutting down the entire OCLC system.

October 1973. Courtship continues as they take the OCLC road show to Evansville for the Indiana State Library Association meeting. Here over evening meals Barbara Evans Markuson and Steve discuss their visions for OCLC's future.

May 1974. The Beams celebrate their April wedding with a trip to the National Computer Show in Chicago. Beehive has invited OCLC to demonstrate Beehive's new computer terminal, designed for OCLC use. Newspaper and government browsers show some interest. Oak Ridge and Chicago librarians stop by for a look.

July 1974. Finding a new position in Columbus for an experienced cataloging assistant is made easy by Steve's contacts. The State Library of Ohio, quite new to OCLC membership, welcomes an experienced user. Then, after only two months, a position opens at Ohio State QUE and Pat experiences Hugh Atkinson's innovative leadership firsthand.

October 1974. Steve leaves OCLC. That move takes the couple to Pittsburgh, Pennsylvania. With the help of PRLC/OCLC acquaintances, Pat quickly finds a position with Pittsburgh Theological Seminary, a library only two months into a commitment with OCLC. From that vantage point she continues to enjoy the growth of OCLC, cataloging on a progression of hardware from Spiras to Beehive to M300 to Wyse to the PC-of-your-choice. Finally 25 years of her archived records are visible to local users with the installation of a local DRA system.

The OCLC Online Union Catalog has meant camping adventures, beautiful trout streams, motorcycle races, touring, and now, life on the road in an eighteen wheeler, with my own Operations Manager, Steve Beam.

## Linda Beauchene
Bismarck, ND

On March 17, 1986, I met a new friend that would change my life forever. That friend was OCLC.

It was my first day. I had just started a new job as a paraprofessional in technical services at a public library. Everything was new. My supervisor began by introducing me to my fellow staffers and showing me around the department. My desk and data-entry terminal were at one end of the L-shaped room near a window. Aaaaaahhh!! A window! This *was* my lucky day.

At the other end of the small room and last on the tour was an impressive-looking computer with an even more impressive keyboard. "This," my supervisor said proudly, "is OCLC." "What does OCLC stand for?" I asked.

And so it started. Days that were filled with materials processing, volunteers, data entry acquisitions, and OCLC. Months passed, then years. OCLC and its Online Union Catalog and I were becoming better acquainted. The days of sitting before her, petrified, were long gone. Instead, a warm feeling of wonder and awe for this machine was being cultivated.

Holding symbols, fixed field elements, 245 fields, delimiters, indicators, collations, subject headings, and so much more became my routine language at work. With its silent online characters, the Online Union Catalog became an unspoken language to me, one for the world to share.

For you see, the OCLC Online Union Catalog doesn't care what color your face is, what kind of car you have, or even what your political views are. All the Catalog cares about is building bibliographic bridges, instead of borders, so that we can learn about each other and the lives we lead. It is an instrument of peace, a force for good. It holds the ability to transform knowledge into wisdom and suffering into triumph.

In searching for a job, I found a career. In searching for my purpose, I found my destiny. In searching for something, I found everything.

Her name is the OCLC Online Union Catalog and she is a citizen of the world. She is the face of every face you've ever seen; she is every emotion anyone has ever felt. She cares inordinately about the world, but is not intrusive. She knows everything about politics, but is not political. Despite all her power, in an electrical instant, she may vanish from our sight. In doing so, she reminds us just how fragile is our connection with each other. But above all, she teaches us that fraternity is one of the supreme gifts we may bestow upon each other.

In the tumult and fabric of life, the OCLC Online Union Catalog steadfastly preserves and honors our collections. She lofts the mighty written word into electronic flight and these words find safe harbor in the sparkle of a librarian's eye and the gratitude of a patron's heart. I love the OCLC Online Union Catalog and its mission to humanity; I thank her for letting each of us share in the dream and vision of her pioneers.

## Peg Bennett
Southern College of Seventh Day Adventists (SDA)
Collegedale, TN

Libraries *are* crucial to education, right? Right. But consider this scenario: scores of one- and two-room schools—no librarians—scant funding. How to organize and maintain suitable libraries relevant to students' needs? An impossible task, right? Wrong! And this is the story...

Southern College librarians had long been anxious to improve these libraries, with collections varying from under 100 to over 5,000. Why would a college be concerned with elementary schools? Southern College is part of a multilevel educational system operated by the Seventh-Day Adventist Church, and each conference (the smallest unit of church organization) provides numerous elementary and secondary schools within its geographical territory—the majority, one- and two-room multigrade elementary schools. Clearly, there was a need for skilled professionals; clearly, too, there were insufficient funds to provide them. Therefore library organization and maintenance has fallen the lot of the teachers, who have scant time or training for the task. Most often, the libraries languished. Enter OCLC.

Since the librarians at Southern College already had a passion to assist the libraries—and since the college library was using the OCLC cataloging subsystem—why not use OCLC as the means of fulfilling that desire? Thus, ANGEL (Adventist Network of General Educational Libraries) was born.

Perhaps a unique service to be provided by a college library, ANGEL selects and orders materials for the schools, not only processing those *new* items, but also the *existing* collections held by each school. One hundred seventy-five schools now belong to the program, and nearly 400,000 items have been processed. Fortunately, many titles are held by several schools, keeping first-time use low. Although titles are at the K-12 level, the hit rate in OCLC is near 90%.

Response was decisively positive, the teachers delighted, the students excited, as ANGEL took wing. Benefits immediately became apparent:

1. Because library materials are organized by current cataloging practices, students learn how to use a library—not only *their* library—but *any* library.

2. Materials are both more rapidly and more easily accessible to students.

3. Students' interest in the library *and* in reading has increased noticeably.

4. Teachers are free to concentrate on classroom duties.

The program continues to gain momentum, and plans include introducing online catalogs into the schools. Even with all the desire, effort and vision of the Southern College librarians, this concept would have remained an impossible dream without OCLC. What does OCLC mean to me? An **O**pportunity to **C**onvey **L**ibrary **C**ruciality—and to thousands of students in the southeastern U.S., **O**pportunities to **C**ultivate **L**ibrary **C**omprehension. Thanks, OCLC!

## Rebecca L. Berg
University of Northern Iowa
Cedar Falls, IA

I work with the OCLC database daily. It is the fundamental tool I need to be successful at my job in an Interlibrary Loan department. But over time I have found that, though my job is made immeasurably easier by using OCLC, it is really the patrons I provide service to that benefit from this immense catalog. In my view, OCLC is really...

...for the adult student who chose English as her field of study. She had planned to do her master's thesis on Emily Dickinson but halfway through her studies she was diagnosed with breast cancer. In short time her ILL needs changed with the dramatic changes in her life. Her final thesis title... "Lumpectomy vs.

Mastectomy." Her requests deal predominantly with articles that offer prognosis tables.

…for the freshman who's got it all figured out. Two weeks before finals he begs our department to borrow a book our library owns. Seems he can't pass his final without this book but failed to consider due dates and waiting periods before he submitted his name to a hold list. I tell him we cannot order an item we own. There is nothing quite as pathetic as watching a confident and cocky nineteen-year-old turn to mush with sheer panic. Pity overtakes me… "Come on," I say, "Let's look it up on my computer. Maybe we can find it somewhere close." We look the book up in OCLC and a quick search of its holdings shows there are four libraries in our area he can try. I give him a printout with deciphered OCLC symbols and send him on his way. I rarely know the outcome. He was given the tools he needed to obtain the book. I guess if I see him back next semester I can ask him. But, then again, just seeing him back may indeed be my answer.

…for the professor who was feeling nostalgic about his past. Wanting to parlay his youthful, bygone interests into a textbook proposal he requested every book title and article notation he had ever saved. Valiant searches on OCLC produce holders for approximately half of the requests. Yet how aggravating to find that in the last twenty-five years libraries of his past acquaintance found his most important and vital information passé and chose to withdraw those very needed items. Via ALA forms, the search continues.

…for the senior who didn't learn as a freshman. After a day and a half spent securing the required signatures for graduation, it seems there is an outstanding paper needed in biology. He needs a book about Monarch butterfly migration of Black Hawk County and he needs it yesterday. A recall of our library's copy will not arrive soon enough. I start to feel those wispy "tough luck buddy" hairs start to stand up on the back of my neck. But anything short of compassion and assistance would be cruel. "Come on," I say, "let's see what my computer says." He smiles and tells me he knows all about what this computer can do… seems he's done this before. Figures…

…for the person…(doesn't matter who as we all know there are sooo many) who presents a request form with the single statement, " I know you will never be able to find this." "Hang on a second," I say as I type in a keyword search with sweaty palms. Come on OCLC, I think, don't fail me now. At few points in one's occupational life are there such simple yet empowering opportunities of triumph. "Was your title… ?" I ask. Not a problem!

**Rebecca Bergeon**
University of Colorado at Boulder
Boulder, CO

Ever since I can remember libraries have been a part of my life. My mother worked in the public library in my hometown in Michigan, and every day after school I went there to wait for my mom. I would do my homework, and then I had permission to peruse the library and read. I learned that libraries could, literally, be the doorway into unknown worlds—a gateway if you will, into all the mysteries and magic places in the worlds of fact and imagination. Libraries have always been, and always will be, a familiar and comforting environment for me. During high school and college I worked in libraries. To have all the knowledge of great minds at one's fingertips seemed to be a form of empowerment.

I now live at 8700 feet in a small mountain town outside of Boulder, Colorado, with my two grown children. I am somewhat removed from the world at large and my exposure often comes through my work. I work in the Interlibrary Loan Lending Department at the University of Colorado. I have never been able to find any other job I enjoy more than working in a library. We use the OCLC ILL Micro Enhancer program to receive requests from many of the 23,000 OCLC libraries in 63 countries. People from around the world: Japan, South Africa, France, Italy, Canada, Denmark, Russia, Australia, Hong Kong and the United States, to name some, have transmitted their patrons' requests to us via OCLC. OCLC has made this possible by listing, for each title searched, the libraries that own that item. CU tries its hardest to retrieve these books and Journal articles from locations and branch libraries all over CU's campus. I take pride in being part of a team whose members do not merely do their jobs, but excel in their work.

We have the opportunity to serve library patrons from all areas and walks of life. Just recently a woman from Iran asked us to send her some articles. Her university could not afford to pay us for the use of the materials so I went ahead and sent the items to her anyway. She wrote me a thank-you note on a beautiful card from her country and we have since become pen pals. An elderly gentleman wrote us a thank-you note for an item we loaned to him, saying that he had had it on his reading list for 35 years and was thrilled to have finally had the opportunity to read the book. Then, of course, there are the other library staff people we communicate with. My personal favorite was the time we sent a message to a library saying that we could not photocopy the article they had requested because the book was too tightly bound to get good photocopy. We sent the abbreviated message "too tight to copy" and they replied "whenever we get too tight to copy we just close the office and head home," which I thought was a great response. I have had E-mail correspondence about OCLC ILL requests from Russia and Australia and conversations with libraries everywhere in an effort to serve their patrons.

Before the OCLC ILL program, resource sharing was cumbersome and untimely. OCLC has changed the course of resource sharing for the world by making ALL of OCLC libraries' holdings accessible to mankind. It has revolutionized the whole concept of Interlibrary Loan.

How has it changed my life? Just as when I was a little girl and had access to the world of ideas and facts and the opportunity to travel the universe by opening a new book, OCLC has put the real and literal world at my fingertips. It has created a wonderful opportunity to communicate with the entire world in a very real, and at times, a very personal way. It has broadened my horizons and has given me the opportunity to be an integral part of a global community by having a database that seems to represent a "world" library catalogue. The possibility to share our library's resources with other libraries and to utilize their resources unavailable to our patrons at home is a major step in the concept of availability of knowledge for all. It has brought into my life a satisfaction and joy that comes from basic human sharing and has enriched my life greatly. Thank you OCLC.

## Wendy D. Bethune
Findlay-Hancock County Public Library
Findlay, OH

The OCLC Online Union Catalog is a tremendous resource for today's libraries. Librarians can utilize this vast database in service to our institutions and patrons as a cost-savings measure and a tool to increase access to information. OCLC is a clear leader in the worldwide movement to increase communication, minimize duplication of effort and contain costs in a world of skyrocketing prices of library materials. We can be proud of this database that we have all built together over the last quarter of a century.

As a reference librarian, my primary concern is meeting the information needs of my library's patrons. It is impossible for my medium-sized library to purchase every item every one of our patrons could ever be interested in. OCLC's Online Catalog allows our library to determine what other libraries have the item(s) our patrons are looking for; we can then direct the patron to another library in our region if they so desire, or place an online interlibrary loan request to make the item available right in our small town. These two functions—the ability to determine what other libraries own and the ability to make those items available to our patrons—are hallmarks of excellence in library service. As we experience shrinking budgets and increasing demands for information, the OCLC database stands out as a wealth of resources we can all participate in and utilize for our patrons' benefit. The OCLC Online Union Catalog is a library for librarians, answering the essential question we all encounter every day: "How can I get the information I (our patrons) need?"

OCLC's database is clearly a leading resource in providing worldwide access to information. Even from my medium-sized library in a fairly rural county in the midwest, my patrons have access to materials located all over the region, the country, and the world. Our local newspaper editor is one of our biggest supporters, having obtained items in his specialized interest area that would never be available to him through any other means. He thinks it's a miracle—we know it's OCLC. Our cooperative efforts in forming and maintaining this database provide a tremendous service not just to our local patrons but to our customers wherever they may be. OCLC's Online Union Catalog gives me a whole new dimension to that question I and reference librarians all over the world ask dozens of times each day: "How may I help you?"

Let's celebrate 25 years of the OCLC Online Union Catalog—hooray to all of us!

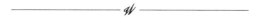

## Linda Bills
Bryn Mawr College; Haverford College; Swarthmore College
Bryn Mawr, PA

"The Modern Union Catalog..."
To the tune of Gilbert and Sullivan's "Modern Major General"

It is the very model of a modern Union catalog
The information's digital, it is no longer analog.
From ancient scrolls of papyrus to "Netted quick-time cinema,"
From crumbling clay tablets through literature millennia,
Whatever form of media your knowledge is inscribed upon
This catalog describes it well and even tells what shelf it's on.
Thirty-five million titles now, from aardvark right through Zenaphon
(So many that they can't be sung, not even in a patter-song).

[Chorus: So many that they can't be sung, not even in a patter-song]

So in the heartland all these bits are gathered and retrievable—
They're rushing all around the world at speeds quite unbelievable.
They babble on in Yiddish, Serbo-Croat and Ukrainian,
Bulgarian and Arabic, Chinese, Urdu, Romanian.
Librarians from near and far contribute facts reMARCable,
Bibli-o-graphic entities—the current and the archival.
Our catalog of knowledge thus grows both in breadth and density—
And everyone can now access this resourceful immensity.

[Chorus: And everyone can now access this resourceful immensity]

With electronic knowledge we've been plucky and adventury
We've changed the paradigm in just a quarter of a century
And now we've trashed the three-by-fives, through which the
patrons had to slog,
And made the very Model of a Modern Union Catalog.

## Ilene M. Black
Trenton State College
Trenton, NJ

Happy Silver Anniversary, OCLC Online Union Catalog! Your twenty-fifth year
of operation is my first year of using OCLC. Learning the ins and outs of the
OCLC Online Union Catalog is a fascinating, challenging business. Take it from
an OCLC rookie!

Ordering from the OCLC Online Union Catalog is like traveling and meeting
people from all over the world. Logging on to the OCLC catalog almost feels as
though I am walking through the doors of other libraries, browsing through their
stacks, poring over their titles, and selecting what I need. When I create a
Workform for borrowing Interlibrary Loan items, it's as if I am having a brief chat

with other library staff from faraway libraries. I like to imagine those other people sitting at their desks in their offices, working on OCLC, coffee at one elbow and phone at the other. Perhaps they look out their window and see palm trees and sunshine, or mountains and snow, or skyscrapers and bustling traffic.

The wave of the future is a paperless office environment. With the OCLC Online Union Catalog, the need for paper is practically nonexistent. Everything you need to know is at your fingertips. What an improvement over flipping through a thick, messy binder, running your finger down a page, and MAYBE locating the title you need! I never worked with the paper copy of the Union List, but I've heard the stories. The world is moving towards automation and electronic information, and the OCLC Online Union Catalog is at the forefront. It sure makes my job much easier!

The OCLC Online Union Catalog means a window to the world of other libraries, institutions where learning is good, where information is the reason we're here. It's about sharing our resources with each other, communicating on a level higher than the letter or telephone. It's a world where our patrons are our priority, and getting them the materials that they need is what we do best, thanks to the OCLC Online Union Catalog. "A valuable tool" mildly describes the OCLC Online Union Catalog. It has totally rewritten the way we acquire materials. It's an innovative, efficient, and reliable source. It's the only way I can imagine, the only way I know.

To sum it up, the OCLC Online Union Catalog is the foyer to a broad vista of information, a virtual plethora of computerized materials. It's the 90s way!

## Robert N. Bland
University of North Carolina at Asheville
Asheville, NC

The work of librarians is in the main a subtle work, painstaking and fundamental, and seldom given to the spectacular which captures the public fancy. From time to time, however, there may come to fruition in our field an achievement dazzling to any with eyes to see. Such, I believe, is the achievement of the OCLC Online Union Catalog.

This remarkable world catalog—now comprising over 35,000,000 records of books, documents, reports, theses, dissertations, and media in libraries across the planet—is a monument to the life of the mind and a bibliographic colossus, but more than that, it is a testament to the spirit of human cooperation. Unprovoked by fear or law, not even inspired by the prize of personal gain, the OCLC Online Union Catalog has grown step by step, record by record to its formidable proportions, simply as the result of the human capacity for good sense and the willingness of thousands to share expertise and effort for the common good. Nothing quite like it in our profession has gone before; nothing quite surpassing it are we likely to see again.

In my own career, I have been involved with the OCLC Online Union Catalog in a number of capacities. As a cataloger, I have been gratified with the efficiency and cost savings this database has brought to libraries, and by the opportunity to share my own original cataloging with others. As a systems librarian, I have been impressed to find consistently high-quality MARC records available from OCLC, which can be processed again and again without error. And as a scholar, I have been thrilled—indeed awed—by the scope of this world bibliographic resource.

Recently, I was reminded again of the immense power and value of the OCLC Online Union Catalog to the scholarly community when, in reading Churchill's history of World War I, I came across his description of an apparently obscure episode concerning the German battle-cruiser "Goeben," which was somewhat mysteriously able to evade the British navy at the beginning of the war, only to reappear and wreak great havoc upon the allies later in the eastern theater. My curiosity piqued by Sir Winston's evident displeasure at the Royal Navy's handling of this matter, I wondered if there were other sources that might shed further light. A single search of the world catalog in FirstSearch turned up a considerable bibliography comprising both German and British publications from 1916 forward, as well as several recent books on the topic. Extraordinary! One wonders what a Hume, a Macaulay, or a Gibbon could have done with such a tool.

And it is of course as a tool, not as a monument, that we should think of the OCLC Online Union Catalog. For my part, it is a source of satisfaction to have played a small part in the creation of this magnificent tool.

———————————— *qv* ————————————

## Kathleen Casteel Blazar
Cleveland Health Sciences Library
Cleveland, OH

Over twenty years ago while attending library school at Case Western Reserve University in Ohio, OCLC was included as part of a library automation course. Were the library school not in Ohio, OCLC with its roots in Ohio most probably would have been overlooked in the course as a viable future automation system for bibliographic control. As part of the course, students were afforded one fifteen-minute session to explore the system. Of course the quarter-hour session was not enough to whet anyone's appetite and any opportunities to further experiment were well-relished.

OCLC has changed from a professionals-only vehicle to a most user-friendly part of the information world. It was not readily apparent years ago why we were painstakingly filling in the blanks of every field in an online workform as we cataloged. Without these efforts information retrieval today would not be the invisibly effortless retrieval to the end-user that it is. The fascination of discovering information replaces the frustration of wondering how to do it. This fascination originally witnessed by an eager library student is now shared by the ultimate user of the information. Gone are the days of "Request impossible" messages and Corporate Author searching only prior to 9:00 A.M. E.T. With the current online prompts and help, the database is easily searched by all users at all times.

OCLC has undergone a metamorphosis unlike any other in the library world. Simply put, the system has changed from a fancy way to make catalog cards for the card catalog, to something in the next century totally devoid of print and available electronically. When OCLC was only part of the technical aspects of the library, it was necessary to sneak into the back technical processing room, coerce a cataloger from a terminal and search for the information for the waiting patron out front. Now with the WorldCat as an end-user system, the patron can perform the search himself and frequently without the assistance of a librarian.

Librarians should be proud of their efforts over the past twenty-five years to create the premier bibliographic database. They have done an excellent job making information readily available worldwide through the OCLC Online Union Catalog. They have done so in a professional world-class way and should endeavor to do so in the future.

## Daniel K. Blewett
Loyola University, Chicago
Chicago, IL

Like many librarians, I first learned about the OCLC Online Union Catalog in my cataloging class in library school at Indiana University. However, it was not until I started working as a student assistant on the Reference Desk that I realized that the OCLC system could be used for reference as well as cataloging functions. Over the years I have grown to understand and value the key role this system can play in the research process.

OCLC has replaced the huge, expensive book catalogs of previous decades as the primary bibliographic aid. As impressive as those tomes are, they are limited in their utility by primarily concentrating on the collections of one institution, and by only being available in a relatively small number of libraries. The OCLC Online Union Catalog is exactly the opposite. It represents the holdings of hundreds of libraries around the world, and can be accessed from millions of individual locations. This greatly increases the number of items that scholars might potentially use.

Perhaps the most impressive feature of the OCLC database is the massive number of bibliographic records it contains, over 35 million at last count. Many of these items do not appear in other printed or electronic reference tools. By using OCLC one can quickly have access to the bibliographic details of more material than one can possibly imagine. This bibliographic control of materials is perhaps the core of librarianship, and greatly aids research. I have accessed OCLC to help patrons complete footnotes and bibliographic citations in books and articles, which has long been a concern of librarians. As more records from special collections, retrospective conversion cataloging projects, and libraries in other countries are loaded into the system, the research value of the OCLC Online Union Catalog increases.

The wide variety of formats found in the Union Catalog is also a great feature. Monographic and serial titles make up the majority of bibliographic records in the catalog, but ephemeral, cartographic, audiovisual, dissertations, manuscript materials, government documents and electronic information resources are also included. All languages are represented, and some foreign alphabets are also used. Searching OCLC replaces the tedious and time-consuming task of searching numerous and more subject- or format-specific printed and electronic tools.

The fact that a wide variety of libraries contribute to the Union Catalog is also a great benefit to researchers. Not only are academic research libraries represented, but so are all types and sizes of public and special libraries. These libraries can contribute records of materials not widely available in other institutions, but which might be useful to someone somewhere else. As the system is not restricted to just the United States, one can become aware of the holdings of some of the major foreign libraries as well.

Since member libraries have attached a location code to a bibliographic record to indicate that they own a particular title, scholars, by knowing what is housed at a particular location, can better organize their research trips. Not every library has its own separate electronic catalog, and not every electronic catalog is accessible via the Internet. Nor is every electronic library catalog easy to search. It is much easier to search the OCLC Online Union Catalog to discover who owns what items, rather than search many different electronic systems.

Many people do not have the time or funds to travel to other institutions to conduct research. Although not directly used by patrons, the linking of OCLC's interlibrary loan system with its bibliographic database makes the sharing of resources among libraries faster and more convenient. This allows more people to do more research at their home institutions. Coupled with this is the ability to access the OCLC databanks via the Internet rather than just from hardwired terminals, allowing for the system to be used from virtually anywhere on the planet, or even in space for that matter. Patrons have frequently expressed their happiness with this capability.

One thing that has greatly increased the research value of the Union Catalog in the last few years has been the refinement of the search engines for OCLC Cataloging, OCLC ILL, PRISM, EPIC, and FirstSearch. The FirstSearch system is very user-friendly, and people can master the basic search commands of all three versions relatively easily. With only minimal instruction, I have been able to teach users how to do their own research on OCLC. This means that that I do not have to do all of their computerized research for them. By using the Subject search feature in FirstSearch one can find items that have the desired keyword(s) in either the title or subject headings fields. This is of great help when trying to find many individual titles that fall under the same subject category, which is the purpose of much bibliographic research. One can also combine a subject keyword with a format keyword (e.g., "sources" or "correspondence") that pulls up citations to primary research materials.

As one can gather from the paragraphs above, the biggest advantage of the OCLC Online Union Catalog, for both patrons and librarians, is the convenience factor. By using just one system, one has quick and easy access to the bibliographic details of millions of items in all formats that could prove useful to research, one can find out where the item is located, and one can find out what other items fall under the same subject heading. This searching can be done either at the library, office, or home. I have been able to demonstrate to patrons that although the Loyola University Library is not the size of Harvard's, one can still conduct extensive research at Loyola with the OCLC system, and that it provides access to a wide variety of important resources. The Union Catalog is such a versatile research time-saver that those who ignore it are just hurting themselves.

A lot of time, money, and effort has been invested in the OCLC system. What started out as a useful bibliographic network for Ohio libraries has grown into a vital international information resource. Several projects are currently underway to improve the contents and capabilities of the database. As a result, the OCLC Online Union Catalog is the world's premier bibliographic research tool. It greatly assists all libraries in fulfilling their primary function, that of meeting the information needs of their communities. I cannot imagine being able to effectively serve the patrons of Loyola University's library system without it.

## Karen Blinn
Marion Public Library
Marion, IN

Once upon a time not so long ago in a nearby place, each town had its own library complete with its own cataloger. These catalogers labored to classify and describe their library's books. The poor catalogers worked in isolated rooms, with only piles of books and the sound of clattering typewriter keys for company. In fact, their standard equipment consisted of 3" x 5" slips of paper, pencils, and the ever-present typewriter (originally a manual but frequently upgraded to electric in later years).

Things continued in this manner for years. Occasionally, a glimmer of hope would break through the gloom when the librarians met each other at their annual conferences. (For these events, the catalogers' directors released them for a day or two to fraternize with other librarians of their ilk.) Murmurs would riffle through the meeting rooms to the effect of, "Oh, if only we could share our cataloging some way. Then each of us wouldn't have to catalog every book for every library!"

As is frequently the case, technology took its time catching up to the needs expressed by the lonely catalogers. Some of the braver members of the group tried sharing printed cataloging records, but these generally came along too late to help much. So, of necessity, the catalogers continued to cherish their 3" x 5" slips.

Finally, in 1971, online computer technology had progressed to the point where dreams and reality could meet. A group of far-sighted librarians from Ohio formed the OCLC Online Union Catalog. Now, from their own libraries, catalogers could use telephone lines to access cataloging records contributed by other members. Each item needed cataloging once! Colleges and larger public libraries immediately jumped at the chance to join this cooperative organization.

Into this melange, our very own librarian from Marion landed when she went off to library school in the early 1980s. There the professors demonstrated the wonders of cataloging with OCLC, while at the same time teaching the traditional 3" x 5" method. This was fortunate since the library she went to serve remained stuck in the paper age and would remain there for several years to come.

Finally, in 1991 Marion's new library opened, complete with three OCLC terminals. Gone was the constant clatter of the typewriter! Not only that but the same size staff could add many times more items to the library's collection each year. Marion's librarian found it so wonderful not to have to measure each book and puzzle over possible subject headings.

Now, every so often, her director stops by to jokingly ask if "she wants to get rid of the terminals and go back to pencils and 3 x 5s." She shouts "No!" And he laughs. Meanwhile, she loves those computers so much that she has moved on to systems administration in addition to OCLC work. Thank goodness for those far-sighted souls who started it all twenty-five years ago!

## H. Leroy Bradway
University of Iowa
Ely, IA

OCLC Online Union Catalog is a gold mine of information for libraries and library users. It enables a library to have accurate data for copy cataloging of its new holdings and to improve cataloging records of its existing collection. It also provides one of the very few up-to-date sources of information for seeking the location of an item. This is vital for researching information from the stone age to the nuclear age, from the sub-cultures of Spain to the local writing of a poet in the neighboring community, from the map of ancient Israel to the score of Beethoven's 5th Symphony or the latest database on population in New York City. As a student, I can find resources for a paper on nutrition in Japan. As a minister, I can research historical and archaeological items in Israel and Egypt or Reformation history in Germany. As a library user, I can receive the proper information for requesting a map, music score, book, or computer score from more than 560 million locations through Interlibrary Loan. OCLC Online Union Catalog enables me to partake of the riches of the world's knowledge. A richness that can make the poorest person, the equal of a king.

## Ross A. Bunnell
University of Oregon
Eugene, OR

> The O C L C
> Data seeking the cast net.
> Now even I fish.

## Danny Burdett
Albion College
Albion, MI

A true story...

The OCLC Online Union Catalog saved my life. You may have heard about it. I fell down a well. Trapped, hundreds of feet below the surface of the earth. It looked rather grim for young Danny. The rescue crews put forth a superhuman effort, but to no avail.

Then someone mentioned the Excavatori. You know, the nomadic tribe of well diggers from Pakistan, chased from their homeland about 100 A.D., all the way to western Europe, where they roamed and dug for the next two centuries. Fortunately, a college professor was one of the nervous throng assembled wellside. He just happened to have done a doctoral dissertation on the Excavatori while at the University of Chicago: *Migrant patterns of the Excavatori, as related to the North American Free Trade Agreement.*

The professor explained that if anyone held the answer to the harrowing problem at hand, it would be the Excavatori. Before crawling down one of their own wells about 300 A.D., never to return (owing to a disagreement with the Gauls over their annual soccer match, which had ended on a controversial penalty kick), the Excavatori had left behind an impressive body of writing, consisting of epic poetry, cookbooks and a sprawling five-volume opus that summed up all their subterranean expertise. But where to find one of the potentially life-saving volumes, written in Urdu? Only a chilling silence met the professor's question.

But then... from amongst the crowd, a librarian spoke. "What about the OCLC Online Union Catalog. 4,000 years of recorded knowledge in 370 languages. If the volumes are out there, I can find them!" A suddenly hopeful crowd cheered her as she sped off to her library. Despite the obscurity of both time and language, she was able to find the appropriate volume: *101 Underground Problems and How to Solve Them.* The indefatigable librarian put through an interlibrary loan request, being sure to place the following admonishment in the borrowing notes, "child trapped in deep well; rush if possible; thanks!"

Unfortunately, the first four libraries in the lender string turned her down. In the meantime, I had begun to gnaw on my little fingers and hallucinate about being an earthworm. It didn't look good.

Fortunately, the last library came through. They sent the book overnight, and the librarian rushed back to the scene. The workers were then able to get me out in no time. The OCLC Online Union Catalog had saved my life.

As true as all of the above may be, I could also say that when I take over interlibrary loan at Albion College over the summer months, I couldn't imagine trying to do the job without the OCLC Online Union Catalog. It's a pretty amazing thing. With its help, I'm able to quickly and efficiently do my work and turn my attention to even more important subjects... like golf.

**Linda Burkey**
Western Illinois University
Macomb, IL

Interlibrary loan log of Western Illinois University—in the year 1996...

In service to the public, I am. Loading OCLC into my RAM.
Patrons polite and not so nice asking, "Can you help me Ma'am?"

"I need this book or that video and oh this article, if you please.
By the way my paper was due last week."

Off to the OCLC terminal I trek. If I can find that book
anywhere—I can find it there.

Scan title—here I go! Off into worlds unknown!
It found a hit... No, no that's not it... Wait... Here it is: yes—that's it!

DHA—oh, my! This library has the book, but will they be able to retrieve it from that little nook.

PRODUCE—SEND—will they be my friend?
Shipped. Yes! They came through in the end.

Now, let's see. There was a photocopy my patron needs.

ULLVIS—who has the right year?
Oh, dear. No one keeps this past a year.

ULSILO—now, we're getting somewhere.
Hey, that library over there. Could you fax this article over here?
Now, that video. SCAN title, DHA—will I ever find a library that will lend videos. PRODUCE—SEND—would you please lend?

Whew! The book, photocopy and video all came in.
Here stands my patron with a grin.

"Thanks, Interlibrary Loan. You've got everything I need.
My professor won't be mean."

"You're Welcome," I say—as I watch my patron stroll out-of-sight to write into the night!

My journey has temporarily come to an end, but I know there will be another patron coming in.

———————————— ✇ ————————————

**Donald H. Byerly**
Chester County Library
West Chester, PA

As a volunteer working in the Technical Services section of our county library, I am immensely grateful for the existence of OCLC. How else could we catalog our holdings quickly and precisely with the same notation used in other libraries in our area and indeed across the nation and around the world?

Even in our relatively small library—small in comparison to those of large universities or cities—the variety of our holdings is immense. New publications arrive daily, spanning the large amount of fiction and biography, and what is to me the unbelievable variety of topics in non-fiction, to say little of maps and audio-visual materials and computer files. Such are the vagaries of human interpretation that without OCLC, two catalogers in separate offices cataloging the same title might easily give it different call numbers. (Witness the different interpretations of the federal income tax code given by different IRS employees!)

Though my duties do not include using OCLC directly, I deal with the library's main computer database, adding, deleting and changing records. The other day through a misunderstanding I deleted a record in the library's main computer that should have stayed in. Catching the error, I printed the record from the screen and explained things to my supervisor. "No problem," he said, "We can recover through OCLC." This was a small thing, but reflects the versatility of OCLC. I was relieved.

Two catalogers in our Technical Services section sit daily at their green-glowing screens accessing OCLC. How comfortable it is to know that all the materials entering our library are catalogued easily, reliably and best of all uniformly.

———————————— ℳ ————————————

## Hilde Calvert, Sandy Duncan, Karin Kwiatkowski, Lisa Johnson, Melinda Sheffield (Interlibrary Loan Team)
Ball State University
Muncie, IN

Ball State University ILL Ode to OCLC...

> OCLC, oh how we love and adore you!
> We never again want to be without you!
> We can't just say it with one little line,
> How you help us serve our all users so fine.
> So let us count the many ways,
> Let us sing the Interlibrary Loan praise.
>
> We wish to make it super clear,
> With OCLC we need have no fear.
> We can fill requests for other places
> And always keep a smile on our faces.
> We find the things our users need,
> With accuracy and lightning speed.
>
> OCLC you have made great strides over the years,
> With automation you have eliminated our headaches and fears.
> From having to send each line at a snail's pace,
> To full-page editing, on with the race!
> Let us not forget the wonderful microenhancer,
> It has made updating much faster and fancier
>
> You let us search with such great ease!
> Three two two one its such a breeze!
> Four four or four three one,
> Push Alt F10 and you are done.
> For name or title or just name,
> This is the basic searching game.

For names such as Smith or Miller or Meyer,
You may want to add a qualifier.
To limit entries and attain more precision,
Use your best judgment and volition.
Select as many qualifiers as you need,
To achieve results at maximum speed.

Patron requests with incomplete citations
May require the keyword search initiation.
That technique is so fabulously magnanimous,
The keyword you use does not need to be ingenious
The system then searches in all of the record
For that keyword and displays results on the spot.

Once your search is complete and you found what you needed,
Display the record and select the holdings best suited.
In the hope of finding lenders both willing and free,
You select a string of five that do not charge a fee.
Complete the workform with all the vital information
Alt F10 to send screen edits, p F11 to produce your creation.

You hope for the best that a lender out yonder,
Has what you asked for and sends it, great wonder!
It is no exaggeration, without OCLC we could not find,
So fast what we look for nor have peace of mind.
There remains no more doubt, when all is said and done,
OCLC, you are the greatest, you are the triumphant one!

## Ann C. Case
Health Science Center Library
Gainesville, FL

I began using OCLC in 1979. We had all the OCLC terminals in one room, and sat and gossiped between entries as we waited for some action on the screen. I remember staring at the screen for so long that when the new record came up I didn't know it and just kept staring. Today if I don't get instant action I get VERY upset!—What's wrong with this thing!

When I came to this library in 1985 there were still terminals dedicated to OCLC and we batched work and went to the OCLC terminal, preferably before and after prime time. There are people in this office from 5:30 a.m. on, and it started with needing to access OCLC during odd hours.

Now we have access from our desks to EVERYthing and toggle back and forth all day long. Less exercise, broader chair bases, but much more efficient work and wonderful access. And I still complain if I don't have split-second access—until I think back to 1979.

The look of an OCLC record has become part of my landscape. I didn't realize this until I found a title, printed off the record and took it to a "civilian."

She looked at that piece of paper like it was written in Sanskrit and said, "What is that?" Only then did I realize that I would have to interpret fields and delimiters to the outside world. I expect my tombstone to read: "100:1 :Case, Ann C. 650::Librarians [x paraprofessional]."

I enjoy introducing the public to the possibilities of OCLC. When I can find exactly the title someone is looking for, and show them that all the information is there on one record—dates, publisher, format, length of volume, whether the title has illustrations, an index, a bibliography.

I was so excited when they begin to give fictional characters name authorities. And there's the ability to answer trivia questions like the late Friday afternoon question of how many movies Elvis made and in what order. OCLC always comes through!

## Terry L. Chiever
San Bernardino Valley Municipal Water District
San Bernardino, CA

As the custodian of a special library, the OCLC Online Union Catalog means that I can create a connection between the past and the future. It means that I can facilitate meetings of great minds, overcoming the barriers of time and place, and it means that I can participate in bringing hope to the future. The total of these activities means that the OCLC Online Union Catalog lets me aid in increasing the well-being of mankind.

To bring life to the past, all I need is a document, such as Wastewater discharges in the Bunker Hill-San Timoteo area, 1934–35 to 1975–76, and access to the OCLC Online Union Catalog's PRISM Cataloging Service. Using these tools, I can immortalize G. Louis Fletcher and give insight into his work as a result of his position as district engineer of the San Bernardino Valley Municipal Water District, the corporate author of the document. I can also bring life to the document itself, which, before introducing it to OCLC's Online Union Catalog, is dead to all but the select few who may remember where it is located. Once the document meets the OCLC Online Union Catalog, it becomes a living source of information because it can be systematically located by anyone who seeks it. Thus, I can create a connection between documents and authors from the past and future use of those documents, using OCLC's Online Union Catalog.

By connecting a document with the OCLC Online Union Catalog, I can facilitate meetings of great minds by bridging time and space. I can make the location of a piece of information, such as Wastewater discharges in the Bunker Hill-San Timoteo area, 1934–35 to 1975–76, known to anyone, anyplace. The OCLC Online Union Catalog makes it possible for people with common goals and interests to work together in spite of time and distance gaps. Individual minds share the product of their work with others when it is made accessible through the OCLC Catalog. Thus, I can be a facilitator of a meeting of the minds using the OCLC Online Union Catalog to record the existence of a piece of information that may be sought by someone else, some other time.

The OCLC Online Union Catalog bridges time and space, bringing the world together, giving us hope. It lets us learn from the past, build on it, and plan for the future, giving us hope. It gives form to the aggregate body of information so that individual pieces of information, such as Wastewater discharges in the Bunker Hill-San Timoteo area, 1934–35 to 1975–76, become purposeful, bringing us hope. As I contribute records to the OCLC Online Union Catalog, I participate in building hope for the future.

The OCLC Online Union Catalog allows me to create a connection between the past and the future, it lets me be a facilitator of a meeting of the minds, and it provides an opportunity for me to participate in building hope for our future. Thus, the OCLC Online Union Catalog lets me join with others in this great philanthropic endeavor—organizing the information of the world!

## Paul E. Clark
Albright College
Reading, PA

At a recent staff meeting, our head cataloger held up a sheet of paper and said whimsically: "What does OCLC mean to us?" After a combination of dull stares and well-intentioned smiles were offered in response, one staff member quietly said: "Well...how would we feel if OCLC didn't exist?" It was at this point that our meeting took a serious turn, and we—as a staff—began to examine all the ways in which the quantity and quality of our work together has been served by OCLC.

Voices were raised immediately...many of them echoing similar themes: how much faster cataloging can be done so that books arrive on the shelves with less delay, how much less cumbersome cataloging now is thanks to OCLC, how much time and budgetary resources are saved because of this technological/informational breakthrough. Several more murmurs about convenience and the loss of onerous repetition in cataloging ran through our group before another quiet question was raised: "Certainly, those are some of the ways in which OCLC helps us, but does that REALLY answer the question?"

Silence descended yet once more. Having taken to heart this tactful accusation of staff parochialism, one of our number chimed in: "If you think about it, the greater uniformity that OCLC offers all of us is only possible because of an amazing cooperative effort that our colleagues committed themselves to a long time ago." Thus, what had started as a self-interested examination of our own needs had expanded into a deeper understanding of the thought and impulse that had given birth to OCLC in the first place.

It was our head cataloger who picked up the torch and continued to light our way: "Can any of us imagine what OCLC—this World of Bibliography—really means to the enterprise of human learning and scholarships?" With that insight, our discussion had moved beyond the practical implication of the workplace and beyond the collective commitment that brought OCLC into being. That phrase,

"World of Bibliography," presented us that day with the visionary possibilities that OCLC truly promises...today and in the future. I doubt that many of our staff meetings will take us that far...across the threshold of what it means to do the work we do.

## Milton G. Clasen
Texas A&M University–Kingsville
Kingsville, TX

Reduction of duplication of effort by catalogers in OCLC libraries is the basis of OCLC's successful 25 years, and that is also the foundation for successful library operations at Texas A&M University-Kingsville during the 13 years it has been with OCLC.

The OCLC Online Union Catalog has made it possible to keep the backlog of new materials awaiting processing to a minimum at this library. Together with dedicated coworkers, it has also given the cataloger time for a special retrospective conversion project for book bibliographical records likely to need local attention. That first included conversion of records for the theses of the university, followed by more unusual books in the bilingual collection and main collection, especially Spanish language books and items published on demand. Many new records were added to the OCLC Catalog, and there also have been numerous opportunities to upgrade and enrich records already in the Catalog, including CIP records.

In 1992, OCLC also granted to this library enhance authorization for books format. The cataloger has used this authorization not only for the special retrospective conversion, but also to correct mistakes and add information to recent bibliographical records in the OCLC Catalog. This has included adding Bilindex (Spanish) subject access points to records for books in Spanish or about Spanish speaking people. As a result of enhanced activity at this library there were several months for which the library owed nothing for OCLC services because of credits to the library's account.

The contributions of one library may not seem to be very significant in a bibliographical database of over 35 million records, but many libraries making these and other kinds of contributions enrich all OCLC libraries. What this library has gained from other library contributions comes from programs large and small. The contribution to serial records by CONSER libraries has made much more information available to our library users than was the case with the brief records in the card catalogs before OCLC records were used. More recently, genre headings have become available for this library's users as a result of the OCLC/L.C. Fiction Project. The Program for Cooperative Cataloging has made more bibliographical records available to use locally. NACO Program libraries contributing authority records have made access points more consistent. Libraries have also contributed to the quality of the database by reporting errors to the OCLC Online Data Quality Control Section. More contents notes contributed by many libraries are now available here.

Interlibrary loan has greatly increased since the library went with OCLC. In part the increase was due to participation by the library in the PAISANO Union List and the lists of which it is a part.

The most important contribution of the OCLC Online Union Catalog, however, is that it has made possible automation for this library. That in turn has helped the university retain its accreditation. That means a great deal for anyone associated with this university.

## Eileen Coan
Stow Public Library
Stow, Ohio

It may never catch on as a slogan for ALA, but the OCLC Online Union Catalog has turned me into a "library slut"—I never say "No!" In a small, underfunded, otherwise nondescript, Midwestern public library, we offer the best customer service for miles. We may not get the bestsellers for a few months after they hit the superstore chains, but we can get a turn-of-the-century treatise on alchemy. We may not be conversant in the National Book Award nominees, but we can get repair manuals for appliances that no longer exist. And, it may take us a while to fill the requests for Oprah's latest life-changing self-help manual, but with the push of a few buttons we can get an obscure L.P. recording of a one-hit wonder.

O.K., it's not as great as chocolate truffles or a full-body massage, but sometimes it's downright fun. When you do a wildcard 3,2,2,1 or take a stab at sca_ti and hit paydirt, it's a rush. Like a good game of Scrabble, you learn to minimize the strokes for maximum points. And it's social too! I've used the Borrowers Notes field to beg and whine, thank profusely, gloat about the Cleveland Indians scores, and barter down a lending fee. With the recent addition of LVIS holdings, I can join the club of librarians with a conscience.

What else can I say? Its not just that it makes my job easier, OCLC is the reason I have a job. When money is tight and we hold onto rebuilt dot-matrix printers, a few thousand dollars a year in online charges, staff time and shipping allows us to fill almost every request that comes along. Thanks to WorldCat and MEDLINE, I've had simple encounters result in a bouquet of flowers and homemade baklava. While my library fits the stereotype of testosterone-free, someday I may even get a date. Happy patrons, popular librarian, end of story.

## Thomas Coipuram, Jr.
Library of Congress
Falls Church, VA

As a library and information science student and as a reference assistant for the Congressional Research Service at the Library of Congress, I frequently use and rely on this electronic union catalog. We use it to identify and locate items that are not part of our collection and refer patrons, who do not have access to the Library of Congress, to libraries in their locality that have these items. The OCLC Online Union Catalog helps us not only to identify a particular item and determine which libraries would have this item in their collection, but also helps us assist the patron in acquiring the item by either directing them to their closest libraries or through an interlibrary loan.

From its almost humble beginnings in the midwest, back in 1967, when the presidents of the colleges and universities in Ohio founded the *Ohio College Library Center* to develop a computerized system in which the libraries in Ohio could share their resources, today OCLC, (now known as the *Online Computer Library Center*), is literally the earth's largest library catalog, listing the holdings of thousands of libraries around the world.

To appreciate this astounding resource and see the practical usefulness of this Online Union Catalog, we must first look at the purpose of having a union catalog. A union catalog by definition is a catalog that lists the holdings of more than one library or collection. This is readily apparent in the existence and growth of the OCLC Online Union Catalog. This ever-growing union of the world's library catalogs is not only a reflection of the unity of libraries and peoples throughout the world, but a promise, now and of a future, where access to knowledge and information can be provided in any language, format or from any time period. This electronic catalog which is literally a world catalog can potentially be used by anyone who is trying to identify and locate an item that may not be in their library collection.

The uniqueness of this Online Union Catalog, as opposed to the collection at the Library of Congress for example, is that the Library of Congress is more of a repository of information and ideas, while the beauty of the OCLC Online Union Catalog is that anyone with a computer can find out where a particular item is located, especially if that library is in the same region or locality of the user. It has become the gateway for library patrons or anyone seeking information to not only access the vast collection of human knowledge in these libraries but as a step towards acquiring these items.

It is in a sense, analogous to the white- or yellow-pages where people are trying to find and locate friends, relatives, businesses, etc. In the same way, this Online Union Catalog is a resource where people can find their favorite books, ideas of interest, and other information sources anywhere in the world by being able to know the holdings of thousands of libraries around the world.

**Janet Colburn**
Sam Houston State University
Houston, TX

In this modern world of technological advances and expansion, no one entity represents the power of knowledge and information as does the OCLC Online Union Catalog. Over the past four years, I have called on OCLC to locate many different types of materials. I can say without a doubt that my expectations have always been exceeded.

One of the greatest benefits I find as a student is the ability to obtain information pertinent to my discipline. Although our library has an adequate amount of holdings for a university its size, the inventory is not exhaustive. There is no greater satisfaction for me than acquiring that one book or article without which my knowledge would be incomplete.

Additionally, as a library assistant in our interlibrary loan department at Sam Houston State University, the OCLC Online Union Catalog provides me with vital implements to carry out my everyday tasks. Our patrons depend on our department to secure their needed materials and I rely heavily on OCLC to help me locate every kind of publication. Helping patrons is the very essence of what we do in the library.

While the OCLC Online Union Catalog has opened up a whole new world for me in the educational and professional areas of my life, words cannot begin to express my gratefulness in terms of what it has accomplished on a personal level. Being the mother of two growing children is a challenging yet rewarding vocation. My daughter has been an avid reader for several years and my son learned to read two years ago. I have been able to share books with them this last year that I read in my childhood over *twenty-five years* ago! Most were books that urged a kind of personal growth and individual discovery that have remained dear in my memory. It was truly a delight I would have never known if the OCLC Online Union Catalog had not been able to locate those materials. I was truly amazed that any computer program could afford such access. The experience brought us closer together as a family. While the statistics on OCLC are favorably overwhelming, I am convinced that its ultimate impact cannot be measured in numbers or figures. The OCLC Online Union Catalog enhances lives.

## Bruce Connolly
Union College
Schenectady, NY

An apology...

As a reference librarian, whether working in a group instruction session or informally with a single student, the message that I try hardest to get across to library users is that they are not alone when they come into the library. We offer the people who come through our doors the opportunity to enter into a partnership—potentially, a very powerful one—in which we match our professional skills and our knowledge of library resources and services with their subject expertise (sometimes just emerging), their need to know, and their willingness to learn from us.

What I also try to communicate to our library users is the notion that their research efforts are in no way bound by the materials available just within the walls of our building. If they can identify a source that they think will further their research project, we can probably put that item into their hands. Libraries, like the people who use them, don't have to be alone.

When I talk with someone about this interdependence that libraries share with one another, I always imagine a stream of energy that flows from my library out across the map, lighting up the points along its route, branching off as it connects with one spot and then another, and rebounding finally to my own library again. I don't actually mention this pleasurable little vision to the person or group I'm working with, for a number of reasons (most of which probably don't need to be spelled out). What might be toughest to explain to someone outside the profession, though, is that the boldest, brightest beam of energy connects directly to Dublin, Ohio.

What does the OCLC Online Union Catalog mean to me? It's the foundation of virtually every service I attempt to provide. It makes nearly everything that I try to accomplish as a professional possible. I take it completely for granted. I remind technical services staff, who insist on talking in terms of "subfield a" and "variable-field formatting" and "dagger something," that they are in mixed company and that that kind of language is not proper. I'm not likely to change. And I apologize.

## Colleen M. Conway
Hope College
Holland, MI

I started library work as a college student in 1974 when I was awarded a job in the Cataloging Office as part of my financial aid package. One of my responsibilities was to receive card packs ordered from the Library of Congress and type the appropriate call numbers and tracings on them. It was here that I met my first electric eraser, and here that I decided that cataloging was a really stupid way to earn a living.

Then we got OCLC.

Since my supervisor treated students as a real resource and allowed us to learn as much as we could, I attended OCLC workshops and actually did retrospective conversions. Better yet, a machine in Ohio processed our card packs and I got to say good-bye to my friend the electric eraser. Cataloging no longer looked like a stupid way to earn a living.

After graduation I was hired by the same college library to manage, among other things, the Interlibrary Loan Office. I placed and filled loan requests using a teletype, typing up a list of what I wanted and hoping someone in the system could help me out. It was in this job that I learned the definition of obsolete machinery (the so-called repairman doesn't even know how to turn it on) and realized that libraries could be inefficient and frustrating places in which to earn a living.

Then we got OCLC for Interlibrary Loan.

Blind requests turned into requests to known owners. The equipment worked. Patrons were happier. My department was more efficient, and a library was starting to look like a cool place to work.

So I went to graduate school.

OCLC skills helped my grade in cataloging class. My OCLC experience helped me get a teaching assistantship. And I got my first job as a cataloger because I had experience with OCLC. It was in this job that I trained and supervised a work-study student who now works as a librarian for OCLC in Ohio.

Then I moved to Michigan. OCLC today is so much a part of the library landscape that my skills are no longer remarkable, in fact they are not even very up-to-date. But I have just finished serving a three-year term as a member of the Executive Board of the Michigan Library Consortium, partly because of my long history with OCLC.

So what does the OCLC Online Union Catalog mean to me? It has played a major role in shaping my career. Without OCLC I would never have chosen library service as a way to earn a living; nor would I have met many of the people I now call friends and colleagues. It has influenced my philosophy: share everything, re-invent nothing, always keep your equipment up-to-date, and remember that even the smallest player contributes something to the game. It may even shape my future. I intend to hang out in libraries for another 25 years, I just hope the OCLC Online Union Catalog will be there too.

## Jo Anne I. Cordis
Central Oregon Community College
Bend, OR

I am *Opal Whiteley: The Unsolved Mystery* written by E. S. Bradburne in 1962 and I live on a shelf in the library of Central Oregon Community College in Bend, Oregon. This has been my home since the mid-sixties when I was purchased. My early life was lonely, hardly ever leaving my home. Oh, a few times a student would check me out, but most of the time I just sat there.

My library joined OCLC in 1982. But because I was so old, my record was not included at this time, only new books were added. Then a most wonderful thing happened to me, changing my life forever. In 1989 my library went through a retrospective conversion and my record become known through the OCLC Online Union Catalog.

Through the Interlibrary loan subsystem, thousands of libraries are connected electronically. Using this system, a small public library in McMinnville, Oregon asked to borrow me in 1990. This was my first trip out of Central Oregon and into the beautiful Willamette Valley. I was cramped from sitting on that shelf for so long and it felt great to have someone reading my pages.

In 1991, a trip to the Oregon coast found me at Seaside Public Library and gave me my first breath of salt air. How I loved the beach! The Pierce County Library in Tacoma, Washington was my first venture outside the state of Oregon.

George Fox College in Newberg, Oregon has a beautiful campus and in 1992 a patron asked me to come there. This was my first visit to another college campus. The Online Union Catalog is opening the world to me.

1993 found me in McMinnville Public Library again. Perhaps my former patron told a friend about my story and said that I should be read and how easy it was to borrow me. Through the ILL system, anyone can request me from my home in Central Oregon. I also traveled to Ft. Vancouver Regional Library in Vancouver, Washington near the mighty Columbia River. My fame was spreading!

The following year was very busy for me. Again I traveled to Washington, this time to Sno-Isle Regional Library in Marysville. And within three months, I was out again. A patron at the North Central Regional Library in Wenatchee, Washington requested my presence. I remember the smell of apple blossoms in this area of central Washington. How I love this new life that the OCLC Online Union Catalog has given me!

The end of 1994 found me with a patron from Davis County Public Library in Farmington, Utah. I have traveled beyond the Pacific Northwest for the first time. What wonderful and exciting places would I visit next?

I was requested twice in 1995 for patrons at Lewis & Clark College in Portland, Oregon. They just couldn't get enough of me there! March of 1996 found me en route to the Ledding Library in Milwaukie, Oregon.

During the past six years, I have been read more than in all the previous years of my life; all due to the OCLC Online Union Catalog. Librarians call this resource sharing, but I call it my travel agency! I now have a social life and it has meant the world to me. There are only twenty-nine libraries in the United States owning my title. Although I am only one record among more than 33 million, I am one of the best. What a life!

## Alan Cordle
New Hanover County Public Library
Wilmington, NC

My first original record...

When my fiancée, Kathleen Halme, was offered a creative-writing professorship at the University of North Carolina at Wilmington I was happy to move to an old Southern, seacoast city, but I was concerned that this small place would not have many options for me. When I got to town, we married in an old church that was used as a stable for horses in the Civil War.

A librarian at New Hanover Public Library took a chance on hiring me as a cataloger; although I'd never had any cataloging experience, I had some library experience working in a huge microforms collection while earning my bachelor's degree. Although I was wary of the whole technical services scene and of OCLC in particular, I quickly became comfortable with performing copy cataloging.

Perhaps I grew too comfortable or I just got tired of the repetition, but I wanted to do some original cataloging. A year went by. Several staff turnovers prevented me from being trained, but something had to give!

Kathleen received good news: she had won a poetry contest that I'd encouraged her to enter, and as a result, her chapbook, *The Everlasting Universe of Things*, was published. She signed a copy for the library, and I told my boss, Charles May, that we could add it to the collection if I was allowed to catalog it. He had taught cataloging for SOLINET for many years, so he proved to be an excellent teacher. He helped me to create #31234869 for my wife's chapbook—my first original record.

I was learning a new skill and loving it—the precision and fussiness suited me more than I'd ever expected. Meanwhile, Kathleen received another call, the one she had been waiting for for ten years: The University of Georgia Press had accepted her full-length book of poetry for publication.

I was excited for her, because this was her dream: to be recognized for her hard work of creating and revising fine poems. Secretly, I was also excited because I thought I'd get to catalog *Every Substance Clothed*.

Then the letdown came. Charles told me that the DLC catalogers would probably catalog it. Well fine, I thought, but they won't come up with any good subject tracings like I did for her chapbook (Finnish Americans—Poetry). Sure enough, they created a pre-publication record, and when the book came out, I was on educational leave, completing my desperately-needed MLS.

As soon as I returned to work, I typed *EVE,SU,CL,* and pulled up the record. There were already over 50 holdings in libraries in the U.S. and Canada. It wasn't the book sales I was excited about; when all 1000 copies printed sell, her royalties will be about $200 total. Rather, I'm so pleased to know her work's being read and that I *could have* cataloged it if those darned DLC catalogers hadn't gotten to it first.

———————————— ⅋ ————————————

### Jane Cothron
Kansas City Public Library
Kansas City, MO

After I graduated with a sparkling new master's degree in Library Science, I went job hunting. Unlike medical doctors who come out of a training process which gives them a thorough grounding in both the theory and practice of their profession, schooling in library science concentrates on the theoretical. My first positions in the field were both part-time, one in the reference area of a community college library and the other as a cataloger in a special library.

At the reference desk I could discuss unusual questions, suggest resources, and ask for suggestions from the other more experienced librarians. As the only cataloger in the special library, however, I had to rely on cataloging textbooks, the OCLC database, and the *Bibliographic Formats and Standards* manual for information about cataloging. Searching the Online Union Catalog was an invaluable training tool: I could not only find existing records for much of the material, but achieved enough familiarity with the MARC records structures to begin creating original records.

Now, as one of four catalogers in a large urban public library, I have others with whom to explore ideas, try out new cataloging solutions, and talk over changes in cataloging styles and forms. Generally, though, after checking the system documentation and discussing the cataloging rules in AACR2, we fall back to discussions about how other institutions are handling the problems—how is everyone else doing it. The OCLC Online Union Catalog which contains over 35 million records is an excellent place to search out the ways information is kept in MARC fields. Using OCLC's database to retrieve and create records links me to the thousands of catalogers, both past and present, who worked to create the utility.

———————————— ⅋ ————————————

### Cathy Cottrell
Ericson Public Library
Boone, IA

**O**nline! What do Seattle, WA; Orange City, IA; Boone, IA; Dublin, OH and Libraries have in common? My experience with OCLC. I heard about OCLC while in high school in Seattle, attended Northwestern College in Orange City and saw how OCLC was used for interlibrary loans. I did not know that I would be at the Ericson Public Library in Boone for 13 years doing ILL on OCLC. I did not realize until now how new OCLC was (but of course it has to be because the use of computers and PC's was just beginning). I have witnessed OCLC growing to become what it is today. I realize that our library has a small number of ILL requests, compared to larger institutions, but having online access to materials for our patrons to borrow, with a database that most of the world has access to just by having a computer and modem, expands our library worldwide.

Connection! It is not only computers and modems that make the connection, it is the people that you meet and have contact with. The OCLC Users Group meetings help me use OCLC more efficiently. One nice Christmas surprise were the cards we received in December from libraries in Colorado thanking us for filling their requests.

Library! OCLC helps our Library be the information center of the community. Having FirstSearch available helps us answer more questions quicker, locate those hard-to-find journal articles and find latest company information for those with job interviews. Using OCLC makes getting the information quicker, and makes our cataloging effort simpler also. The Library is where a citizen comes and says, "you can do all that?" We are able to smile and say that we can, knowing that OCLC makes it all possible.

Cooperation! If I could I would thank all the libraries connected to OCLC. It is somewhat uncomfortable for librarians to send books around the country/world and expect they will come back. It takes an extra effort to look for requests and prepare them for shipping. I say "thank you" to OCLC for providing an opportunity to borrow items from other libraries and make patrons here in Boone excited that we found that book that was out-of-print or that article that was needed for research from a periodical that we did not have. To be able to say that we can request material for a patron makes serving the public easier. This is made possible by libraries saying "yes" to participating in interlibrary loans. The patrons at Ericson Public Library and I thank you!

———————————— ⁊ ————————————

**June M. Courtney**
Reading Public Library
Reading, PA

My first contact with OCLC came when I first took cataloging courses in both undergraduate school and later in graduate school. Upon receiving my master's, I worked for over twelve years as a reference librarian with very little use of OCLC. The OCLC terminals were always in the technical services or cataloging departments of libraries for which I worked. They were far away from the reference department and only used by the reference librarian responsible for interlibrary loan. I eventually became a backup to the interlibrary loan librarian and used OCLC whenever he or she was away from work to keep ILL going.

In 1991, I had the opportunity to become the head of a technical services department, and at that time the OCLC Online Union Catalog really came alive for me. As it had been years since I had done any cataloging work, I decided to go back to school and once again take cataloging courses. I enrolled at Drexel University and took the cataloging courses that seemed most relevant to my current situation. Cataloging courses taken while actually working as a cataloger help to bring practical experience to the learning situation. Everything made more sense as I could immediately see it at work. I once used to think that all I ever wanted to be was a reference librarian. I have always enjoyed the thrill and challenge of searching for and finding information. I now have also learned that I enjoy enabling one library's patrons to find books by cataloging them. I enjoy searching the OCLC Online Union Catalog—trying to find the right record and, if need be, creating the record to be placed in the OCLC catalog and shared with many.

OCLC, to me, has become a window to books everywhere. I can find a record to help me catalog a book and I can find other libraries who own the book. I can create a record for a book that is unique to my library, and help someone find a book anywhere in the United States, Canada and many other countries.

My desire for the future is to perfect my skills as a cataloger and to create more original cataloging records. OCLC gave me my first real chance to work daily with computers in libraries. Before there was an automated card catalog, there was searching on OCLC. It enabled the library to avoid the tedious typing of catalog cards and speed up their production by having OCLC send them to us.

Although today many things are automated, the OCLC Online Union Catalog is still there for us as we transfer those records to our automated system and do away with the card catalog. Unfortunately it has also eliminated many positions as automation now does that which once required many people. But although there are fewer jobs, there are still challenges there. We now must monitor the system for errors and improve the records we see.

The shape of the future has changed and the challenges have changed. We now need to catalog the Internet in addition to books, videos, films, audiocassettes, serials, computer files, multimedia, archival materials, sound recordings, scores and maps. To meet the future, I and many others will continue to use the OCLC Online Union Catalog and its educational opportunities to help us improve the quality of cataloging.

**Elizabeth S. Crosby**
Robert Packer Hospital
Sayre, PA

To those of us once groping our way and struggling with paperwork, OCLC is more than a helping hand. It is an essential element in today's world of technology. As a fairly new user and a latecomer in this new world, I am enjoying the challenge and having a great deal of **F*U*N**!

**F**ast............

To have within reach, a methodized system as this, which gives you the ability to get information as quickly as a few keystrokes is a real treat. We are able to proceed rapidly and glide along in progressive steps, almost unaware of how much we owe to the system.

**U**nique.........

OCLC provides us with a means of opening more widely, the resources of collections all over the world. I am impressed with the creativeness and originality that puts at our command the vast treasures of literature and the sciences. It certainly exceeds any preconceived notion I might have had when first introduced to it, and gives the sharing of information wings of flight.

**N**eed.........

Communication, no matter what form, cannot be acquired in any form of perfection, except by continued practice. My position requires that I have OCLC. I **need** this to succeed, and so I approached it with a positive attitude! I am reminded of a quote Lou Holtz, famed Notre Dame coach, "Ability is what you're capable of doing. Motivation determines what you do. Attitude determines how well you do it." To the unpracticed, it is often a case of attitude.

Ready accessibility of the multitude of information available is essential today. Indeed, who can appreciate the real extent of the efficiency of OCLC except those of us who use it daily.

**Jetta Carol Culpepper**
Murray State University Libraries
Murray, KY

The OCLC Online Union Catalog has significantly influenced three areas in this regional academic library: cataloging, interlibrary loans, and acquisitions. To report this, let's go back to the 1970s but not for nostalgia. A glance into the paper slinging and work-intensive environment of these departments reveals partially how OCLC has changed librarianship. In response, library management turned to a new emphasis. Several careers were reshaped when teaching of orientation classes and offering patrons greater accessibility to information became the real world and no longer a dream. The library, sometimes referred to as the "storehouse of knowledge," gravitated toward becoming a more welcoming and outgoing facilitator in the educational process.

I recall working in the cataloging department of the Murray State University library. A half-dozen students and two clerks worked frantically to alphabetize and file thousands of the Library of Congress proof slips. The clang and rattle of those metal trays echoed across the lower floor of the library as another half-dozen students and a clerk speedily searched for specific slips to be photocopied on catalog card paper stock. Across the bibliography room, a third pool of workers searched volumes of the *National Union Catalogs*. Their fingers hurt as they used lead pencils to hastily copy cataloging entries on 5" by 7" notepads.

In the cataloging department, four catalogers assigned call numbers and checked work for errors in copying entries or pulling proof slips. Breaks afforded time to write original comprehensive catalog entries for thousands of resources not otherwise cataloged. This work was passed to typists whose endurance exceeded that of the typewriters. The pace and near assembly line style of work were monitored for quality and quantity of output. Patrons needed better access to a backlog of unprocessed acquisitions. Interlibrary loan and acquisitions personnel walked circles around the card catalog as they carefully checked holdings before completing their respective ordering routines.

What did OCLC do to change this laborious and stressful environment? The OCLC Online Union Catalog enabled the phasing out of proof slips and the *National Union Catalogs* as sources of cataloging. Less original cataloging was necessary. Reclassification of holdings into the Library of Congress system would have taken many decades without OCLC. The OCLC records in this institution are presently utilized in the local online public access catalog (OPAC).

Competition with the public for standing space while waiting for card trays at the catalog stopped. Interlibrary loan personnel simultaneously search holdings of this and other libraries on the OCLC Catalog. Acquisitions personnel check the OPAC from terminals in their department.

Librarians who previously would have been assigned to these departments are teaching library orientation, maintaining a continuous reference service, making collection analyses, and giving tours.

Welcome to the Murray State University library. Librarians teach research and learning skills which open doors to the values of the collection. Patrons may gain access to holdings files in other libraries. We are glad to help you. Do you have a question?

———————————— ⚓ ————————————

**Patrick S. Daly**
Western Maryland College
Westminster, MD

Comprehensive. If one had to describe the OCLC Online Union Catalog in a single word, I cannot think of a word more fitting than "comprehensive." With more than 35 million bibliographic records spanning 4,000 years of recorded knowledge, the OCLC Online Union Catalog has easily become the largest database of its kind. To me, this means that OCLC represents the most reliable reference tool available. Having this immense database available literally at my fingertips has proven invaluable to both me and our library patrons. Because I work in interlibrary loan, I receive a variety of reference questions. I've developed a mantra in responding to those questions: "If we don't own it, I can tell you who does." For the students who have waited until the last minute (students don't do that, do they?) and thus do not have the time to wait for an interlibrary loan, having the holdings information available is indispensable. I simply direct them to a nearby library that has the material they need. Of course, OCLC has become an integral part of my job in other ways as well. For those pesky faculty members who ask for books written by 19th century German existentialist philosophers (in German!), OCLC once again comes through like a true champion. With three simple keystrokes, I am told which ONE library in the world actually owns the book. I do not even know where I would BEGIN to find this information were it not for OCLC. Quite simply, the OCLC Online Union Catalog is composed of an abundance of priceless information. Like so many of those books for which OCLC has bibliographic records, the OCLC Online Union Catalog breathes a life of its own. It does much more than make my job easier; the catalog makes my job POSSIBLE. For these reasons, I say THANK YOU, OCLC!

## LeAnn Lindquist Dean
University of Minnesota, Morris
Morris, MN

Contemplation of the role that the OCLC Online Union Catalog plays in my professional life as a librarian brings to mind three metaphors—gateway, key, and bridge. I continue to be as excited about the online catalog now as I was over twenty years ago when I first viewed this electronic wonder. Here was the gateway from the collection and library at hand to the resources of the world! It was not an obscure gateway characterized by the twists, turns, and obstacles encountered in searching print union catalogs and bibliographies, but one straightforward listing accessible from a machine on my desk. It took me from the "here and now" to the "there and possible." In another sense, the Online Union Catalog was the key to quality and consistency in collection records management. In addition to providing a gateway for finding what other libraries owned, it provided a methodology to make a local collection more useable by enhancing the quality of its records. This was true, first, in the case of printed paper card records, and later, for electronic records. Thirdly, the Online Union Catalog provided a bridge from information at hand in an immediate physical sense, to information available ten miles or ten thousand miles away. The bridge spanned gulfs of physical distance, time, technical sophistication, and format.

All of the metaphorical allusions point to one assertion. The Online Union Catalog was a pioneer effort in overcoming barriers—barriers to good service on a local level and to the exchange of information on a national and global level. This affected me personally on two levels as well. On the immediate level, it provided efficient methodology of finding information—specific bibliographic and location information that was accurate and easily available. On another level, however, the existence of this powerful tool over the course of the past twenty years, played a role in my "sense of self" as a librarian. I could do a better job of cataloging, selecting resources, providing reference service, providing interlibrary loan service, and managing a library. In that sense, the OCLC Online Union Catalog was not just a gateway, a key, or a bridge to information. It played a role in overcoming the gulf between the librarian I was and the librarian I strived to be. Thus, the OCLC Online Union Catalog has played a significant role in my life and the life of other librarians over the course of the last twenty-five years. The past-tense approach is misleading, however. It is just as exciting to contemplate what its role will be in the future, for it is not a stagnant endeavor, but has changed and continues to change. It will play a dominant role in the future as well in the lives of all of us who are engaged in the process of transforming information into knowledge.

## John Allen Delivuk
Geneva College
Beaver Falls, PA

To me, the OCLC Online Union Catalog means joy and efficiency. I enjoy cataloging accurately and efficiently. The OCLC Online Union Catalog helps me by making available the world's largest online database of cataloging records. It contains authority records to help me catalog accurately. In addition, OCLC constantly works to improve the database and make it more accurate. Thanks to the OCLC Online Union Catalog, I can catalog accurately and efficiently in less time.

I enjoy helping students and faculty. The Union Catalog adds to the joy of my reference work. Because of FirstSearch, I can provide subject access to millions of books and other materials that are of great help to students, faculty and the wider community. It adds to the joy by giving me more resources to meet the needs of library users. Within seconds, I can find information on almost any book title and most audiovisual titles and order them via interlibrary loan.

The OCLC cataloging database gives me the joy of sharing with other librarians. No longer do I catalog merely for one library. Instead, by original cataloging and enriching records with contents notes and Library of Congress classification numbers, I have the pleasure of helping other libraries throughout the world to build better databases. These improved databases help library patrons.

The Online Union Catalog gives me the joy of dependable technology. An excellent computer software and telecommunications system distributes the OCLC Online Union Catalog. OCLC's system has very few breakdowns, performs quickly and effectively, and usually communicates flawlessly with the local equipment.

The cataloging system has increased my joy by decreasing my drudgery. Because it has made local automated catalogs possible, it has eliminated the tedious task of proofing cards, filing cards and checking filing. OCLC has further helped by its excellent telephone support. I find that support normally answers my technical and cataloging questions quickly and accurately. I like the OCLC staff not only for their technical efficiency, but also for the relationships that I have developed with some OCLC staff, especially Kathy Kie, the Independent representative.

The OCLC Online Union Catalog has added to the joy of my scholarship. I have used the catalog to find and borrow rare resources that I needed to improve the exactness and range of my scholarly research.

Finally, the OCLC catalog gives me the joy of gratitude. Experience has taught me that work is hard. When others make my job easier and better, it is because they have worked hard to make it easier. Thousands of persons have worked and continue to work to make the OCLC Online Union Catalog a fast, effective, dependable system for cataloging, reference and interlibrary loan. Allow me to convey my sincerest thanks to all of you for making my job easier and more fun.

## Emmett Denny
State Library of Florida
Tallahassee, FL

Long before our present concept of the information superhighway, I was employed as a library technical assistant at Florida State University. My responsibilities included proofreading records before they were produced in the OCLC Online Union Catalog. As a recent library school graduate, I was aware of the global nature of OCLC. In retrospect, the OCLC catalogers working in the early 1980s were pioneers of a technological movement that would bring about a global bibliographic network with the capability of providing instantaneous dissemination. When we pressed our produce or update keys, we were creating and sharing with OCLC members an electronic synopsis of man's written, visual and/or spoken output of recorded knowledge.

Today, at the State Library of Florida, I am creating OCLC records for databases, electronic journals, government documents and computer software. The State Library of Florida's contribution to the lofty goal of universal bibliographic control falls primarily in the domain of state government documents. Our catalogers are providing librarians, researchers, and scholars all over the world information about what is being published by the state government of Florida. As we continue to catalog and produce our retrospective holdings in the OCLC Online Union Catalog, we are providing valuable information on the historical evolution of Florida government.

This ability of the OCLC cataloging system to describe and disseminate information in a uniform and logical manner continues to impress me. When I observe one of my bibliographic records being accepted into the OCLC Online Union Catalog, I am proud that my work is part of the total record of this enormous database. And although my records are literally at times a bleep on a computer screen, I can liken myself to a late twentieth-century version of the anonymous scribe that toiled during ancient and medieval times.

I believe that one day historians will examine the evolution of databases to get a sense of what was being discovered and learned by society during specific periods of time. As we move inexorably toward bibliographic record number 40 million, I am satisfied that my contribution to this output is permanently retained much like those who chiseled the hieroglyphs on the temples of ancient Egypt. This internal feeling of satisfaction is why I strive for the highest standards of quality in every record I enter into the OCLC Online Union Catalog.

My continuing, yet anonymous presence in the building of the OCLC Online Union Catalog makes me a ghost in the machine. Perhaps only a cataloger can understand why this gives me a tremendous feeling of accomplishment. Creating bibliographic records for OCLC makes me an active participant in the international information community.

### Edward Dodds
Disciples of Christ Historical Society
Nashville, TN

I appreciate the fact that the OCLC Online Union Catalog makes millions of books available worldwide to persons who otherwise would not have access to material which can be lifechanging. However, in my personal situation, the OCLC Union Catalog is important because the process established in order to enter the Disciples of Christ Historical Society holdings has become the backbone of advances into technology based library and archival practices.

One of the most significant religious collections in American Protestantism, the Disciples of Christ Historical Society was founded in 1941 for the purpose of gathering, preserving, and making available the large trove of materials relating to various early 19th Century reform groups stemming from the work of Thomas and Alexander Campbell and Barton Stone; namely, the Christian Church (Disciples of Christ), the Christian Churches and Churches of Christ.

Since its inception the Disciples of Christ Historical Society has encouraged the creation, publication, and dissemination of accurate historical materials by means of the maintenance of the world's largest collected library and archives of Campbell-Stone Movement materials consisting of 33,800 volumes; 17,000 biographical files; 10,000 congregational records; 1,000 audiovisual items; personal paper collections; and nearly a dozen unique indices including a 400,000 card catalog. The participation in the OCLC Union Catalog made the Society's library available internationally. Because of the successful precedent of the OCLC electronic catalog, utilization of electronic mail and the establishment of a World Wide Web home page to provide rapid information turnaround have been undertaken.

Yet many of the patrons of the Disciples of Christ Historical Society library cannot personally access our archival holdings; they cannot at present view an index without visiting our facilities' card catalog. Because many of the churches we serve are halfway around the world from Nashville, this is a practical impossibility for most. However, since OCLC can provide MARC records which can be specialized at our institution, our Board has supported the efforts of the staff to pursue an on-site electronic catalog which will be coupled to an Internet server making an index available to many who otherwise would be unaware of the riches contained in our holdings. Perhaps one day we may even be able to digitize and deliver via E-mail—because of our OCLC Union Catalog experience, we are not afraid to dream.

## Wan Ab. Kadir Bin Wan Dollah
University of Malaya
Kuala Lumpur, Malaysia

OCLC is an acronym of "Online Computer Library Center," originally known as Ohio College Library Center when it was first conceived in 1967. OCLC Online Union Catalog, which is the essence of OCLC services, began operation in 1971.

Since OCLC came into existence, it has offered a wide range of services including a source for cataloging, reference services, interlibrary loan, retrospective conversion and union listing.

The implementation of the Integrated Computerised Library System at the University of Malaya (ILMU) in 1992 has given me the opportunity to make use of online facilities in my library operations. The use of OCLC ensures productivity and enhances work flow, as well as improving user services. During the past few years, it cannot be denied that OCLC products and services have given me more value for my money. Since it is a nonprofit membership organization, the services offered are charged at a minimum rate.

It is very meaningful for me to deal with the OCLC Online Union Catalog because I can increase access to information without increasing library costs. It provides me with a huge bibliographic database and library information networks worldwide. As of June 30, 1995, there were a total of 31,126,380 records in various formats covered in the OCLC Online Union Catalog, which gives me an excellent success rate for cataloging. I can find about 90 percent of any catalog records in OCLC Online Union Catalog, which can save a lot of time when doing original cataloging. In short, OCLC can increase cataloging efficiency where it can affect the effectiveness of the University of Malaya Library as a whole.

OCLC cataloging services also can increase my staff's productivity where OCLC cataloging library have moved to PRISM service. PRISM characteristics offer keyword searching, full-screen editing, improved response time, searching capabilities and the ability to extract bibliographic records into our local system.

Furthermore, it can reduce staff training, where the staff is able to learn from the screen and not from training institutions that require higher expenditures as well as being time-consuming.

My library also can maintain a high quality of records for materials available, since OCLC records are of uniformly high standards. AACR rules and US-MARC coding practices are followed to ascertain the quality of records.

OCLC Online Union Catalog is a very useful tool for me as a librarian, in order to provide effective library services. I can conclude that the silver anniversary of OCLC Online Union Catalog is the celebration of cooperation and commitment for all, particularly for those involved in library and information services.

**Kirk Doran**
Shenandoah University
Winchester, VA

The OCLC Online Union Catalog exemplifies sharp contrasts between our human accomplishments and limitations. The Catalog stores more diversity with more uniformity than any other bibliographic database. Without it, the world's library materials would be dissipated among thousands of isolated catalogs, unknown and inaccessible to most people. We have designed hardware and software that far exceed the power of our brains to organize or remember data. We cannot even conceptualize the 35 million records in the OCLC Online Union Catalog, let alone fathom all the works they represent. Yet, without human creativity, a trait computers sorely lack, the database would have nothing to represent.

The OCLC Catalog's representational nature reminds us that computers were originally used to automate traditional library jobs. But now, computer networks are spearheading a huge paradigm shift toward merging full-text and multimedia with bibliographic databases. Following the lead of the 856 field's link to electronic sources, other fields of MARC records may cease to merely represent the card catalog tracings of the past, and become direct links to actual sources. The OCLC Online Union Catalog is both a framework for theoretical control and a gateway to substantive access. But the largest bibliographic utility worldwide is thus far dwarfed by what it does not contain. Despite the sleekest streamlining of automation, cataloging is still a time-consuming chore for human intellect. Computers are poor at interpreting content, making lateral leaps, identifying relationships between ideas, and defining "aboutness." Cataloging everything in the world's libraries, let alone making all texts, images, and sounds available online, is a daunting race against time and deterioration in the face of an unprecedented J-curve in information output.

The evolution of the OCLC Online Union Catalog mirrors the evolution of MARC records, fighting fiercely the limitations of bibliographic control. The confines of language to describe content persist despite exhaustive authority work. Hidden misspellings thwart the most ingenious keyword searches. The univocal results of classification force restrictive decisions. Quotes, pictures, and tunes elude the MARC record's descriptive abilities. Even some of the longest serial records lack adequate subject headings. Here is a seam where the boundaries of MARC records meet the coverage of periodical indexes, indexes that are listed in the records' 510 fields. Why not create a link between them?

Apart from its potential for more expansive networking, the OCLC Online Union Catalog is already an incomparable reference tool that allows billions of different keyword searches. When we respond creatively to reference questions with our own questions for the Catalog, it can deliver the most elusive answer. Cataloging on OCLC, however, is less exciting. MARC records remain cluttered, unappealingly single-spaced, machine-looking entities, stuffed with codes whose sometimes unsearchable surfeit defies common sense. Simplification and clarity would benefit all librarians.

Finally, the OCLC Online Union Catalog contrasts our lasting heritage with our mortality. It is a monument to humanity's boundless imagination and the fleeting existence of each individual. It can locate in seconds more than one person could read or absorb in a lifetime. It is a metaphor for our transcultural and multilingual global community, and symbolic of our separate lives, imperfect and incomplete, but always striving.

———————————— *⸙* ————————————

## Shirley Dorman
Ohio University
Athens, OH

OCLC Online Union Catalog means to me that it's the world's largest and most comprehensive database of bibliographic information, containing the merged catalogs of libraries around the world, and serving in 370 different languages. OCLC makes available to libraries and their patrons resources that no single library could possess.

OCLC establishes, maintains, and operates a computerized library network and promotes the evolution of library use, of libraries themselves, and of librarianship, and provides processes and products for the benefit of library users and library patrons, and reduces the rate of rise of library per-unit costs. This global network provides a worldwide flow of information for libraries and their users.

From statistics, I can see the growth of OCLC: 1994 was another record-breaking year for OCLC in almost every category from membership to system use to financials. Since 23 years ago, OCLC has grown from 54 academic libraries in Ohio to more than 23,000 libraries in 63 countries and territories.

I have enjoyed searching on PRISM; it is the most heavily used cataloging and resource-sharing system in the world; my working in a library really can put this to good use.

———————————— *⸙* ————————————

## Scott Downing
East Texas State University Library
Commerce, TX

(With apologies to T.S. Eliot)

> O. C. Elsie, the union cat, the PURRfect online friend
> Of I-L-L librarians, who borrow and who lend.
> "Page up (F5) page down (F4)" the I-L-Ler's wail,
> "Either check the union lists or be thrown in jail."

> Both borrower and lender be.
> I hope they do not charge a fee.
> But if they do my IFM
> Will speed my payment back to them.

O. C. Elsie, the electronic cat, resides inside her electronic house.
Before she can logon today she must FirstSearch for her mouse.

"Produce and send and IFM" the I-L-Ler's roar.
With the OCLC cat, watch their fill rates soar.
3,2,2,1 can be such fun, and 4,4, has its place.
Just some of the many ways to search this database.

Produce and send, again and again.
GOB, BAC, and FOR and order one more.
"Oh database, oh interface," the I-L-Ler's shout.
O. C. Elsie, the union cat is there to help them out.
Mccavity, the mystery cat, can be anywhere.
But when an I-L-Ler calls, Elsie is right there!

**Suzanne du Vair**
Wisconsin Department of Natural Resources Research Library
Monona, WI

The OCLC Online Union Catalog is fast becoming one of the most important information resources in the world. Just as we must preserve our natural resources in order to maintain quality of life on earth, so we must preserve our human heritage. Rich cultural experiences provide a foundation for creativity in the "global village." Access to information and ideas was once very difficult due to lack of telecommunications and lack of electronic data storage. Now, with the assistance of databases such as the OCLC Catalog, people all over the world are able to tap into and to help create a "global culture." The fact that the Catalog "spans 4,000 years of recorded knowledge in 370 languages" proves this point vividly.

Having worked in interlibrary loan for the past four years, I understand the tremendous need for resource sharing. No one can own every available bit of information, or necessarily access it either, but if we are to improve the lot of humans, we must learn to share what we know so that we can find out what we want to know. The OCLC Online Union Catalog provides much-needed information about all kinds of subjects in a variety of media. Because we use one medium does not mean that another is no longer viable. Print and electronic media can and do coexist. They enhance each other. This is important to note because different countries develop at different rates and, in many cases, their forms of communication are affected by their national economies.

Often, researchers are looking for esoteric items that aren't always available for purchase through most commercial vendors. Sometimes all the researchers really want is an accurate citation, publisher information or a list of holdings. With its wealth of information, this is where the OCLC Catalog comes in. It's fast. It's efficient. It's borderless. (It also makes library workers look good.) New modifications by OCLC, such as ILL fee management and pre-cataloging information for new acquisitions, make it easier to maintain accuracy in library work. Alliance with the Internet creates a wider audience for the Catalog and for OCLC products in general.

In conclusion, the OCLC Online Union Catalog remains a reliable resource for people who are highly specialized in their work, or for people who are simply curious. By meeting the needs of more people in more places, the OCLC Online Union Catalog has a bright future indeed.

**Linda F. Dyke**
Bucks County Free Library
Doylestown, PA

Ode to the OCLC Online Union Catalog...

> Chorus (essayed by the author and fellow DPB Technical Services cataloguers):
>
> We love you, OCLC, for your authors and your books,
> For your /vis and /rec -prompt searches, for your DLC input;
> When our bosses and our patrons load us down with stuff to add,
> Your resources let us tackle the most arcane doodad.

### I. The Materials

> Bill Gates' new CD-ROM, Frommer's latest title change,
> Granny's vintage Fanny Farmer, the vicar's history of the Grange,
> K-Mart's marked-down children's flicks, our fav'rite rock group's first CD,
> And, of course, the many "Gov docs" sent to our deposit'ry.

> Chorus (as above)

### II. The Librarians

> Our patrons keep us hopping, with their needs and with their gifts,
> And woe betide us if our service is anything but swift;
> We're out here on the front line, where all the action is—
> Thank God for OCLC, " 'cause it helps our Techies whiz."

> Chorus (as above)

### III. Interlibrary Loan

> We sail daily through the waters of the wide OCL-Sea,
> Where we use its finding aids to track our patrons' every need;
> From a college out in Texas to a lender in Peru,
> Our want lists cross the ether and their wishes soon come true.

> Chorus (as above)

IV. The Patrons

We're the stuff libr'ies are built on—their reason and their rhyme,
And we count on them to get us our materials on time;
We know nothing of the Techies, or the folks in ILL,
You say **OCLC** makes it work? Then we wish the buggers well!

Chorus (as above)

## Valerie Edmonds
Mercer University
Macon, GA

**OCLC means all the world to me!** As a reference librarian, heavily involved in library instruction, I talk about the vast amount of information to be found through OCLC to over 3000 students every year, yet I still find it difficult to fully comprehend all of the cooperative work it has taken, and continues to take, to produce this rich database. OCLC opens up the world to allow all of us to know about books and other cataloged items that can be found in libraries not only in the U.S. but in so many other places in the world.

I started my library career as a para-professional managing periodicals. The practical applications of OCLC, verifying titles, tracing title changes, and updating records were very valuable to me then. When I entered graduate school, I was able to get permission to take my cataloging class at the Mercer library, getting hands-on experience under the tutelage of our cataloger Miriam Hudgins. Miriam taught me the intricacies of original cataloging and even allowed me to process two original records. I don't think any other experience would have enabled me to gain as much respect as I have for the integrity of OCLC records.

As my professional career progressed, I served for two years as Interlibrary Loan librarian where I learned firsthand how essential OCLC is to this remarkable library service. I often wonder how many people know that books and periodical articles can be borrowed from all over the U.S. and the world at minimal cost. I remember the first time I requested a book from a European library and received it. This communication affirmed that others in faraway places share interests and concerns with us. Our relatively small library sometimes receives requests from foreign countries letting us know that items in our collection are of value to them. And how do librarians locate all these treasures? Through OCLC!

Perhaps the most important part of my career is as reference librarian and teacher because it allows me to pass on what I know about finding and selecting the material which, if chosen wisely and studied carefully, can lead to wisdom and learning. OCLC can eliminate the restrictions of space and time that used to force scholars to spend hours, days and sometimes years traveling the world to find the library material they needed for their research. OCLC is the incredible system that can bring the world of knowledge to all who wish to explore it.

## Jerri R. Eldridge

University of Missouri—Columbia
Columbia, MO

As a regular user of the OCLC Online Union Catalog, its services are of great value to me, primarily as it relates to my job at the University of Missouri—Columbia Ellis Library. I am currently the theses/dissertation cataloger for the library at the university. It is my job to check theses/dissertations and to catalog according to AACR2 rules. As part of my job, I also assign subject headings to our theses/dissertations. Since Library of Congress subject headings do not relate consistently with theses/dissertation subject matter, I rely heavily on the OCLC Online Union Catalog for searching of related subject matter that may be used for these manuscripts. My careful selection of subjects for the theses/dissertations prove to be of great value to our patrons since our theses/dissertations are heavily used by faculty and students. Without good subject accessibility, the manuscripts would prove to be of little use.

I also use the online catalog for searching records for cataloging of DLC copy, authority checking and verifying, and previously in another position used it for subject authority control at the University.

I value OCLC Online Union Catalog very much. It helps greatly in my work and gives me a feeling of satisfaction, knowing the records that I input are good, accurate records not only for the accessibility of our faculty, staff and students but for others as well, who may need access to related works. It is hard to imagine life without the Online Union Catalog. I'm sure there are quite a few people who use it daily, whose work depends greatly on it and its accessibility makes all cataloging much better.

## Jo Anne C. Ellis

Central New York Library Resources Council
Syracuse, NY

The word I most often use to describe the OCLC Online Union Catalog is "magic." To anyone who, like me, remembers what interlibrary loan and technical services were like before OCLC, this is hardly an exaggeration. (Okay, here she goes again…pushing book trucks twelve miles uphill in a blinding snowstorm…)

Interlibrary loan used to be based as much on guesswork as on actual identification of holding libraries. If you were lucky you'd find locations in *National Union Catalog* or another etched-in-stone reference tool. Of course, you wouldn't know if a lender still *had* the item until you typed an ALA form and sent it off with childlike optimism. Often you'd need to repeat the process all the time thinking that there must be a better way.

In the mid-70s, I met the better way. The technical services staff, as sick of typing catalog cards as I was fed up with ALA forms, installed an OCLC workstation, and the ILL staff got to use it—for one hour a day. Impossible! How could we do in an hour what took two people much of the day?

I learned to search the Online Union Catalog, originally created by the Ohio College Library Consortium. With the database opened up to libraries around the country, people wouldn't have to re-invent so many wheels with original cataloging. Our library added its symbol to a record and magically ordered catalog cards for our 30 members—no more typing and duplicating thousands of card sets a year!

The first holdings displays were, by today's standards, unsophisticated and unwieldy. The symbols were not arranged by state or in alphabetical order. Search keys gave limited access points. Still, the giant leap forward was pure, grade-A magic. I think this must have been the way early audiences saw the first movies: not with the jaded view that the technology needed to he improved, but with wonder that the effect could be accomplished at all.

When I returned to ILL in 1990, I was amazed that the database was so much bigger, with more languages and formats represented than I remembered. The holdings were arranged in a more user-friendly way, and it was now possible to translate a cataloging record into an ILL request sent to five libraries, with a few keystrokes!

When I became a cataloger for my consortium, I continued to marvel at the scope and the richness of the OCLC Online Union Catalog. Our members' specialized holdings range from medical festschrifts to histories of funeral customs. I usually find even the most unusual titles in the catalog. If I can't find an exact match, there's almost always a record that's close enough to model a new record on.

The OCLC Online Union Catalog is an example of cooperative cataloging in every sense of the word. The willingness of catalogers to share their records with the world confirms my long-held belief: What helps one library helps all libraries.

**Luis J. Escobar**
Colorado State University
Fort Collins, CO

When I work on the OCLC Online Union Catalog, two images of Alexander the Great come to my mind. The first is the regard ancient scholars had for this man, out of gratitude and admiration for his founding the Great Library of Alexandria in Egypt. OCLC is to the modern scholar what the Great Library at Alexandria was to ancient scholars. As such, the OCLC Online Union Catalog is a monumental milestone in the history of human learning and knowledge.

In our rise to global preeminence our nation has not only developed into a prosperous community, it has also accumulated the greatest store of wisdom in history. No culture has ever paid such tribute to the value of learning as has the United States, a value which is evident in even the humblest of college libraries of this nation. Incredibly, as if this were not enough, OCLC gathers into one the individually magnificent libraries of the United States. In conjunction with the Interlibrary Loan system (another magnificent communal achievement!) American and visiting scholars at the most parochial of learning institutions have the Great Library of the United States at their fingertips.

OCLC will also always be for me a romantic and philosophical experience. As I examine the record of a volume unique to the Library of Congress, I cannot help but remember Thomas Jefferson donating his library to the American people after the War of 1812. In the course of compiling a bibliography of European paintings destroyed in the World Wars, I cannot help thinking of the cultural and scholarly treasures encountered by American soldiers on the battlefields of Europe, Africa, Asia, and Latin America. When I come across the record of a CIA *Who's Who in North Vietnam*, I cannot help thinking of the somber reports of our intelligence agencies and diplomats, documenting the ravages of the Cold War across our hapless globe. But also, I cannot help but reflect upon the tender sentiments of scholars around the globe, exchanging learned tomes as tokens of good will—often defying the official hostility of national antagonisms—which I, an unknown graduate student, may then scrutinize and savor in the quiet sanctuary of my university library.

The other Alexandrine image which comes to my mind when consulting OCLC is the legend of the Gordian knot. When Alexander cut the fabled Gordian knot, he is said to have wept, for he believed that he had conquered the entire world, and there was nothing left to conquer. So too have I, in my scholarly lust for knowledge, entertained the conceited dissatisfaction of exhausting human knowledge regarding a particular subject in OCLC. "Is that all?" I mumble at OCLC's computer display. OCLC may be the stack pass to the Great Library of the United States, but it will still not get me into the national archives of Paraguay, or the files of the Chinese police in Tibet. For such arcane challenges, I will have to tear myself away from OCLC's computer display.

———————————— ❦ ————————————

## Robert H. Estep
Rice University
Houston, TX

Although I began cataloging at an OCLC-free institution, I was nevertheless aware of its dragon-like presence and horizonless ethos from the very beginning, having heard tales of the glorious occasion of its birth (attendant pangs and all) from the veterans among my comrades. That they missed their old friend was evident, for these anecdotes were often delivered with the merest hint of nostalgic tears moistening their eyes.

When I left to come to Rice, I was therefore eager to hear more concerning this OCLC creature. I was promptly chastised for an insufficiently reverential tone of inquiry. I suppose my gaffe was tantamount to asking, "Does your grandmother still cheat at mah-jong?" At any rate, my neophyte's ignorance was deemed forgivable and thus, on the morning that Fondren Library hove into view, I was well-armed with rumors, old-timers' advice, thrice-blessed medallions for tribute and garlands of garlic just in case.

After a quick jotting of passwords, commands (pleas, threats) and with an admirable Ariadne peering over my shoulder, I was free to explore.

\* \* \*

Now, one of the more curious affectations I have grown fond of in librarians of long acquaintance is the excessive anthropomorphizing of anything (objects, concepts) having to do with technology. Their own workspaces, for instance. Far from being ergonomic modules shuttling them into the spookily hygienic future, they more often resemble a seething parliament of opinionated, contentious demigods and goddesses. Some benevolent, sweet-tempered, soft-witted, spectacularly powerful. Others secretive, sullen, hostile, malevolent. All in all, a sort of doll's house clash of titans.

* * *

Five years later, I realize that I have begun to cultivate a similar affectation.

Namely, that OCLC is a city. A somewhat medieval city. Late 13th-century, say, happily untouched by disaster (although denominational skirmishes and fratricidal muggings buzz the air like pollen in prime season). A city, like any other, built by mortals yet curiously designed to be deathless. Inhabitants as diverse as imagination allows. Ancients living beside newborns, all waiting to be admired or mocked but, above all, waiting to be used.

A sleepless city with neither center nor outskirts, where the agents of feudal factions venture out solo, forever encroaching on each other's turf, their household graffito daubed on far-flung 040s. A city crawling with magpies and thieves, searching for what they need and, upon finding it, claiming it, carrying its ghost away to be tickled, molded, clipped, or stretched to their own obscure and delicate liking.

There is a perpetual playfulness to what is, if not deadly serious, certainly no laughing matter. A rivalry from neighborhood to neighborhood, with the ever-changing orthodoxies of "trust no one" versus "when in Rome..." Thus, there is grudging respect or outright awe upon discovering some wild treasure neatly and accurately display-cased. And, though few will admit it, there is also much merriment to be made at the expense of one's neighbors and their occasional missteps. Never forgetting, of course, that one cataloger's shack is another's palace.

And the city's off-switch? A pleasant illusion. It never sleeps.

───────────── ℳ ─────────────

## Kim Eunju
Korean Educational Development Institute
Seoul, Korea

During our life, we meet many new things continuously. Sometimes they provide us various experiences whether it is valuable or not.

The process of meeting between OCLC and I is not only the meeting of another experience but also the meeting of another colleague beyond space and time. The process of meeting with the OCLC Online Union Catalog database is a similar process of human development.

When our library prepared for library automation, we needed a system to input our bibliographic data. I think that most librarians will be faced with a similar situation to perform the library automation for their own library. Especially, constructing the retrospective database is a really heavy load to librarians.

At that time, I heard about CAT CD450 from my professor and I recommended it to my boss for saving time and effort to key in the data. So we downloaded from your data to cumulate our database. It was very useful to us. It is the first time to meet OCLC.

And then OCLC helped us input the no-hit record of our library by the MICROCON service. Then we began to participate in the PRISM service for online cataloging of our new materials.

Nowadays we prepare for sailing the sea of INFORMATION called OCLC. From the sea, we will get many fluent resources and much valuable information. There is another "global village" in the OCLC Online Union Catalog.

As we meet with our colleagues every morning in the same office, we can meet our colleagues who work all over the world through the database. The OCLC database is not owned by OCLC but owned by all participants. Therefore we have to think that the development and enrichment of the database is in charge of all the participants... because the development of OCLC is the development of ourselves.

As if I heard about all the services of OCLC from my professor, I teach university students about the library corporation including the automation. Now I talk about OCLC's activities and services with my students so they will meet OCLC.

**Tatiana Falk**
University of Michigan
Ann Arbor, MI

I'm an assistant in the interlibrary loan office of a major research university library. As impressive as our collection is, our three-person borrowing operation still receives well over 20,000 requests each year for material that our library system doesn't own. Our access to the holdings of the OCLC Online Union Catalog means that I can do my job!

OCLC is our "first resort" source for over 90% of the materials our patrons order. We are able to fill the vast majority of these requests from OCLC member libraries. Rapid service is our patrons' primary concern, and the OCLC Online Union Catalog enables us to serve them quickly. It's easy for me to locate records for patrons' materials because there are so many ways to search. The new custom holdings display has helped us to save time. We have several reciprocal agreements with other university libraries across the country. The rapid display of our chosen partners' holdings allows for quick selection of an appropriate lender string.

The cooperative attitude of the libraries who create the records in the catalog, combined with their willingness to share resources, makes it possible for us to fill the majority of our patrons' requests. Patrons often come to us saying, "I don't know what library owns this book" or "I've checked all the other library catalogs on MIRLYN (our OPAC) and this newspaper isn't anywhere." When we tell them that we have instant access to the holdings of thousands of libraries through OCLC, not just the dozen or so that patrons can access through our OPAC, their eyes widen in amazement.

The OCLC Online Union Catalog has had a great impact on our work. The large number of records for materials held by only a few libraries, or even by only one location—small-town newspapers, technical reports, or even rare editions of musical scores—are often the most helpful records in the catalog. When we are able to obtain these items for our patrons, they're grateful that such a service exists. "I can't believe you were able to get this!" Although we smile and thank them for their compliments, we really can't take all the credit—it's the presence of those records in OCLC that makes my work easier.

## Barbara A. Farina
Grossmont College
El Cajon, CA

Way back in 1978, when I started working in the technical services department at Grossmont College, my first task was participating in a "Dusty Book Inventory." These were books waiting for cards to be mailed to us, not to mention the carts and carts of government documents waiting for original cataloging. After six months and a million sneezes, I escaped to the circulation department, but eventually I came back to my first love, technical services.

I became the non-print technician. At that time, we had about 1,000 classical records to catalog, along with the carts of government documents still waiting for original cataloging. Our cataloging librarian, Dick Johnson, was a wizard at getting the most information on a "P" slip, but it was still a laborious job.

But then came OCLC Online. What a godsend that was. I became the technical services Sherlock Holmes. I really enjoyed searching out the difficult and sometimes seemingly impossible. By the end of that first year, we had completely caught up on the government documents and had made a good dent in the classical records. Since that time, we have never had more than one cart waiting for cataloging.

Now I am the learning resource center systems specialist. I am still in cataloging, my true love, and am proud to say that with OCLC's help, our book turnaround, from the time material is received until it is out on the shelves, is no more that three weeks, tops.

It has been a long time since we were introduced to the first Online OCLC system. I have seen the system evolve into what it is today. The new enhancements are wonderful, and I especially appreciate being able to create bibliographic records from existing records in any format. OCLC has always done the very best in updating its system to keep up with new technology. The materials they publish are excellent, and the bulletins and news updates keep us well informed as part of the OCLC family.

Three cheers for OCLC.

## Robert Farnsworth
University of North Florida
Jacksonville, FL

Over the past fifteen years, I have found that the OCLC Online Union Catalog has meant many things to me—most of which can be compared to a series of doors leading into different rooms or experiences.

The first door OCLC opened to me was the door into using a computer. Yes, I was one of those who asked, "Will it explode if I hit the wrong key?" Fortunately, nothing ever exploded or gave me real cause for alarm. As a result, I have been able to face other computers and help colleagues to feel more secure in using the machines.

Another door that was opened for me was the door into changing careers. I was a teacher for many years—and was in need of a change to a new field. With the help of my part-time cataloging experience on OCLC, I was able to obtain a new job—and a career—that I still hold and love in our Library.

The third door that OCLC opened was the door to widespread access to libraries (something which still astounds me). As I worked on my master's degree, then on my doctorate, I was able to obtain many wonderful books through the Interlibrary Loan system without huge expense. Plus I was able to spend more time on my research and class studies.

The fourth door that was opened was the door to telephone customer service. Several times when I was alone and couldn't figure out something on the system there was always someone—regular service help or a technician—who was able to help me get through my problems. And though I know some of my situations were probably hilarious, I was never made to feel that I was dumb or incapable. On the contrary, OCLC's phone team workers are masters at calming people down and restoring their self-esteem. Now I try to follow this good example when I'm on the phone with patrons.

The fifth door that was opened was the door to the world. I still am fascinated by the many languages that OCLC deals with. And seeing those languages in the same cataloging format that I am used to has brought me to a greater awareness that all catalogers—no matter where they are in the world, no matter what their particular political outlook—are people who are attempting to help other people expand knowledge.

Thus, over the years, and through these doors, OCLC has come to mean a lot to me personally. Time and time again I have seen it is truly a "people's computer system." No matter that machines are involved, it is the people who work for OCLC, and the people who use the system, that are really important. By its existence and efficiency, OCLC proves a remarkable fact—we can be a world of people helping people.

Thanks, OCLC!

**Dana M. Feil**
Smithsonian Institution
Washington, DC

The OCLC Online Union Catalog helped launch my federal library career in a big way. It provided a training tool for library cataloging and for various federal library protocol.

In 1992, I had been working as a medical laboratory technologist for over ten years. I had just returned to work part-time after an absence of several years to be home with my children. I needed full-time employment with retirement and other benefits, and I wanted to begin a new career in library work.

Since we live around the corner from a prominent federal agency with a library, I decided to see about the possibility of working there. I attended an open house held at the facility every third year, signed up as a volunteer, and was called in a few weeks later.

I worked as a volunteer all that summer, and when a job opening became available, I applied and was appointed to the position as a library technician in cataloging.

I was trained in cataloging rules and protocol using the OCLC Online Union Catalog. The uniformity of different formats (before format integration) made it much easier than otherwise to learn the basic cataloging rules and how they apply to different types of materials being cataloged.

I also learned many computer skills that apply to other computer applications and types of work: creating macro keys, downloading and uploading files, etc. I also learned a lot about how LANs are connected and how they operate.

In conclusion, I credit OCLC Online Union Catalog with the enthusiasm I have for the work I do.

———————————— *//* ————————————

### Renate S. Ferree
Bridgeport Public Library
Fairfield, CT

For many years, the OCLC Online Union Catalog has been my constant and trusted companion. Together we have fought—but not won!—the battle against the ever-increasing onslaught of uncataloged—and uncatalogable?—materials. It has been my friend and confidant. (Nobody needs to know you got the author's name wrong. Just use the "loc" and "rep" commands!)

The Online Union Catalog has been my beacon of hope. (Maybe I'll finally find that Beethoven symphony today!) It has greeted me every morning with more or less meaningful messages. It has connected me with the world (Nice to know that OCLC is down in Great Britain today because of maintenance) and filled my heart with envy. (I bet the weather at the ALA midwinter conference in San Antonio is much better than here!)

The OCLC Online Union Catalog has been my source of:

1. anger (Wouldn't you think that 2 years is enough time for somebody else to buy and catalog that book?),

2. frustration (What do you mean by: "Check the results of your last work"? I haven't done anything yet!),

3. information (Creative typing has provided me with materials in languages I didn't know existed.),

4. joy (Bless that person who finally entered that awful serial with the 5 title changes!), and

5. modest pride (My CD entry looks just as professional as the DLC ones, if I may say so myself!).

The OCLC Online Union Catalog has made me feel:

a. superior (Those dummies don't know the difference between a subtype and a series title!),

b. inferior (I never entered a video with 45 lines!),

c. impatient (Come on, gimme that record! I don't have all day!), and

d. nosy (I wonder who those dummies are? See a.).

In short: THE OCLC ONLINE UNION CATALOG IS THE CENTER OF MY CATALOGING UNIVERSE.

Just like in the real universe there are new stars to discover (That "acd" command does wonders for me!) and black holes to avoid (How can you log me off after I worked ½ hour on this record—OK, I took a little coffee break—but still, isn't that excessive punishment?) There are novae (see: Format integration) and comets and nebulae and lots and lots of unknowns (see also: Format integration). So let's boldly go where no man has gone before!

## Ann Fields
Ft. Myers Lee County Public Library System
Ft. Myers, FL

I have always loved to search for things. Winning the Easter egg hunt in kindergarten was the highlight of my youth. For the past nine and a half years I have had the time of my life searching on OCLC. For most of those years I have served as interlibrary loan coordinator for the Ft. Myers Lee County Library System. We are located in southwest Florida with a population of nearly 400,000—of which approximately 43% are library card members.

I was with OCLC before PRISM and marveled at it then. But my hunts have become so much easier and more successful with PRISM enhancements such as scan title and keyword searching. And now with customs holdings building and building, our staff can practically go on automatic pilot when requesting interlibrary loans.

For me, OCLC is fun and fulfilling. It delivers a multitude of materials for our patrons' various needs and has put me in touch with persons from every walk of life. Imagine you are an aspiring actress who needs an out-of-print play script to audition for a part. Through ILL, OCLC locates and delivers the script and wins the coveted part for our patron. Genealogists who used to travel far and wide to trace their family trees, now have genealogical materials delivered to their closest branch. A patron requests huge maps of old Russia known only to be held at the Library of Congress. An online OCLC request allows delivery of the oversized documents in cylindrical containers that would rival UPS. And then there is the patron who makes a special trip to our office to say that an obituary obtained through ILL from an old issue of an out of state newspaper has reunited him with a relative he's been seeking for 36 years. How can this job not be fulfilling? Is there very much OCLC can't locate in the catalogued world? I don't think so.

This month the New York Public Library asked us to fax them an article from an older edition of our local newspaper. Talk about the mouse helping the lion… our very own Aesop's fable!

I guess the biggest thrill of my Interlibrary loan career is when noted children's author, Verna Aardema, of *Why Mosquitoes Buzz in People's Ears* and many other African folk tales, was featured in a meet-the-author series.

Because she had used ILL and OCLC to obtain many books from which she fashioned her stories, she asked me to pose for a picture in the title, *A Bookworm Who Hatched*. I am immortalized on page 15 of OCLC# 27725774. And, yes, credit where credit is due, OCLC is featured on page 21.

OCLC has provided our library system, our patrons and myself with unsurpassed service and satisfaction. Jumping back to that illustrious Easter egg hunt of my youth, let me conclude with an addendum to an old proverb… Don't put all your eggs in one basket, unless that basket is OCLC. It will make you a winner every time!

--------------------------------- *w* ---------------------------------

## Meredith A. Finley
Dayton and Montgomery County Public Library
Beavercreek, OH

In the early seventies, OCLC, a name synonymous with college libraries, was coming to Dayton & Montgomery County Public Library. I was petrified and not a willing participant. After studying the OCLC manual, learning about fixed fields, tags, first and second indicators, and practicing on the department's one terminal, the three catalogers, myself included, were ready for the Big Day. Little did we realize the Big Day was only the first of a series. On this first Big Day, cards were produced for the main library and its 18 branches. Our first effort was not perfect.

From that first Big Day, I was hooked. OCLC cataloging was like solving a puzzle—I'd fill in the blanks until a complete picture appears. Using OCLC for original or copy cataloging was easier than typing copy for original cataloging or correcting LC proofs. One of the earliest commands much appreciated was the "new" command. I really loved this command until I produced an original record with the subject "bears" instead of "lions." During the seventies and early eighties when our library was not automated, cards were a necessity. OCLC improved the 049 field—multiple symbols could now be added to this field. Before this 049 field improvement, only one main or branch symbol at a time could be input. Any interruption or lapse of brain power could cause multiple or no sets of cards.

During the past two decades, OCLC has improved not only software but hardware as well; terminals have changed to workstations. Along with the M310 came full page editing, expanded function keys and user-defined function keys—these were great for the non-typist. OCLC has always kept up with the times by supporting both non-automated and automated libraries. During the eighties Dayton Public became automated (cards are no longer a problem); the export function is used to transfer records from OCLC's immense database. The majority of records needed for books (including foreign language materials and GPO publications) can be found in OCLC.

OCLC has helped the Catalog staff keep up with the increasing volume of work. In 1995, the Catalog Department released 136,468 books and 53,862 AV items. There are now 6 OCLC terminals, 4 copy catalogers (2 for books, 2 for AV), 2 original catalogers (1 for books, 1 for AV), 6 support staff, and 1 supervisor. In 1973 (the first year with OCLC), the Catalog Department released 72,538 books and 4,081 phonographs (AV items). In that year, there were 1 OCLC terminal, 1 copy cataloger, 2 original catalogers (1 for books, 1 for serials), 10 support staff and 2 supervisors. Currently our Catalog Department processes books and AV items within two weeks.

It seems as if one of my hobbies is falling. Twice, a broken ankle has landed me in a wheelchair (I have cerebral palsy and cannot use crutches). Co-workers, OCLC, and DMM's automated system enabled me to continue working.

## Joel Fishman
Allegheny County Law Library
Pittsburgh, PA

OCLC Online Union Catalog, what a friend to me,
Consisting of 35 million records of various types,
Oh what a sight to see!
Begun in 1971, now twenty-five years old, and growing each year,
The collection is extensive and deep,
Easy to search and easy to find,
Makes a librarian's job relaxing at times.

Seeking authors and titles by the score,
To fill a need for evermore,
Looking for authors like Binney, Selden, and Stillingfleet,
This system can't be beat.
Searching history long forgotten,
To answer questions woe begotten,
Patrons are astounded, you see,
When I can find an answer for thee.

Need a book, article, score, or map?
Take a little trip through the online cat,
Locate a title the patron does not know about,
Borrow it from Harvard, Berkeley, or a lesser-known spot,
ILL can be so useful.

FirstSearch is a new reference tool,
Accessing bibliographic databases too.
Loaded on a local OPAC,
Working like a Z39,
Going to make it home on time.
By finding and ordering a necessary article,
Sent by fax or E-mail, the very next day
To make a patron happy in every way.

Can't forget the networks too,
People working hard just for you.
Keeping costs at a reasonable rate,
So OCLC you can't hate.

Oh, 25 years and still counting,
OCLC, the corporate giant,
Is making library work, oh so pliant.
So librarians give a cheer,
OCLC is here.

———————————— ℐ ————————————

## Connie Foster
Western Kentucky University
Bowling Green, KY

What do you associate with the word window? Add an "s" and you have Bill Gates and megabucks. Perhaps the response, "I don't do windows." Or maybe a moment of opportunity. In the context of OCLC and its phenomenal growth, I immediately think of Frederick Kilgour and his vision, his window of opportunity that opened a connection to and view of the world of information resources. What OCLC is today comes from its modest Ohio beginnings and the early leadership of Kilgour. This twenty-fifth anniversary adds a silver lining to the efforts of past and present leaders and staff who have propelled OCLC into the position of the world's foremost bibliographic utility.

As a serials librarian, I eagerly awaited our library's link to the world in the late 1980s. To have at my fingertips catalog records of obscure and popular titles, to browse similar records to assign call numbers or subject tracings, to view authority records, by checking holdings symbols to see if our institution would benefit from certain esoteric gifts about to be donated by a professor—these are a few examples of one person's log-on results. As if that weren't enough, along came "scan title" to enable additional search capabilities for problematic titles, qualifiers by types of materials, and many more enhancements to provide more successful searches and editing capabilities.

Although administrators struggle with library budgets to accommodate new workstations, software, and other enhancements, OCLC softens the changes with incentives and prods us out of our tendencies toward status quo. With the recent announcement of a windows environment, I look forward to transferring my mouse coordination skills to yet another computer terminal until I can have one workstation for all technical services functions.

As faculty and students engage in research, the exciting access to FirstSearch and the promise of indexing resources on the Internet provide new and better windows on the world for scholarly purposes. These quests are tempered with the reality that finding it through FirstSearch or on OCLC does not mean one can have immediate access to the document.

As Kilgour's window changed into a house of glass, the technological furniture actually decreased. Mainframes no longer occupy entire floors of data centers; magnetic tapes are now pocket-sized cartridges for data storage and retrieval; cumbersome coaxial cables transform into sleek fiber optics. Such is the paradox of hardware miniaturization that enables a bibliographic utility to experience exponential growth in records added, transactions completed for interlibrary lending, and strategic enhancements planned. More important, however, is the leadership, the quality staff, the communication, and the desire to improve constant access to library resources. With partnerships, collaborative arrangements, and ever-changing technologies, OCLC holds the promise of a golden twenty-first century in information access. Happy anniversary!

## Stephen P. Foster
Central Michigan University Libraries
Mt. Pleasant, MI

The OCLC Online Union Catalog has evolved into much more than just another massive computer database. OCLC is now an inseparable part of libraries and the OCLC Catalog is an extraordinary cultural achievement that combines the best of human creative capacities for technical ingenuity and social cooperation. From that achievement many people in many places have benefited. Librarians, perhaps, are the most knowledgeable of what OCLC is and does, but the OCLC Online Union Catalog's significance extends far beyond them.

For a librarian, the OCLC Online Union Catalog is, first and foremost, a monument to the possibilities for long-range projects of shared expertise. Begun in Ohio as an academic, cooperative adventure, the OCLC Catalog has in a quarter of a century become a vast international bibliographic utility, comprised of the work of thousands of librarians, each attempting to create those important records that provide access to knowledge. At a time in which the richness and diversity of human experience is becoming increasingly recognized and appreciated, the catalog compiles the bibliographic records for and the holdings of works of the many of the world's libraries (great and small) and facilitates access to them for people in the most diverse of communities.

For a scholar, the OCLC Online Union Catalog is an important piece of research infrastructure, a remarkable, unprecedented bibliographical representation of global knowledge and human creativity in all of its intellectual forms—including books, serials, music, archives, and computer files. Its existence enhances the already rich and persistent human capacity for enlarging the understanding and communicating information. Historically, the OCLC Online Union Catalog comprises a vast bibliographic document that captures nearly three thousand years of human intellectual and artistic accomplishment. It forms an electronic catalog of works of every imaginable subject in many different languages, including all of the major languages of the world.

For a participant in and beneficiary of a technological revolution, the OCLC Online Union Catalog is an example of the development and use of technology that can serve and enrich many different kinds of communities and people. The technology that created the Catalog enables libraries, and the people who use them, to be linked together and more fully share the fruits of knowledge. The Catalog's history of rapid, international expansion provides promise of an even greater expansion of access to human knowledge.

For a citizen in a democratic society, the OCLC Online Union Catalog is both a manifestation and symbol of the power of shared information. As we recently watched the dictatorships of eastern Europe crumble, we were reminded that the perpetuation of free and democratic societies greatly depends on the unimpeded, open flow of knowledge and information. A ubiquitous international knowledge-utility like the OCLC Online Union Catalog makes the constriction and control of information and knowledge increasingly difficult, and inhibits the designs and operations of aspiring dictators and tyrants. Certainly, the OCLC Online Union Catalog has expanded in many ways unforeseen by its creators twenty-five years ago: its existence reflects creativity and cooperation at its best.

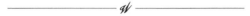

## Jennifer Frankel
Salem Public Library
Salem, OR

In an era of technological change in the library, the OCLC Online Union Catalog represents both the precursor to and destiny of the late 20th Century library. As a librarian who has entered the field in the mid-1990s, this integral placement of the OCLC Online Union Catalog helps me to see my own destiny in the profession. As the online coordinator at the Salem (OR) Public Library, my duties include not only the Online Union Catalog, but also online services such as DIALOG and Internet applications such as Netscape. The Online Union Catalog is the model that I would like to see the Internet emulate: good, reliable information at a low price. The Internet is touted as the great equalizer of libraries: small libraries can expand their collection by leaps and bounds with just the addition of a PC and an Internet connection. The OCLC Online Union Catalog proved to do the same thing 20 years ago. As Fred Kilgour stated in *American Libraries*: "We do things to libraries, not for them" and "We want to make resources more available to users of libraries, and to reduce the unit costs."* Although the Internet has started along this road, it has a long way to go to reach the level of the Online Union Catalog. The confidence I have in myself as a librarian is never as strong as when I bring patrons over to our OCLC terminal in the reference area. Whether they want an item through ILL or just want to know if their favorite author has a new book out, I am sure that I can give them the correct and complete answer through the Online Union Catalog. As a new librarian dealing with emerging technologies, the confidence I receive through the Online Union Catalog is invaluable.

Just as the Online Union Catalog shows the way to new technologies, it also will always be the quintessential cooperative library system. It is created, maintained and used by librarians who have an interest in open and affordable access to information. As the Internet becomes increasingly privatized and online services charge upwards of $300 per hour to use, my confidence that they will be a viable tool for libraries and their patrons to use diminishes. I am sure that the OCLC Online Union Catalog, because of its roots in libraries, will always be affordable and accessible to all libraries, from the large, urban university library to the small, rural public library. Every library I have ever been in has had a use for it.

I look forward to a long and interesting career in librarianship and I am confident that I will be using the OCLC Online Union Catalog every step of the way.

*Plotnik, Art. "OCLC for You—and ME?!" *American Libraries* Vol. 7, No. 5, May, 1996, p. 263.

**Tracy Fritz**
Wilmer, Cutter & Pickering
Washington, D.C.

My relationship with the OCLC Online Union Catalog has not been a fleeting affair. It has been at my service, and I at its mercy ever since I started working in a law library and became accustomed to its daily pace of pandemonium. On the contrary, over the years we have evolved into loyal companions; I am astounded by its ceaseless ability to locate the most obscure of documents, it continues to soldier on, ready for the next showdown.

Does it seem a little odd to someone outside the library community to carry on an association so tinged with gratitude and indebtedness to something as abstract as an online system? Perhaps. I believe, however, that admiration for OCLC is in direct proportion to the degree of which one had to use its print alternative, the *National Union Catalog*. This bold endeavor, to photocopy cataloging and holding entries of major libraries across the U.S. and Canada, was certainly an ambitious attempt at establishing a global collection originating in North America. The initial printed catalog was published in 1942. It then produced a five-year supplement followed by another cumulation spanning the years 1948 to 1952. Suffice to say, this system could hardly attempt to keep pace with the needs of today's libraries and library users. The volume of publishing, and as a consequence, rate of cataloging, has increased at least, ten-thousand-fold. The alternative therefore, had to be more accommodating to growth and accessibility. Technology aside, perhaps one of the most distinguishing and unique qualities that OCLC has over its predecessor is collaboration. Unlike any other library database, the users of OCLC are also the authors of its content. It truly is a universal effort based and dependent on cooperation, meticulousness and above all, knowledge of cataloging standards. I withhold no emphasis when stressing that last attribute.

Once again, in order to truly appreciate and comprehend the contribution of OCLC in the cataloging domain, one has to revert back to the days when it was not an alternative. Thankfully, I'm unable to do this, since I am not a cataloger, and I became a librarian long after the birth of OCLC. However, I have taken a cataloging class, so I am somewhat qualified to commiserate on the tedium and laboriousness involved in original cataloging. Apart from graduation, one of the main incentives that helped me through the course was the knowledge that the term, "copy cataloging" was widely practiced. This resource didn't diminish my desire to learn, but rather reinforced my belief that the mission of librarianship didn't end when only the patrons were served. It is a field where expertise is always shared, and teamwork is the norm. This isn't part of some lofty mission statement, it is a reality, one made possible by OCLC.

# Wendie H. Gabay
Reconstructionist Rabbinical College
Wyncote, PA

Utilizing OCLC to its fullest capacity enables me to serve all of my users' information needs. Despite the small size of our collection, OCLC proves that the Mordecai M. Kaplan Library of the Reconstructionist Rabbinical College is a major resource to libraries whose collections are of much greater proportions. In addition, in certain subject areas, our collection reaches levels of greater intensity than other libraries whose collections have reached acclaim in the academic world. I recently conducted a study comparing our strengths with those of several well-known Judaica collections. As a result, we discovered the relationship of our small library and its holdings to larger institutions. In most cases, our collection intensity in designated subject areas proved (via the OCLC holding statistics) to be on a par with or even stronger than the institutions known to be of great stature. The ability to achieve the research level of collection strength was by virtue of a retrospective conversion project coupled with a non-uniform interest of member libraries toward retrospective conversion projects.

By operating OCLC's vast database, I am able to fulfill 99.5% of my patrons' requests through interlibrary loan. The desired title is often in the hands of our users in as little as two days. The OCLC database has allowed us to generate countless bibliographies for our students and faculty in many subject areas, including those fields in which our library does not collect.

We also play an active role as a lender in the OCLC interlibrary loan system. We have served as a resource for such fine institutions as NASA, the Food and Drug Administration, Harvard University, the College of William and Mary, Notre Dame University and the University of Lund in Sweden.

We provide our clientele with the most up-to-date information available via OCLC, as well as with the most ancient of texts. By using OCLC's authority file, we have uncovered the various identities held by authors which had previously been unknown to us. The information contained in an OCLC MARC record is quite valuable and answers many reference questions for both librarians and end users. It reveals the genre of a work, the language in which it appears, and the original language in which the work was written. For many books, a synopsis is included in the MARC record, as well as the contents of an individual volume of a book, periodical, or sound recording. We are able to determine the research value of a serial due to the fact that the OCLC record contains information about where a serial is indexed.

Skillful use of the treasures found in the OCLC system enables even a small library working under severe budgetary constraints to expand its collection way beyond the walls of the institution. Thanks to OCLC, the Mordecai M. Kaplan Library has been able to reach levels of user satisfaction which previously were never even dreamed of. It also proves that the value of an OCLC supplier is not always determined by size and reputation. The multifaceted nature of OCLC enables the experienced professional to be a productive member of the academic community.

## Joseph A. Gabriel

Harvard University Graduate School of Education
Cambridge, MA

As a user of OCLC for the past 17 years, the Online Union Catalog has much significance to me. As a librarian, it has become the source for information on all topics in most languages for the printed word. In addition, it is a place to find non-print formats such as records, CDs, tapes, computer files, and visual material. Recent advances in searching now allow the user to search by title, subject, author, keyword, publisher and place. The Online Catalog was also the place where I learned to understand how the MARC format benefited the world of research by organizing information in a logical and searchable method. As a cataloger, I helped contribute to the goal of providing access to information by describing a book or item according to the standards set up by OCLC.

In addition, the OCLC Online Union Catalog helped me to locate information. Using the display holdings option, I could see where in my area a book was held. Using OCLC interlibrary loan features provided access to material not in my area. The Online Union Catalog has helped to unify the library community worldwide, to eliminate barriers and to foster cooperation.

In effect, the OCLC Online Union Catalog has become the national online bibliographic library. With over 35 million records, the OCLC Online Union Catalog provides a clear path to a jungle of information. It has provided a record of scholarly achievement of our past for future generations. As a librarian and a past student, I am proud to have been part of the process.

## Barbara Gewirtz

Manpower Demonstration Research Corporation
New York, NY

You might say I've grown up with OCLC. I started as a librarian at the Hebrew Union College-Jewish Institute of Religion in August of 1976, and as I learned to catalog, I also learned the OCLC system. HUC-JIR made the bold decision to join OCLC, even though as a Judaica library, a large chunk of the collection—which contained a number of different languages—at that time could not be cataloged on the system. But the director of the library felt that as a scholarly Ohio library, it should support this fledging system.

Four years later, I left Ohio for marriage and a job in a research institute where all cataloging was original and the librarians typed the cards. I was lost without OCLC! (I left that job six months later). My first son was born shortly after and my second son in 1984, and from then on, when I returned to work, I always took OCLC with me. First, in a small education library, I learned about the dial access option right on my desktop p.c. (with my new daughter occasionally frolicking in her playpen next to the LB1027s). After six years happily cataloging education material, I joined the staff of a social welfare policy research organization, and was asked to organize the library, which was "the black hole" of the organization. What a challenge! My predecessor had been doing original cataloging in Dewey and Sears subject headings, while *her* predecessor cataloged the collection using her own system. I had the task of merging these disparate schemes—but how? OCLC dial access, of course, since our collection, as well as the budget, was rather small. But first I had to convince an administration supervisor who knew nothing about cataloging, that OCLC was my only option. It took about a year but then OCLC at MDRC was launched!

Everyone was surprised at how useful having the OCLC database on hand proved to be. First, I was delighted to discover just how much of the literature of social welfare policy was already in the system. Cataloging was a snap! Furthermore, OCLC has proven to be a marvelous bibliographic aid to a "one-person library" librarian. I'm often asked what a particular author has written, what is the first name of someone and who wrote the book called... . My staff calls me a miracle-worker—all that information and I rarely leave my desk!

The world of librarianship has changed dramatically since those early years in Ohio; now I'm dealing with issues such as online catalog versus continuing our card catalog and other automation issues: finding more space (everyone's dilemma, certainly); and how to turn this into a two-person library someday. But one thing is certain, OCLC will always be there at my desk, making my work-day a little simpler.

## Joanne Gilliam
Cleveland Public Library
Cleveland, OH

"A-l-l A-b-o-a-r-d!"

The conductor of the future, wearing a hat emblazoned with an OCLC logo, sounded the call in 1971.

"Not for me," said I.

I was a novice professional librarian who had typed her way to a shoe box full of 3" x 5" cards via cataloging courses. I felt that my future was to be found in library environments in which the OCLC database was not going to have an impact.

I managed to avoid the terminable terminal by practicing my craft in a small liberal arts college and then in a private secondary school.

Many, many a time, while helping students and teachers, I was frustrated by not having the resources available to locate the needed information. Secondly, my suitability as a proving ground for Tylenol was assured every time I opened the door on my cataloging backlog.

Then, as if walking in a spring garden past opening hyacinths, I sniffed a pleasant intellectual fragrance. I discovered that the sweetness of greater capability was within my grasp when I began working as a substitute in a public library and sat down to use the dreaded OCLC terminal. I was able to deliver greater service to patrons by using OCLC to locate elusive material. The look of joy on the borrower's face warmed even my cold heart toward the avenue that had allowed me and my institution to provide greater service.

Working now in the technical services department of a large public library, I benefit from records imported to our database. I return the favor, and contribute original cataloging for others to share.

The train has stayed on track even when the roadbed took on startling changes. This little engine could and did. Oh yes, it started by chug, chugging along, but it has picked up speed and passengers.

One of the people now on board used to practice avoidance. Either advancing age or an intellectual renaissance has clearly showed the benefits of cooperation. Give thought to riding with us, even if we encounter a tunnel or two. The train stops at a myriad of stations and we'd love the company.

## Ann Gilmore
Springfield Greene County Library
Springfield, MO

"What do you know about OCLC?" my Director asked.

"OCLC? Practically nothing," I responded.

"Well, you need to learn," he replied. "We're going online next spring."

That was the fall of 1976. In the months to follow, I would remember that day when I walked out of his office, and stumbled down the stairs to the Technical Services Department. My confused mind was in a state of turmoil, as I attempted to comprehend the unknown OCLC and its effects upon my department in the "not so distant future."

Hours, days, and weeks quickly turned into months as we tried to learn about OCLC, worked on a profile, and set up training sessions with BCR. This, in addition, to work as usual, only seemed to add to the apprehension and uncertainty of the future. The impact that OCLC would have on the Technical Services Department and the entire library system was of great concern.

In May, 1977, we were officially introduced to the world of OCLC, and our lives were changed forever.

The OCLC Online Union Catalog meant many changes immediately.

One of the first steps was to discontinue our subscription to the LC Proof-slips. No longer did those long narrow boxes arrive in our department requiring hours of time to sort out the titles that we would probably purchase. Then hours of time were spent interfiling those into the many drawers of previously received slips. When the new titles arrived, proof-slip files were searched. Titles that weren't matched would be set aside for NUC searching or original cataloging.

Another drastic change was the elimination of the Xerox copier. This also eliminated the need for the Public Service Staff to "race downstairs trying to locate the fire," because the fires ceased to occur. The temperature setting on the copier had to be set as high as possible because we had used card stock. This resulted in many fires and scorched card stock. My assistant and I became quite proficient at cleaning drums, clearing card stock jams, etc.

Many hours were spent typing, sorting, and alphabetizing catalog cards. This was no longer necessary as the catalog cards arrived from OCLC sorted by location and alphabetized—ready to file.

Withdrawal symptoms were very evident in the department, as the processing procedures changed or were eliminated. However, the staff recovered quickly and moved forward.

Last year our library processed over 75,000 items. The OCLC database supplied cataloging records for approximately 95% of those materials.

Almost 19 years have passed since that day that I had to admit that I knew "practically nothing about OCLC."

Today we are, and will continue to be a staunch supporter of the OCLC Online Union Catalog.

What does the OCLC Online Union Catalog mean to me? In addition to NO MORE of the previously mentioned procedures or processes, it means quality and quantity, accuracy and dependability. Perhaps it can be summed up in four words—"Online Consistent Loving Care."

## Cassandra S. Gissendanner
University of South Carolina
Columbia, SC

During the past twenty-five years, I have utilized library resources as a student, as a catalog librarian, as a teacher, and as a "regular" customer. In all instances, I have found the OCLC Online Union Catalog to be the library's greatest asset.

Before OCLC was created, the library world was one in which searches for bibliographic and holdings data for cataloging and interlibrary loan purposes required long, tedious hours of delving into numerous books; electric erasers left smudged and torn catalog cards; revision of typing consumed vast quantities of time; and alphabetizing and filing catalog cards continued ad infinitum. With the advent of the Ohio College Library Center, a new sense of pride enveloped all libraries affiliated with it. "Cooperation, collaboration, and resource sharing" became bywords. As the system developed into OCLC, libraries made "connections." What began as a network of state libraries soon became a network of national libraries, and now exists as a network of international libraries allowing access to 35 million records for information located in 560 million places, written in 370 languages and dating from 2000 BC.

Like me, many librarians first came in contact with OCLC in the mid-70s. My library went online with OCLC via SOLINET in 1976. Immediately, the cataloging backlog began to dwindle as appropriate records were found with amazing speed. Revision of cataloging data decreased in time consumption, leaving more time available to deal with difficult cataloging problems and maintenance tasks which had been deferred for years. Suddenly, a record could be searched, cataloged, and revised within minutes instead of hours. Later, the addition of series, name, and subject authority files enabled accurate, consistent records to be provided even more quickly. As catalogers realized that their cataloging was being outsourced to the rest of the nation and to the world, motivation to produce the best record possible increased. As the cataloger's sphere of influence and recognition widened with OCLC, so did quality and service.

Shortly after going online, I discovered the ease with which I could determine if another library held a work which I needed for research. In other words, interlibrary loan was facilitated by this new system. Materials from all over the nation were just keystrokes away. Colleagues in the public service areas of the library discovered that they were empowered to give prompt, efficient service to faculty, students, and other people in search of vital information.

Now, as we contemplate the future of information and technology, we realize that the OCLC Online Union Catalog virtually opened the "gateway" to the world of information sharing, where projects like PromptCat, OCLC Selection, FirstSearch, and Galileo could be conceived. Gazing beyond today, we realize that because of the OCLC Online Union Catalog, the only limits on the access to information are the limits of our own imaginations.

## Michal R. Glaser
University of Texas at Austin
Austin, TX

I began my career in libraries at a time when the most reliable library resource was its staff of long-term employees. Coupled with the collection itself, they were, in fact, our library's database—our authorities of bibliographic information. This capable staff made their own decisions about bibliographic access to our cataloged materials. However, with the help of the OCLC Online Union Catalog, the jobs of our librarians and staff were greatly enhanced. The shared cataloging information and online authority file were a wonderful improvement.

Not only was OCLC new to our particular library, but so was I. I came to my position at this academic library with limited library experience, except for having worked in a corporate library setting. And here I was, in a clerical position in the serials receiving unit of a university library. While some of my experience proved to be useful, I had a lot to learn. Least of which was the library jargon associated with my new job. Such terms as "serial," "monograph," and "series"; "added entry," "subject heading," and "successive entry"; "RETROCON," "MARC format," and "OCLC" all seemed rather confusing. My first days were somewhat trying. Meeting fellow employees, learning new tasks, and understanding the department jargon kept me very occupied.

During this time, I encountered my first title change. I was informed that one of my periodicals would have to be recataloged so that our records and card catalog would be accurate. Questions needed to be answered concerning its publication history, previous title and linking notes. Had the title really ceased? Was the new title a successive entry or something with no connections to a former title?

"We have a wonderful resource for answering these types of questions" said my supervisor. "OCLC!"

"Go See Elsie?" I thought. "Why would Elsie, the librarian in charge of archives, be an authority on title changes?"

You see, I had just toured the archives department and had met a helpful librarian named Elsie. I had not yet visited the cataloging department where our OCLC terminals were located. I had not even heard of "OCLC."

So off I went, to talk to our authority on title changes, and—hopefully—to get some answers to my questions. Needless to say, the misunderstanding became clear rather quickly, and everyone was amused. Elsie graciously referred me back to my supervisor, who then gave me my first lesson with our online resource, OCLC.

From such humorous beginnings to the present time, I realize how much I have come to depend on OCLC in order to do my job. It truly is a most "wonderful resource" in this age of shared information. The searching, downloading, and cataloging capabilities provide an information link unsurpassed.

So much has changed in 25 years. OCLC has added PRISM and library card catalogs have been replaced by online systems. However, I can't help but smile every time I pass an OCLC terminal and think back to those "Go See Elsie" days at the University of Nebraska.

## Edna Golan
Technion–Israel Institute Of Technology
Technion City–Haifa, Israel

In 1970, I started working as a librarian in the physics department library of Technion–Israel Institute of Technology, Israel.

Our main tools for scientific information retrieval were INSPEC—*Physics Abstracts* and *Current Contents*—all in print form.

A few years later, I attended a lecture at the Annual Israel Librarians Conference. The lecturer told us about a big revolutionary project that had started in the United States. We were told about one big online catalog that was beginning its operation, and that many academic libraries contributed their holdings to this united catalog. We were also told how all the academic libraries benefit from this united net.

For us librarians in Israel, it seemed as far away as the moon. As we all know, a tremendous revolution took place in the world—one which is very relevant to librarians and their users: the Internet. All of a sudden, the world became a village. Information became accessible so easily and quickly. The academic libraries in Israel joined the revolution with enthusiasm.

Now I come to the main point of our essay: The wonderful tool, "OCLC Online Union Catalog."

To think that a few years ago we lived without OCLC, is unbelievable.

Our library users are: regular staff members; faculty members; students to second degree—master of science; and students to third degree—doctor of science.

To serve our users, we enter OCLC through FirstSearch. The best advantage of FirstSearch is its friendliness. Once you have entered, it leads you step by step. No previous knowledge is needed. It is very useful to librarians and users as well. It supplies us with valuable bibliographical information. The most important item for our users is the INSPEC, which starts in 1969 and is updated regularly. The fact that it starts in 1969 is very important—it saves a lot of precious time to our users. We the librarians frequently search the books catalog. The librarians in our library encourage especially the young students, to second and third degree, to use the FirstSearch service for all kinds of scientific information needed. Our professors do not need encouragement—they use it in their office.

The Middle East is the cradle of human written history. The first archives were excavated in this corner of the world. Now we, the people in Israel, retrieve information online from the U.S. in the new world. How symbolic.

## Carol Goodson
West Georgia College Library
Carrollton, GA

I remember only too well the first time I was really aware of OCLC: I'd just finished my MLS, and was on the verge of leaving the university library in New York where I worked during Library School. Someone mentioned that the library was joining this new network, OCLC; I blurted out, in words which make me blush whenever I remember the incident: "Why on earth would *we* (meaning "we sophisticated New Yorkers") want to join a computer network of libraries in OHIO!" All I can say is that I've gotten a lot more humble since then.

I soon departed for my new public library job in the Midwest, and had no further contact with OCLC until I moved to Georgia in 1980 and began a position which involved locating materials on the system, mainly for rural public libraries too small to be on OCLC themselves, but who wanted to get materials for their users via Interlibrary Loan. I was introduced to OCLC searching on my very first day, but my reaction this time was *quite* different. I had never used a computer before, so I was totally awestruck as I discovered for the first time the thrill and sense of power that came with being able to search the holdings of libraries all over the world. Because of my fascination, I quickly became a rather expert OCLC searcher. I must confess that I was rather proud of my new skills, but even more, I enjoyed the satisfaction of knowing that I was indirectly helping people in isolated, often poor areas of our state to get access to the best materials on any subject—access equal to that available to the richest, most educated and privileged person anywhere in the world.

In my next job, I learned to use the ILL subsystem and by then I had become a fervent advocate of OCLC. I read everything about Frederick Kilgour I could get; he was and still is one of my professional heroes, an individual with the kind of vision I never had, but which I envied and admired. Later, as director of a tiny academic library in Nashville, my first goal was convincing the college administration that we could not possibly do without OCLC, and within a year I was on a plane to Atlanta to work out the details at SOLINET.

As an academic librarian on the tenure track—caught up, like it or not, in the world of "publish or perish"—I do some writing. I am currently working on a book, and it hasn't been easy giving up all my weekends. However, I was driving to my office to work on it one rainy Saturday morning, when a sudden thought instantly changed my mood from gloomy to ecstatic: MY NAME IS GOING TO BE IN OCLC! Talk about immortality: that's as good as it gets.

**Dorothy Peyton Gray**
Los Angeles County Metropolitan Transportation Authority
Los Angeles, CA

Thanks to the OCLC Online Union Catalog, I feel confident when I advertise our special library services to our employees with the motto: "If we can't find it—it doesn't exist!"

**Ann T. Greer**
Southern College
Collegedale, TN

All within the space of less than thirty minutes, despair turned to jubilee.

When she walked into my office, I saw the mental pain reflected in the crevices around her mouth, and the wrinkled lines on her forehead. She needed not to tell me because I had seen that look many times before on a multitude of faces. But she explained, as did all the others before her, that she had waited too late to start on her class assignment.

I quizzed her about what she had in mind; then, logged onto OCLC. I talked through the process of selecting the proper database; entering appropriate search labels; and scanning the list of records.

Her face began to loosen.

She leaned over further to peer into the monitor. A quick giggle told me that she was elated when I chose "print."

References in hand, she skipped out of my office without despair. Jubilee lingered. And that's what the OCLC Online Union Catalog means to me.

**Dusty Gres**
Ohoopee Regional Library System
Vidalia, GA

The OCLC Online Union Catalog means the world to me—literally. In my area of rural southeastern Georgia, we provide the world's supermarkets with a very famous product: the Vidalia sweet onion. In my library, I provide the people of my area with a very important product, the world's information—through OCLC.

Farmers need information. They need information about weather, soil, seeds, and markets. They need information about where to send their product and how to send their product, and how to convince others to buy their product. They need information on new types of products and services to make their farms productive.

All these things are found in the millions of books, serials, and other media in the OCLC records. I can quickly and easily find a source for needed information, and I can request it and receive it in a short time—and time, even for producers who have to wait for the seasons to pass for their product, is very important.

This door to information is open, not only to the farmers but also to all the farm workers; through bookmobile delivery, we reach out to farm workers and provide them materials for enrichment, education and an important touch of home, in their own language. For through my library's access to OCLC, we have access to books in the languages of the world—many of which are being spoken right there in the farm camp.

Just as important, and certainly not to be left out, are all the other people in this area: a surprising cross section of humanity. We have engineers from a nearby nuclear power plant; we have university instructors and college students; we have local industries who manufacture products whose diversity ranges from oxford shirts to seals and gaskets for space vehicles; and we have people who just want to read a good book they heard about from a friend. These people, all of them, are offered the information materials of the world—through their library and OCLC.

## Linda Smith Griffin
Louisiana State University
Baton Rouge, LA

The OCLC Online Union Catalog is the world's largest and most comprehensive bibliographic utility. The primary goals of OCLC are, resource sharing and reducing the cost of information. I was introduced to OCLC in 1985. At that time, I was not aware of the tremendous influence this bibliographic utility would ultimately have on my professional career choice.

In 1985, I applied for a temporary entry level Library Associate position with the LSU Libraries, an academic research library. Prior to this time, my only library experience was working as a student assistant for the State Library of Louisiana in the Recorder of State Documents Office. When I interviewed for the library associate position, the acronym OCLC was mentioned frequently. I was perplexed as to what the acronym stood for and what it did for libraries. As much as I tried, I could not remember whether I had encountered this acronym during my work for the Recorder of State Documents Office. I was convinced the interviewer was speaking an unfamiliar language. For example, she would say "we conduct **3,2,2,1, 4,3,1** or **4,4** searches using OCLC..." Not readily comprehending what the numerical phrases meant, and really wanting the job, I decided to look as attentive as possible, hoping my non-verbal communication skills were sending positive messages. A week later, I was offered the job. To this day, I am convinced the only reason I was offered the position was because no one else had managed to look as attentive as I did. Shortly thereafter, the unfamiliar numerical phrases were incorporated into my daily work flow.

The principal reason I was hired was to help reduce an insurmountable DLC and member copy monographic backlog. During that time, the previously mentioned search key formats were one of the primary means of accessing the bibliographic records online. As time progressed and I became a better searcher, my productivity and output increased dramatically. Inevitably, I was offered a permanent position and received several promotions.

I currently catalog complex bibliographic serials and monographic titles in all formats. I rely heavily upon the OCLC Online Union Catalog to help me untangle and resolve a web of complex bibliographic problems. Serial unique aspects of serials cataloging involved title changes, mergers, splits, and reunions. These relationships may comprise two, three, five or ten different records, depending on the nature of the serial. In fact, I once encountered a serial title which involved nearly twenty (20) bibliographic records. The magnificence of it all was in locating all twenty (20) records, with the appropriate linking fields, in the OCLC database. Having access to the OCLC database saved time, energy, frustration, and not to mention a week's supply of Valiums.

The OCLC Online Union Catalog has greatly impacted how libraries and other information providers acquire, collect, preserve and disseminate information. From member libraries inputting catalog records to interlibrary loan transactions, the flow of information would be greatly impeded if the OCLC Online Union Catalog did not exist.

## Dorothy A. Griffith
Norristown Public Library
Norristown, PA

What the OCLC Online Union Catalog means to our library…

"If you can't find what you are seeking in our library, we will get it for you." OCLC has helped us live up to this promise, our library motto, since the mid 1970s. If a library user asked us for a new book, we usually purchased it on demand. By using OCLC for cataloging information, we were and still are able to get the book into the borrowers' hands quickly.

OCLC has certainly meant help to our library in achieving our goals. We started out as a small town library. In 1966 we merged with the county library to form the Montgomery County–Norristown Public Library. By 1978 we had so pleased the public with our motto, and with the help of OCLC, that we were able to move from our headquarters, an old church building. At that time, we were overflowing with books and personnel into adjacent buildings up and down the street. We had achieved another goal with a block-long building built especially for us by the county.

Soon we turned to OCLC again for help in getting everything the public needed. We began to use the OCLC interlibrary loan system. We had been laboriously typing forms in order to obtain materials needed, but suddenly we could borrow online. Gone were the frustrating delays caused by the return of forms for unfilled requests. Gone, too, was the necessity for sending new forms to different locations until available materials were found. With the OCLC system, we could put a chain of symbols into a workform on-screen and wait as the request moved from library to library until it was filled and shipped to us.

Conversely, other libraries on the OCLC system borrowed from us using the same method. Then, using OCLC's microenhancer, we were able to batch their requests and download them to our printer. So fast and efficient was this method that we became the largest supplier of interlibrary loan materials by a public library in the state of Pennsylvania. According to statistics released by our state, we have retained that honor year after year up to the present time. Other public libraries may be larger and serve more branch libraries, but we consistently do more true interlibrary lending. We couldn't do it without OCLC.

More recently, we have made use of EPIC for some difficult information requests. PRISM subject searching has sometimes been truly amazing. One patron asked about an author's correspondence with a critic. He was shocked and impressed when I asked him whether he was inquiring about the letter in a file folder in an Oregon university or the one in the collected papers in a Chicago library.

In short, OCLC has helped us to meet the standards we have set for our library. It has helped us to live up to our motto, taking care of just about every conceivable need for our borrowers in a timely and efficient manner. It has helped us to assist other libraries with interlibrary loans in locations near and far. It has eradicated distances, bringing us closer to other educational institutions. And finally, as it celebrates its twenty-fifth birthday, it has not rested on its laurels. Every year it introduces new enhancements to its programs. And every year it gets better and better.

## Elaine Griner
Brenau University
Gainesville, GA

As a "Jill-of-all-trades" librarian, the OCLC Online Union Catalog is my favorite toolbox. I use it every day to help me accomplish the many tasks required by my job.

As a cataloger, the OCLC Online Union Catalog is my source of MARC records, authority files, and other types of verification information. I use it to catalog all types of materials by updating the MARC records with our library holding symbol, and then exporting the MARC records for use in our local bibliographic utility. Authority files are checked as needed. I also search the OCLC Online Union Catalog in various ways to glean information about difficult-to-catalog items and/or items which have been cataloged in more than one way.

I use the OCLC Online Union Catalog to aid me at the reference desk. Specific requests for items can be verified and located. This information is then used to help patrons use other libraries in the area and/or make interlibrary loan requests based on correct, valid information. An astounding number of our students make use of this service. Interlibrary loan activity in our library has increased 200% in the last two years alone. Information gathered from this activity is used in book and serial acquisitions to make sure that the library collection adequately supports the needs of the university community.

Perhaps my most unusual and sometimes favorite use of the OCLC Online Union Catalog is as a teaching tool! Frequently, a university representative will bring a prospective student to the library and give me a chance to speak with the candidate. While explaining the library resources, I always let them know that nearly anything can be accessed by that student because of the OCLC Online Union Catalog. I explain that the OCLC Online Union Catalog is a worldwide database and that, through interlibrary loan, the student may have access to materials almost anywhere in the world! This information is quite impressive to students (and their parents). I feel that it opens their "academic eyes" to the fact that libraries are not simply isolated buildings with rows and rows of books and periodicals. They soon begin to realize that libraries are cooperative sharing ventures, and a vast majority of this sharing activity is supported and nurtured by the OCLC Online Union Catalog.

**Brad Grissom**
University of Kentucky
Lexington, KY

The Online Union Catalog is the single most important artifact of my professional life: the proverbial stranded-on-a-desert-island companion. As OCLC celebrates the twenty-fifth anniversary of the OCLC Online Union Catalog, I find myself in the twentieth year of my acquaintance with and use of it. It was in the spring semester of 1976, during an internship in the catalog department at the University of Kentucky, that I began manipulating bibliographic records in search, edit, and input modes at the bank of old Beehive terminals, to produce local catalog cards. I was learning the principles of catalog construction, and it was not difficult to see that this huge card-printing database was itself a special kind of catalog: the bibliographic distillation of a certain universe of recorded, collected, and held information. It wasn't called the OCLC Online Union Catalog back then, and it was merely the two-millionth record that was added that spring, but one could see the possibilities.

Fast forward twenty years to the spring of 1996. The OCLC Online Union Catalog nears its 35-millionth volume. (I tried hard once to get one of those milestones, but fell short.) A cascade of formats has enriched the OCLC Catalog, including authoritative CONSER records for serial publications. The magical interlibrary loan subsystem begins to celebrate its millions of transactions. The dread AACR2R is assimilated without a hitch. The no-nonsense authority file establishes itself as a mini-encyclopedia of who, what, and where. I am now in the business of interpreting the local catalog, and my access to its mighty parent is through something called PRISM, with keyword access. (Why, one can even scan titles there!) In a pinch, from home I can tap into the OCLC Catalog's identical twin on FirstSearch, where it bears the imposing name WorldCat. To my cataloging classes, I point to Dartmouth's terra cotta cone from ca. 2150 BC (once the oldest item in the OCLC Catalog) to next fall's trade publications. The most vexing reference questions are often easy work in this august array of descriptions.

My best moments with my desert-island pal, the OCLC Online Union Catalog, have been personal. I like to fill my NCAA men's basketball brackets each spring with OCLC symbols. This year, my 20th, I got to track KUK's run past CSJ, VPI, UUM, EWF, AUM, and SYB.

**Fantaye Hagos**
St. Mary University
San Antonio, TX

Readers of Alvin Toffler's *Future Shock* should be familiar with the concept of economic, political, social and technological transformation. Whether these changes are for better or worse depends on individual understandings.

Alarmists make our environments worse by disseminating their pessimistic views that Armageddon is around the corner. They make our environment hostile and unlivable. They convince us that every square inch of our environment is mined with explosives.

But we should never surrender our visions to our fears. Truly our future can yet be a bright one leading us to an undreamed threshold of peace and tranquillity.

The OCLC ONLINE UNION CATALOG is a reliable, resource sharing system which saves me countless minutes, endless labor and the distraction of unneeded information. It is my boon companion. It keeps me abreast of new databases, journals and documents. It helps me to stay current with advances in library technology.

The OCLC ONLINE UNION CATALOG introduces me to the mechanics of searching national and regional bibliographic records. I enjoy the liberty and privilege of interlibrary and serials control. I am delighted by the technical and reference services I obtain from other libraries.

The OCLC ONLINE UNION CATALOG provides ears, eyes and heart to keep me alive and in touch with different fields of knowledge. It guides me to great ideas from Socrates to Machiavelli, to political upheavals from the Caesars to Lani Guinier, from Rush Limbaugh to Hillary Clinton, from Clarence Thomas to Dan Quayle. It is like a central nervous system responding to my needs and interests in a coordinated pattern. OCLC ONLINE UNION CATALOG is not the Tower of Babel. But it is the repository of global memories. It is a simple and understandable universal language. It is a facilitator of my daily problems, an encyclopedic brain which makes my daily work easier, simpler, more comfortable and painless. It instantly puts me in touch with national, regional and world information while I sit at my computer chair. It is the barometer of my life which provides me information I need and like. I feel as if I have eaten my breakfast in Tokyo, my lunch in London and my dinner in Ohio.

The OCLC ONLINE UNION CATALOG quenches my intellectual curiosity. It is not a hex. It should not be feared like the triskaidekaphobia. The OCLC ONLINE UNION CATALOG is a system which yields the sweet honey of knowledge to aid us in living better now and in the future.

I am confident that there will come a day when the OCLC ONLINE UNION CATALOG will be available to every household and office providing us by the mere press of a button with information we need for our daily activities.

I commend you, OCLC ONLINE UNION CATALOG, for your reliability, dependability and sharing of resources. I raise a toast to you on your 25th anniversary. As we approach the new century, may the bonds of global cooperation and interpersonal networking be strengthened and increased.

**Rosemary Hahn**
Washington University Law Library
St. Louis, MO

When I first began working in an academic library's cataloging department in 1967, there was no OCLC. Original cataloging was done for all new books except those for which we received printed cards from the Library of Congress. Searching for retrospective copy was done in LC/NUC book catalogs, a time-consuming, often frustrating task involving tiny print and inadequate photocopiers. Once a master card was typed, it had to be copied and tracings had to be overtyped. The authority file was a wooden cabinet full of 3" x 5" cards.

Today I do original cataloging only when no library among the thousands on OCLC has cataloged the title. I search authority headings online. The OCLC authority file makes it easy for library users worldwide to verify a specific author, series, corporate body, or uniform title and thereby to use headings which other libraries can locate. When I attach our library's holding symbol to an OCLC bibliographic record, our holding of the title becomes available to libraries around the world for access purposes.

The result of these massive changes in less than 30 years means, first of all, that my job is both easier and more interesting. I have the satisfaction of knowing that the existence of and access to titles is becoming more global every day. No longer will patrons of small, rural libraries in this country or of underfunded libraries in third-world countries be denied information—because of the existence of OCLC, everyone, everywhere can access this wealth of knowledge.

**Danelle Hall**
Oklahoma City University
Oklahoma City, OK

tennessee williams robert frost jane austen elizabeth barrett browning great britain
wyoming new york tennessee west virginia oklahoma texas california oregon utah
catalan urdu serbo croatian vietnamese yiddish arizona new hampshire maine
wisconsin south dakota montana idaho michigan illinois kansas emile zola mark twain
south carolina france florida bulgarian thai ukranian greek norwegian william wordsworth
louis bromfield aamilne chinese japanese latin portuguese iowa indiana

A WORLD OF INFORMATION
A WEALTH OF LANGUAGES
THE RICHES OF MANY VIEWPOINTS AND BELIEFS
CATALOGS FROM ALL OF THE STATES OF OUR UNION
CATALOGS FROM OTHER COUNTRIES
THE INTELLECTUAL RICHES OF THE WORLD THROUGH A FEW
KEYSTROKES

## Nancy S. Halpert
New Canaan Library
New Canaan, CT

Some twenty-five years ago when I was a member of the reference department of a university library, one of my responsibilities was handling interlibrary loan. Dealing with the numerous requests for book and periodical material made by students and faculty took a large share of my time. I recall that this service was one of the most appreciated offered by the library. The necessary procedures, however, were cumbersome, to say the least. Requests to other libraries were made by mail, using the required ALA forms, after verifying the titles in the *National Union Catalog,* or in the case of periodicals, in the Union List of Serials. After the establishment of a local library system, I was able to obtain material from the local area by telephone, but this proved so time-consuming that it was necessary to hire a student assistant. OCLC may be observing its 25th anniversary, but its existence was unknown to me or anyone else at the university at that time.

As a reference librarian for the past 17 years at the New Canaan, CT Library, I have had the responsibility for Interlibrary Loan only for the past six or seven years, quite some time after our library became part of OCLC. Thinking back on the two situations, I can truly say there is no comparison. The speed, efficiency, and accuracy of OCLC has given a completely different dimension to ILL service, still one of the most appreciated of the library's many services. In addition, since we are fortunate to have the OCLC terminal located right at the Information (Reference) Desk, it proves its value as a service tool over and over during the course of a day, as all of us in the Reference Department use it to provide bibliographic information to telephone callers, whose inquiries come from surrounding communities as well as from our own library members. With the addition of FirstSearch, which patrons as well as staff members utilize, the OCLC system has become indispensable. Congratulations on your first Twenty-Five Years!

## Susan Hamilton
Starkville-Oktibbeha Library System
Starkville, MS

As I sit at my PC monitor and watch as information appears on my screen in seconds (not hours or days) I, like so many others, take for granted the convenience and ease with which I can access information.

When I first became employed at the Starkville Public Library in 1978, gathering information was indeed a time-consuming job involving mountains of paperwork. I can remember being relieved that I was not the interlibrary loan librarian, buried underneath it all. How in the world did she keep it all straight?

When I became interlibrary loan librarian in the early 1990s, I didn't have quite the job others did in the past, but I still had to rely on the Mississippi Library Commission to do OCLC searches for me. Our library is a relatively new member of GAC, and the first time I completed a search and actually put in a request for a book, I was fascinated and overjoyed with the OCLC Online Union Catalog. The wealth of information seems endless and the ability it gives us to serve our patrons is invaluable.

So much new material is published yearly in so many different fields that our library system could not possibly store or maintain a collection as large as the 35 million records that are currently contained on the OCLC Online Union Catalog. Two million new records are added annually, and as each new source is added, the information is available for not just the patrons of one community, but for millions all over the world to access! The OCLC Online Union Catalog now houses 35 million records and has over 560 million location listings. Who would have imagined it 25 years ago when it was first put into operation?

Although a library should be so much more than an information superhighway, and too much emphasis is sometimes put on efficiency, the ability to retrieve information as quickly and accurately as possible leaves more time for personal interaction. As we move toward the next century, it will be interesting to see what advances the OCLC Online Union Catalog will make in the next 25 years!

———————————— ⅋ ————————————

**Ashley Hanson**
Connecticut College
New London, CT

I remember my first class in library school. It was a summer class at the University of Rhode Island. Summer classes are miserable at best. While everyone else is off at the beach, I was studying for my "Foundations of Library Science" test. The professor did his best to make it exciting and he actually did manage to grab my attention, despite all the distractions pulling at my twenty-three year old self. One day after a particularly fascinating class I found myself facing the entrance to my workplace with a sense of awe. This was no longer a concrete building with lots of musty books, yellowing 3" x 5" cards and aging old women who recited call numbers like mantras. This was "The Library!" Suddenly, I saw my workplace in a shining, new light. It seemed so grand and worldly. But the best was yet to come…Then God created OCLC.

In "Foundations" OCLC was just a vague notion. It wasn't until later, while taking cataloging, that I actually was able to learn and use this magical tool. At first it all seemed mind boggling. How in the world was I going to remember 3,2,2,1 or 4,3,1? And why are the commas so important? Slowly, the foreign language of searching the OCLC Online Union Catalog became part of my own. I even became indignant when "scan title" was introduced. "Scan title" is for sissies.

Now, when I pass by the massive green volumes of the NUC, I say a silent prayer to the library gods. "Thank you for inventing OCLC before I entered the library work force." I cannot imagine doing interlibrary loan before the OCLC Online Union Catalog. Occasionally, I get an scholarly elderly patron that informs me of a volume's location. "According to the *National Union Catalog…*," she says sternly while peering over her glasses. I thank her kindly and look it up on OCLC, 3,2,2,1 or 4,3,1. I suppose I might have stronger arms if the NUC were still the ILL tool of choice, but I am certain fewer patrons would be happy with my service.

The library is truly a magic place and I have not lost that sense of awe as I walk in the door each day. At the beginning of my career, the OCLC Online Union Catalog provided me with a sense of disbelief. As I learned it, it became a necessity. Now it feels like a place to come home to as other aspects of my job grow and change so rapidly. The OCLC Online Union Catalog now provides me with a sense of comfort. Thank you, OCLC.

## Junie Hao
Olathe Public Library
Olathe, KS

OCLC Online Union Catalog means sharing to me. When I first entered the field of cataloging just one year ago as a new MLS graduate, it was the feeling of sharing that overcame my fear of being overwhelmed in the ocean of cataloging rules, interpretations, manuals, and handbooks, not mentioning the tremendous variety of materials that I received daily. It was the OCLC Online Union Catalog that provided me a reliable, efficient, comprehensive vehicle and got me started to navigate in the treasure of human knowledge.

The Catalog's quality and standards have long been recognized and praised by libraries through the world. It is such a cooperative effort that created the largest, most comprehensive bibliographic resources that no single library could ever possess. It is nurtured and cherished through the whole library community thereafter. I often heard tales of "old days" before the OCLC Online Union Catalog and feel lucky to connect with it when technologies and this database itself have reached to their developed stage today with more sophistication and comprehensives. Ever since the very beginning, the Online Union Catalog provided a supporting backbone to my daily work. It networks a team of library staff, especially a highly well-trained and experienced cataloging crew working in different sites through all the United States and the world. Through the network, the Catalog brings together professional expertise in cataloging and in all subject areas, even in various languages. I am always fascinated to find that there is always someone out there concern what I concern and care what I care. My dilemmas, puzzles and questions are listened to and ready to be shared with. It is this kind of sharing and support that makes me confident and competent on my job. The OCLC Online Union Catalog is like a true friend whom I have known for years and whom I know I can always count on. Meanwhile, it facilitates the best means of continuous education as well as a learning tool for my cataloging practice and in many other areas. I was amazed to envision a broad boulevard right in front of me through the Union Catalog toward professional growth. By the endeavor of keeping up with the quality and standard with the Union Catalog, I am confident to say I am making myself a better cataloging librarian everyday.

Working with Online Union Catalog is also a shared experience in terms of participation and contribution from individuals like myself. Inviting input, update and report from participating libraries makes the Catalog more of a shared endeavor. The fact of being able to making contributions to benefit others outside my own institution makes my cataloging practice even more meaningful. Remembering the day when I entered my very first record into the OCLC Online Union Catalog, it certainly made my day.

Today, along with celebrating the 25 years of library cooperation with the Catalog, I celebrate the first anniversary of my professional librarianship. I am very proud of being part of the whole picture that I have looked upon. Thanks to the collaborative wisdom of the whole library community that makes the Catalog possible, thousands of libraries of all types through the world benefit from it tremendously as rewards. Needless to say, with OCLC playing the leading role as technologies rapidly evolve and develop in information organization and retrieval, the OCLC Online Union Catalog will grow prosperously in every respect. There is no doubt in my mind, you and I will, too, grow together with it—the OCLC Online Union CATALOG!

**Barbro Harris**
Victoria University of Wellington
Wellington, New Zealand

I am a Reference Librarian at Victoria University in Wellington, the Capital City of Aotearoa/New Zealand.

I have been a librarian long enough to recall the heady days in the late seventies when we began searching online. That awesome wealth of knowledge in an instant!

The 'cost per minute' awareness created a new sense of pressure in a profession that had largely been spared the attentions of burnout or stress researchers. Distance was suddenly broken when one was as up-to-date as those "overseas."

The next milestone was CD ROM on which we let our users loose by themselves and found that they could actually master their own searching reasonably well even if we 'librarianishly' often didn't approve of the way in which they got there.

And now OCLC FirstSearch. Users no longer need to come near us! It is the perfect system; easy enough for our users to hack away at with good results, while still having some secret tricks in reserve for us librarians and which, when revealed or demonstrated, made us feel clever and needed. The OCLC Union Catalog was from the outset very heavily used, especially by those in the humanities who had so long felt that the Super Highways held little for them!

> In our department we juggle several hats;
> We help find information for our users, at all levels.
> We are responsible for interlibrary loans/document delivery.
> We organize and deliver our user education programmes.
> We maintain the Reference Collection.

The boundaries between these areas are fluid and the functions interrelated. But in all areas, OCLC has made our life easier.

Very seldom do we conduct a reference interview without accessing OCLC. A large proportion of interlibrary loan work includes OCLC Online Union Catalog access. Demonstration of OCLC databases and often the Union Catalog in particular is an integral part of our postgraduate and faculty training sessions. Monitoring new items is essential for the maintenance and development of a relevant reference collection, again assisted by the Union Catalog.

Ours was never "a just in case" library, even before the phrase was coined, or Conspectus told us so. Identifying collection strengths elsewhere is of great help to us as well as a means of advising postgraduates and academics where to go for further study or research.

Finally, I am on a personal level, grateful to the Union Catalog. Born and educated in Sweden, I belong to an often neglected linguistic majority: NON-ENGLISH. The inclusion of significant numbers of "foreign" language records enables me to keep in touch with my linguistic and literary roots. The same goes for other "new" New Zealanders. Living in this distant land, they value the bridge to their cultural pasts.

We talk about "libraries without walls," of the "virtual library." Clichés, yes, but true of course! To share access to collections, rather than withholding privileged knowledge is a step towards a more equitable redistribution of information wealth. The OCLC Online Union Catalog has opened the gate!

## Susan Hartman
Pathfinder Regional Library Service System
Grand Junction, CO

It was a slow day at the Littleville Public Library. Maybe today Adriane would have time to tackle that "to do" stack. But first things first; when the library is only open 20 hours a week, time is important.

Adriane sat down at her new computer. When the state had offered a chance at the FirstSearch pilot project, a local businessman had loaned a computer to the library so they could try this new strategy. Adriane could now find materials that her patrons wanted, even when all they had was a subject and an idea. She could even tell if books were available in-state! If the materials were at the college in the nearby town, patrons often went there instead of using interlibrary loan. After the FirstSearch pilot project ended, two patrons had made generous donations so the library could buy its own computer and continue using FirstSearch.

Adriane logged on to FirstSearch and found records for the items her patrons wanted. Only three weren't available in-state. Next, go into ACLIN, the state-wide database, to see if the items are on the shelf, then print the forms and fax them. Adriane wondered what she ever did without computers, especially when Mr. Yokomoto came in looking for books in Japanese. With OCLC and FirstSearch, no problem now!

Adriane faxed the requests to libraries around the state, following protocols of course, then faxed the last three to the system office. They would put them on the OCLC ILL subsystem for her and in about ten days she would have the books for her patrons. Next Adriane checked out and boxed two books to loan to other libraries; the system often contacted her with several requests from OCLC, asking if she could loan them.

Adriane then boxed five books and two videos to send to the system office for cataloging. These were the items not in the OCLC database that the system would add and catalog for her. She also added a list of new books. The system would send her labels and the catalog cards would come from OCLC shortly—ready to file. Adriane was thankful for that time-saver.

When things settled down and she was comfortable with the new computer and the Internet, Adriane would ask the system to set up her computer so she could catalog her own materials using OCLC. (They're testing that procedure with other libraries now.) Then Adriane would only need to send the books she couldn't find and the experts would add them to the OCLC database.

With modern technology—and OCLC—the small one-person library now has the same capabilities as the big libraries. The Littleville Public Library is no longer that "poor little library down the road," but a true partner in the library world—and patrons in rural areas can get the same level of service as patrons in the cities. "Empowerment…Yesss," thought Adriane as she turned off the computer and prepared to close the library for the day.

**Sharon Herr**
Ohio Northern University
Ada, OH

The OCLC Online Union Catalog has been an important part of every milestone in my career.

When I entered the library profession in 1974, I chose Ohio Northern University because its library was one of the original 54 libraries which began using the OCLC Online Union Catalog in 1971. I felt that there was no better place to learn or opportunity to be on the cutting edge than at an OCLC library. The opportunity was irresistible to me. My first position was that of Science Librarian which included duties in cataloging and interlibrary loan. Having been a student assistant who typed catalog cards in the 1960s, I was truly enthralled with the leap forward made in the collaborative cataloging that took place in the online union catalog. Even before the interlibrary loan system was started, the OCLC Online Union Catalog was invaluable for providing holdings information needed to fill interlibrary loan requests.

When I changed positions in 1978 and became the library's cataloger, the OCLC Online Union Catalog was indispensable in eliminating a cataloging backlog of gift material from the 1940s and 1950s. The late 1970s and early 1980s brought the announcement of the Library of Congress's intention to implement an online public access catalog (opac) and close the card catalog. Our visionary director got us started on a retrospective conversion project assuring me that one day we, too, would have an opac. The Online Union Catalog was our repository for getting the cataloging for our holdings in machine-readable form. It was an exciting 8-year in-house project during which I saw the OCLC database grow in depth and breadth.

When we implemented our online public access catalog in 1992, getting our records from OCLC, processing them for authority control and merging them into a union catalog with our law library (also an OCLC member) was a breeze.

The OCLC Online Union Catalog has been instrumental in every leap this library has taken and I don't believe I could have had such a rewarding career without it.

## Norma J. Hervey
Luther College
Decorah, IA

A miracle. It was 1972, I had just finished my MLS degree and confronted the challenges of cataloging backlogs of some twenty-five years in a small church-related university with limited funds. Visiting Akron, my BA institution, I saw the OCLC miracle which, unfortunately, was in Ohio. *Why* was I in New York?

By 1974, I was training at SUNY with Glen and Mary; in spite of a January snowstorm which grounded all planes, I was airborne even after the grueling trip from western NY to Albany via bus from Buffalo to Rochester, by train from Rochester to Albany where we arrived at 2 a.m., one day late, minus 20 degrees Fahrenheit. Six months later, we had virtually no backlog and were reclassifying. I haven't had to look back again until now!

My next position, catalog librarian in a major state university, which had not yet addressed a significant lack of staff over a number of years during which time the collection had tripled, offered new challenges. The card catalog was the worst I had ever seen. But, the opportunities offered by OCLC promised an escape from the morass. AMIGOS, was there for us.

When I left, a vision for total resolution of those problems, a promise fulfilled by those who came after—with the help of OCLC. I went on to tackle problems resulting from reclassification with local modifications and rapid changes of staff. Seven years later, I moved on but, by then, there was an online catalog, a marvelous ILL system, and retrospective conversion was nearly complete. The folks at MINITEX lit the way.

Next position? Library director. Now what did OCLC have to offer me? Naturally, there were similarities, a network, BCR, ILL, tapes for the first online catalog, retrospective conversion, statistical support—but there were also new opportunities. Needs of my library focused on automation, staff development, and collection development! Where else but to OCLC! Staff training opportunities continued to be provided by OCLC at national conferences and BCR. The most exciting area now was building collections. We established a liaison structure to work with academic departments and used OCLC to assess our collections, compare them with those of other high-quality liberal arts colleges and to buy. The collection, even after assiduous weeding, grew. Again, OCLC came through. Today OCLC offers international access, CJK, multiple catalog and ILL record holders, access to patron searching, online indices, and more. Tomorrow's expectations are that change will continue ever more rapidly *and* that OCLC and its networks will be there for us! OCLC has been there for me now for the past twenty-four years. To think I once wondered what a MARC record might be and, more importantly, what difference it would make to me. My good fortune in entering this profession as visionaries like Fred Kilgour created solutions to age-old problems cannot be measured. I am indeed fortunate as are my fellow users.

**Judy Siehl Hill**
Butler University
Indianapolis, IN

Cataloging in the year Five P.O. (Pre-OCLC)...

It seemed like a normal day. I was sitting at my OCLC terminal entering an original record for a musical score, when suddenly I was transported back to the year 5 P.O. (Pre-OCLC). I opened my eyes and, to my horror, found myself frantically searching the NUCs to find the L.C. card number for an obscure German text. I had already gone through the first three sets, since our library did not have the Mansell accumulation. At last, just when I was on the verge of re-christening the author, I stumbled on the correct spelling for his surname and found several books with the same title. Egad! Not one of them was the right edition.

As if in a dream, I found myself ordering what I hoped was the matching card set. I typed the L.C. card number on the order form and added it to the pile of forms I had already accumulated. I put the book on a shelf in the cataloging room to gather dust for four or five months until the Library of Congress sent the card set.

With a sigh, I got to work on the L.C. card sets that had arrived in the morning's mail. I tried matching the cards to the books but found that—as usual—the cards didn't always match the books. It didn't seem to matter that the L.C. card number in the book and on the card itself were exactly the same. To add to my frustration, several of the card sets had the right author and title, but the wrong publishing information. Finally, I marked the corrections that the student assistant needed to make on each of the cards.

When she saw all the changes she would have to make, she groaned. "Why do I have to use the electric eraser? Wouldn't it be easier just to type the whole card set from scratch?" she wondered.

It was finally time to do some original cataloging, even though I didn't have the information I needed to establish the added entries correctly. As I sat there, rubbing my aching head, I thought, "There has to be a better way!" I closed my eyes in despair.

When I opened them again, I was sitting in front of my OCLC terminal cutting the correct name from an authority record and pasting it into the bibliographical record I was creating. After validating the information, I updated the record and exported it into our local system. This score could be picked up today by the professor.

**John D. Hill**
Spalding University
Clarksville, IN

To understand my views toward OCLC, you have to understand a little about me. I have always been a "book person," but in a way that goes beyond simply enjoying reading. I have always not only liked books, but also the libraries in which they were found. However, my feelings come not merely from the quantity of books provided. I admire the order and organization that keeps a library from being just a chaotic large pile of books, but instead allows pieces of interest to be found. With this system, a library becomes more than just the sum of its collection, just as a living being is greater than the elements of which it is formed.

My delight for libraries continued to grow upon discovering—while a child in a small rural town—that my local library card allowed me to visit other libraries in the area. However, while this provided me with increased reading material, it did not give me any means of finding a particular book besides a long car ride. Luckily, since that time, the many other libraries I have experienced, both as an employee and as a patron, have been in some form of library system. Working in libraries in Illinois made me aware of the potential in a system that interconnected libraries of all sizes, in spite of being limited in scope to a single state. Similarly, I found the interconnected library systems of the three major universities in the Triangle area in North Carolina extremely useful during my time as a student there.

My firsthand experience with OCLC, however, has come with my most recent library position in the interlibrary loan department of a small private university. Here OCLC serves as the main means of conducting interlibrary loan, connecting us with our primary partners in the city and the state. In addition, it allows us to search the entire nation and much of the world for harder to find items. It is this experience working within the framework and scope of this system that, when asked "what OCLC means to me," aims my perspective not at the present, but into the future. I see OCLC supplying the basis for a completely interconnected global library system, connecting providers and users throughout the world. This vision parallels many predictions for the future of the Internet and the World Wide Web. However, OCLC would supply a system of order and organization for the increasingly chaotic sea of electronic information. In addition, another, and some may say a more important, role exists for OCLC. For no matter how the system may change to handle the growth of the electronic exchange of data and literature, it will remain a meeting place for those interested in items whose large size or small demand would keep them out of this electronic exchange. Consequently, in spite of what those focusing on the web might say, OCLC will only gain in importance as libraries continue to move into the "information age."

**Lisa Hines**
Rice University
Houston, TX

In essence, the OCLC Online Union Catalog means *the world* to me. Not only can I find bibliographic data on materials ancient and modern, I can also communicate around the world instantly with other libraries via the interlibrary loan subsystem. I was rather surprised to receive a request one day from Centralna Tehniska in Ljubljana, Slovenia, which I believe was the first request I have seen electronically from an East European country. With the vast amount of material entered into OCLC, and with all the subscribing libraries, the world is really at your fingertips!

For me, OCLC is a *challenge* to research. While searching requests for patrons as well as doing a little creative searching for myself, I find it overwhelming (in a good way) the number of items entered on a topic. I enjoy locating obscure items that patrons have submitted, while also coming up with topics myself and entering different search strategies. When I became interested in the politics of Northern Ireland, I found records and holders for items that I thought might not be available in the U.S.! I could sit in front of OCLC for days and never lack for something to search—which makes using OCLC fun to work with!

Also, OCLC is a *valuable* resource in the information society—not only in our everyday work such as cataloging records, searching for items, and filling ILL requests but also in special projects. Take the Omaha Project, for example. About 30,000 stolen items, many rare, were able to find their proper homes with the assistance of OCLC. In fact, if I remember correctly from the film about the project, the use of OCLC helped the FBI finish the case sooner than expected!

As much as I love finding information, I have seen how patrons seem to enjoy using OCLC, as evidenced in their experiences using WorldCat. Sometimes patrons will bring to the ILL department a record that they themselves have found on OCLC! Remember the cliché, "It's a small world"? I rather think it is a big world, and OCLC just brings it closer to home!

**Eloise R. Hitchcock**
Tennessee Technological University
Cookeville, TN

The OCLC Online Union Catalog means that libraries worldwide are able to provide access to the recorded knowledge of humankind. This incredible achievement not only exemplifies the fulfillment of the profession's basic goals, it is a monument to global cooperation. Librarians have worked together in creating the world's largest bibliographic database. This accomplishment has allowed libraries to be among the first to participate in the electronic information age, and to become a major presence on the information superhighway. As a librarian, the OCLC Online Union Catalog is a valuable tool for executing the responsibilities of my profession. The database represents the collective desire to bring together information and information seekers.

The ability to retrieve bibliographic information is strengthened by the creation and continuous development of the database. Throughout the world, subject experts are contributing to the advancement of the OCLC Online Union Catalog. Even the smallest libraries input records for unique materials and gain from the shared expertise of the database membership. Collection development activities are enhanced by the capacity to examine records and analyze holdings data. Acquisition of new titles is expedited through verifying bibliographic information and utilizing records for order processing. Furthermore, the OCLC database is essential to the concept of access versus holdings prevalent in today's environment of fiscal austerity and expanded access to materials. Sharing of resources through interlibrary loan services could not be effective without a database to provide holdings details as well as the means of communicating requests through the ILL subsystem. More than 560 million locations containing 4,000 years of knowledge are made available to every participating library around the globe. The OCLC Online Union Catalog is the virtual library without walls. Internationally, researchers of all types benefit from access to this vast resource.

Librarians are often cautioned that they will be left behind on the information superhighway and our mission to provide information access will become obsolete. Contrarily, the creation of the OCLC Online Union Catalog 25 years ago has proven to be a visionary accomplishment. Online catalogs, most built through OCLC participation, were among the first databases to appear on the Internet and have enhanced the perception of the Internet as a tool of value to society. As a librarian, library user, faculty member, and student, I have greatly benefited from the services provided through the use of the OCLC Online Union Catalog. It has been meaningful to me in helping to realize, to the best of my ability, a commitment to the ideals of librarianship.

## Michael Ho
East Texas State University
Commerce, TX

Years ago cataloging was considered boring and clerical. Ever since the introduction of OCLC Online Union Catalog, things have changed dramatically. To me, as a catalog librarian, the OCLC Catalog means POWER, acronym of Progress, Opportunity, Worldwide Involvement, Efficiency and Resource.

**PROGRESS.** In the last two decades, we saw libraries go online local one after another, breaking out from the shackle of limited entries, labor intensive filing and unsightly drawers of smelly catalog cards. Nowadays, people can enjoy state-of-the-art computer systems for bibliographic information, which in fact evolved from a host database like OCLC.

**OPPORTUNITY.** Before joining OCLC, the catalog in my library was overloaded with unconventional practice. To change is not easy because it would mean opposition to those who held their belief dearly. When OCLC came along, an invincible force began to form. The importance of conformation gave us no choice except to clean up and to accept standardization. I am glad that I had the opportunity, brought about by OCLC, to update the irregularities and to preserve the integrity of a later local online catalog.

**WORLDWIDE INVOLVEMENT.** Knowledge has no boundaries. Research nowadays often takes the form of international cooperation. Multiculturalism also has a greater place in the society. People around the world feel the pressing need for a global information exchange. It is in a right direction that OCLC has incorporated bibliographic MARC records from foreign countries. Because of the international participation, records for foreign publications are now easily available, which in turn save the cataloger a lot of time on searching, verifying and creating.

**EFFICIENCY.** With its flexibility and multiple access approaches available, the OCLC Online Union Catalog can be searched by anyone without cataloging experience, a big contrast to the NUC we once relied on. With an online system, the same job can be done much faster with less people. Time-consuming original cataloging has been reduced tremendously because the system provides most of the records.

**RESOURCE.** Consistency and accuracy are the primary concerns of catalogers. As the OCLC Catalog is under the surveillance of numerous professionals and provides authority records for verifications, quality control is greatly enhanced. Most of the time we resort to the catalog for resolving conflicts. The database of more than 35 million bibliographic records is also a good source for information.

My long years of working with OCLC Online Union Catalog have made me believe that these five forces (Progress, Opportunity, Worldwide Involvement, Efficiency and Resource) have formed POWER, not only just an acronym but also the actual power, that has moved many libraries into a new era of online cataloging. To cope with the impact, I find my role constantly changed. The world of cataloging is now more exciting and challenging. I am proud of the milestone in the development of bibliographic information. Yet this is not the end, because the OCLC Online Union Catalog will continue to improve and grow. I am optimistic about the future of OCLC connection, and I appreciate the vision of the founding fathers and the commitment of those that keep the work going.

## Lynne Hobbs

Prince William Public Library System
Woodbridge, VA

Long, long ago, so long ago it is almost lost in the mists of time (or twenty-five years ago if you want to be really specific), all the animals of the world were lost in the Forest of Confusion. There were no Bibliographic Standards to guide their way, no sturdy General Material Designations to stem the floods of information that periodically inundated their domain. They needed help, and lo, their pleas were heard. The Good Fairy of Information floated down from the Halls of Enlightenment (i.e., Ohio) and gave them counsel.

"You must build the Omnipotent Castle of Light and Clarity," she instructed them.

The denizens of the Forest looked at each other in dismay. They were willing to buckle down and work like beavers (or squirrels, rabbits, or bears), but they hadn't a clue as to what the Good Fairy meant. Some of the smaller animals were sniggering and poking each other in the ribs, muttering "omnipotent, omnipotent," so the Good Fairy cuffed them smartly and explained.

"You first must Fix your Fields," she proclaimed. "Then you will set up Constants and Variables. It follows as the night the day, the order of Formats and Standards, but beware ye of Duplicates. Thus will the Castle be built."

Well, now that she had made it all crystal clear, the animals set to work with willing paws and gladsome hearts. In no time at all, they had constructed a veritable Tower of Babel, tidily made of Records, thirty-five million in all, stacked one upon the other reaching to the heavens.

The Omnipotent Castle of Light and Clarity was a superb sight, but the animals soon realized they were hardly better off than before, what with having sore paws from all the construction, and vertigo from the height. They grumbled to each other and furtively looked around for a handy petard upon which to hoist the Good Fairy.

"Silence!" thundered the G.F. "All is well."

As the animals stopped, literally in their tracks, they could hear noises from afar. Construction equipment rumbled through the trees and sunlight beckoned.

"We spied your magnificent Castle," boomed the construction foreman. "Please, join us now in our Quest for Knowledge."

It was a glorious day indeed, for the Omnipotent Castle of Light and Clarity was connected at last to the Information Highway.

And as you travel down that marvelous Highway, remember who made all this possible, and give thanks to the Good Fairy and all her willing workers.

## Marjorie C. Hoeft
Blue Mountain Community College Library
Pendleton, OR

"Just imagine little green men and women marching to Ohio. It takes a few seconds," my PACNET trainer informed me. The monitor suddenly flashed, revealing the bib record of my first search. For me, the cataloging librarian at Blue Mountain Community College, that search marked the end of the traditional and the beginning of electronic communication. I was simultaneously filled with excitement and fear.

Could I learn the required skills and use them to improve on the familiar old ways? Could I give up carefully kept authority card files, the electric typewriter, and finally, the ultimate sacrifice, the sacrosanct card catalog? It was a turning point in my library career, an intimidating challenge that would propel me and other librarians in my region to share our ideas about where technology was taking us. Conservatives all, we needed convincing that we could share resources. But change was in the wind. Together, we took the first tentative steps toward resource sharing.

Because I was the only librarian in the district who cataloged on OCLC, other libraries began to contract with Blue Mountain Community College for my cataloging services. Each library had to obtain its own OCLC profile and institution symbol. Then the librarians began to bring box after box of books, a veritable Himalaya, to the BMCC Library for processing and adding to OCLC.

The OCLC tapeload capability would make possible the creation of a shared database.

In 1990, BMCC, together with public and school libraries formed a local library district, whose coordinator selected a consultant to help design a locally shared system. Once the system had been installed, the patrons of small libraries in remote sections of the counties learned that they could not only find out what other libraries much larger than their own held, they could also borrow anything, from Zane Grey to Xanadu, and receive it at their local libraries via courier. They could make interlibrary loan requests for materials held in the local district, the entire United States, or even the world itself, wherever an OCLC affiliation existed. What unlimited choice!

It was an achievement that eliminated the isolation that had been an accepted part of Eastern Oregon life. OCLC had been, throughout the transitional period, the facilitator of this miracle. Its unfailing user support, clearly written manuals, training sessions and aggressive research had been the backbone and mainstay of this remarkable occurrence.

Now the electronic cataloging process, evolving and never static, has become an integral part of my modus operandi. Gone is my fear, replaced by confidence and pride that I have participated in an event that has bridged human technology in a galactic span from electric typewriter to the Internet, that serves human information needs in undreamed of ways. To OCLC belongs the credit for this splendid resource that serves us all, and reminds us to be grateful that, even while we sleep, the little green men and women wait our bidding, at the touch of keystroke—forever.

—————————— *∛* ——————————

## Virginia Elizabeth Hollandsworth
David Lipscomb University Library
Nashville, TN

The OCLC Online Union Catalog has enabled our library to be connected with thousands of libraries around the world and to seek information not readily available to us. It has been most effective in retrieving books and articles for students and faculty research. Each day our library receives requests for information other libraries retain. Without OCLC the process could take weeks. The OCLC Online Union Catalog cuts stand-by time almost completely and makes pertinent information available immediately. The OCLC Online Union Catalog also allows our library to send books and periodicals to other libraries and universities who need our materials. This is a service that our reference department takes great pride in carrying out each day. Without OCLC our faculty, staff, and students would have to wait on materials for months or turn to other sources that might have less-valued information, and we could not perform our library operations effectively.

—————————— *∛* ——————————

## Victoria Ann Horst

Newberry College
Newberry, SC

I work as the Public Services Librarian in a small, four-year liberal arts church school. Our collection has been carefully developed over the 140 years of our existence to support the curriculum that is being offered here—a rich mixture of arts, philosophy and science courses designed to give our students the tools necessary to develop into well informed thinking, caring people.

The "problem" we have is that we have students and faculty who are intellectually curious. They are interested in pursuing research in areas where our collection is not well developed. The OCLC Online Union Catalog means that I can provide these patrons access to the contents of what amounts to the largest library in the world. This is more than using the Internet to peek into the OPACs of one or two university libraries. I have the ability to judge fairly accurately the level of human knowledge and activity on any particular subject.

Me having access to the OCLC Online Union Catalog to do research for my patrons could probably be compared to giving a few average ten-year-olds permission to help themselves at the world's largest candy store—the feeling of power, that super feeling of this-is-so-cool-what-looks-good-today that has not gone away even though I have been using the catalog for almost two years. What is especially fun for me is being able to provide an item that the patron will never have imagined existed, or believed to be impossible to obtain with an ease and speed that makes the process look almost magical. The OCLC Online Union Catalog makes me look intelligent, professional and competent—and I am very fond of that, especially when it is so much fun.

Having access to the OCLC Online Union Catalog when I am fulfilling my role as the Interlibrary Loan Librarian means that I am able to accurately identify who owns what I am looking for and request that item—all in one-, two-, or three-minute sessions even if patrons are not positively sure of what they want. And this process works two ways. I am able to share my resources with patrons from all over the United States, and more recently Canada—people who would never have known there is such a place as Newberry, South Carolina if they had not read it on a book plate in the book they got on Interlibrary Loan, from me.

So, the OCLC Online Union Catalog lets me do my work quickly and accurately. It has always helped me look good even at the beginning of my career when I was not completely sure how to search it effectively. Now that I have become a more accomplished searcher, I am often surprised and pleased at the material I am able to finesse from the huge amount of material available. What else could I want?

## Stephanie Hranjec

University of Rochester
Pittsford, NY

OCLC is like a magic and unlimited window into the world of different media, a kaleidoscopic screen that constantly changes its colors and shapes. Within seconds, electromagnetic waves transport me into the scene of libraries and publishers, and set me on the shelves among different kinds of literature; I am informed about the newest publications in New York City, Virginia or California, what the people in Europe like to read, what Pavarotti sang under the blue Italian sky in Verona, and the fabulous and fascinating world in which Jane Austen's heroes lived.

Titles flying on the screen reflect the state of affairs of the human species, its troubles and problems: famine in Africa, violence in the streets, adolescents' fears, drugs, crime, the economic situation, war in the Balkans, the Earth's environment. But they also show the faith in people, new scientific discoveries, a new medicine as a hope for millions, a trust in God and family, and the preparation for the upcoming Olympic Games. They tell me a story about a recently-found new Shakespearean masterpiece and the most current sports results. What an amazing world is the OCLC kaleidoscope!

OCLC also means technological advancement in the field of library science and the cooperation of libraries and librarians all over the world, despite all political, racial and religious barriers. We all try to reach our common goal: to represent as best as possible the textual, vocal, and visual communication of past, present and future generations of our multi-cultural world.

Just as the heart is the vital organ of our bodies, so OCLC is at the center of thousands of libraries worldwide, connecting us all via its services. The proof of this lies for me in every MARC record, for there, in the center of each fixed field, is "Srce," which is a code for "source," but which in my mother language* means "HEART."

*Slovenian language

———————————— ✔ ————————————

**Norman Huckle**
University of Nevada–Reno
Reno, NV

The OCLC Online Union Catalog means a great deal to me since I work in the document delivery department at my library. When I started in my position in ILL six years ago, my library was on RLIN and we used the RLIN ILL subsystem. In the summer of 1992, my library changed over to OCLC. Immediately there was a big change in the work flow in our office. Literally overnight, I no longer had to use Ontyme, E-mail, or ALA forms to order needed items. OCLC made it possible for us to order nearly 95% of our ILL's on one system. Impact from these sudden changes caused us to go from one computer in the office to three. One computer was our dedicated line for OCLC borrowing, the other machine had dial-in access to OCLC for lending, and the third was used for E-mail and word processing. Since our borrowing activity was mainly on one machine, we trained student assistants and other staff to process and borrow items for ILL. In 1995, all three machines were given access to OCLC over the library's LAN to the OCLC comptroller. In 1996, we plan to add a fourth machine for a half-time library assistant to be hired.

In the summer of 1994, the library administration made a dramatic change in our ILL policies. We instituted a new policy for rush and non-rush requests for copies. We started charging ten cents a page for non-rush copies and twenty cents a page for copies needed within forty-eight hours, and we no longer passed charges on to our patron if there were lending charges for books borrowed. That summer, to entice faculty to use the service and to show we could obtain items quickly, our dean attended department meetings on campus and gave out coupons for free delivery of an article needed within forty-eight hours. As we all know in ILL, commercial vendors don't own all the journal titles that you need to get quickly, so we often find ourselves turning to other academic libraries for rush delivery. I gained a new appreciation for libraries that union listed. Each time someone turned in one of those coupons, I was able to find a library that held the item by checking their union list and asking the lending library to fax it to me. The fact is that the library's union list has helped us achieve the goals that have been established with our new policies.

OCLC has demonstrated over and over again that it is the best when it comes to verifying requests and finding a library or vendor to send it quickly. That's what it means to me!

———————————— ⑴ ————————————

### Zhang Huiping
Beijing Forestry University
Beijing, China

OCLC is the largest catalog database in the world, and now that it is in an incredible developing speed on the information highway, there are more and more library staffs enjoying the convenience and benefit of it.

As for myself, a researcher of Beijing Forestry University Library, I believe that OCLC is a great treasury of information for every researcher, every student, and everyone who wants to use it. I enjoy the high quality service of this magic system, too, in my office and in my home. Although my library has not yet entered into the organization, I believe that we will be a member of OCLC in the near future. Then it will make my work more efficient and higher quality. I will do my research work though OCLC with the information of more than 63 countries. It is really a great resource for human beings.

I will try to use it to serve the people in my university in researching and teaching works. I think it will make them more efficient and more fruitful. Everybody will be thankful for the help of it, and for the help of the information highway. And I also have the confidence that my colleagues and I will deliver our own information and database on forestry to OCLC and to the world. Then we will work together and be a real union.

———————————— ⑴ ————————————

**Ingrid C. Hunt**
University of Central Florida
Orlando, FL

A techno-peasant on the information highway in the domain of OCLC...

The traffic on the Information Superhighway is ferocious, and for most of us techno-peasants it seems to be chaotic. We have difficulty following or even finding directions to the various points of interest hidden in its hinterland.

Like pioneers we stumble and fumble and hope to find our fortune. But we need help in our search for special morsels of knowledge and guidance to the various sites where bits may be available. However, the vast frontier into which the Information Highway System extends, is hazardous territory because often we seem to spin our wheels in this wilderness.

Sprawled in the green grass of home, people desire the fruits of neighboring orchards; where can a special tidbit be found, and how willing is the owner to share it? Who can help make contact? Well, there are scouts out there with links to the inhabitants of hinterland. They are called servers, and one particularly friendly server identifies itself as OCLC.

The OCLC bibliographic database connects libraries around the world and helps them to make information available to one and all by walking one's fingers over the keyboard of a computer. The wealth of information thus accessible dates back to 2000 BC and can be retrieved in seconds. At the speed of light OCLC's tongue flicks out and finds morsels stored in thousands of libraries in 63 countries. This outright classy library catalog originated 25 years ago in the state of Ohio and has become to libraries as E-mail is to Internet. To all who are in search of documented information, OCLC is the server whose name will go into history and whose praise is humming through the wires of the Information Highways and Byways.

Need a special, obscure, rare publication? Ask OCLC; it'll give you a location, no matter how far away that may be. If it exists, OCLC can find it, identify it, and help to access it. Like the needle on a compass, it will point the searcher in the right direction and help the peasant to find a needle in a haystack. In various formats this unique store of knowledge spans four millennia and makes its information available through hundreds of thousands of miles of telecommunications lines to researchers caught in the World Wide Web.

If humanity has learned it and documented it, it is sure to be found in some library; and the route to this library leads through the domain of OCLC, a wonderful oasis in the hinterland of the Information Highway System.

**Terence K. Huwe**
University of California
Berkeley, CA

More than metadata: OCLC and the seeds of Cyberspace...

The current debate about digital media and commerce, like so many "events" in the marketplace, has a giddy feel to it. The spin is on "digital libraries," "metadata," and direct lines between author to consumer. Certainly, there is no doubt that the information economy is growing up in a hurry. New technologies are providing solutions to longstanding access and usability challenges.

Yet like so many librarians and bibliophiles, I find inspiration in the library profession's strategies for digital technologies. After all, the seeds of cyberspace were planted by librarians and their allies with the creation of the MARC format. Those seeds sprang to life when OCLC launched the OCLC Online Union Catalog in 1971.

For many OCLC Online Union Catalog users, OCLC symbolizes time savings and reduced labor, but at second glance, it offers much more. Indeed, its history could teach other professions a thing or two about information resources management. OCLC was ahead of its time in conceiving a living union catalog, with expandable fields and a focus on shared development. A quarter century later, we can see a surprising correlation between librarians' professional practices and modern management-speak about information technology.

For example, groupware was pioneered by Xerox PARC and brought to market by Lotus Notes. Its backbone application is document sharing. More than a decade earlier, OCLC made it possible for a cataloger at Yale to take a Berkeley record and tailor it to special needs in New Haven. How about collaborating over time and distance? Let's say that same Berkeley cataloger likes extensive note-making in the 505 field, and so does someone at Mcgill in Montreal. It's collaboration and shared brainpower on a transnational level, and it started in 1971. No wonder librarians have already taken the lead in the sensible organization of the Internet and the World Wide Web. Twenty-five years of experience with OCLC metadata has been an excellent preparation for the access engineers of Cyberspace.

But the most compelling legacy of the OCLC Online Union Catalog is its early demonstration that technology should bring people together. While the "raised floor" computer environments of the sixties kept end-user collaboration in the rumble seat, OCLC let users do it their way: collaborating and sharing tips, with plenty arguments over standards, to be sure. By ceding control of the content to a global professional cadre, OCLC created high performance practices that predate the "Reengineering" movement, the "Total Quality Movement," and technologies of collaboration by decades.

As metadata and the resources they describe move closer together and become one, union cataloging can be a durable and guiding influence. This, then, is the legacy of OCLC: collaborative computing, groupwork across time and space, and a lasting commitment to making information accessible and understandable to readers and researchers everywhere.

**Betty Jo Hvistendahl**
Trinity Bible College
Ellendale, ND

The OCLC Online Union Catalog means many things to me. First of all, it means being able to access records from libraries all over the world. This access is very important to a small college library such as ours. Since we cannot afford to purchase an unlimited number of books, periodicals and other materials, it is very advantageous to be able to get them from other libraries. Our faculty and students are often doing research on topics not covered in our library. They really appreciate being able to get these books from others. We are also glad to supply books to other libraries, especially those in our region who do not have special religious collections. We also have many older books that other libraries do not have because we inherited a collection from the state college that previously occupied this campus.

It is also useful to be able to catalog books over the OCLC terminal. This has saved us many hours in cataloging and making labels for books. We no longer have to order our cards from another source and wait so long for them to come. It is a very convenient way to update our holdings. Also, we can use it to find out if a certain book is being held by other libraries. When one cannot afford to purchase a book, either personally, or for the library, sometimes one can obtain the book and get the needed information through ILL. Being able to purchase our holdings on tape is a definite advantage, too, for automating our library.

The OCLC online service has been very useful in retrospective conversion of all our collection from Dewey to Library of Congress. My memory goes back to the time when I came back in 1980 to be the cataloger at Trinity again. We had previously considered changing our books from Dewey to LC, but thought it would be an insurmountable task, since I had no experience with LC. We are very happy with the OCLC classification now that we have converted all our books. Many of our special collections are much more accessible to our patrons because of the LC system. All in all, using the online catalog has been the thing that has made it all happen for us.

## Soo Y. Ihm
University of Missouri—Columbia
Columbia, MO

On August 26, 1971, the Ohio College Library Center Online Union Catalog put the concept of shared cataloging into practice. This radically changed the face of librarianship forever. Originally conceived as a consortium of 49 academic libraries in Ohio by Frederick G. Kilgour, OCLC expanded beyond its intended bounds and, as a result, changed its name to the Online Computer Library Center. Despite this change, OCLC's purpose remained the same: to better serve libraries and their patrons by allowing libraries to share cataloging information.

OCLC has played a large part in my work at the University of Missouri-Columbia law library. As the university's libraries are changing their online catalog to that of the Innovative Interfaces (III) system, we are undertaking a retrospective conversion project. My role has been to update the library's holdings and bibliographic records. OCLC has been instrumental, since it has helped me correct records varying from the slightly inaccurate to the grossly incorrect.

The number and diversity of OCLC's records have been an asset in my work. This bibliographic utility includes 35 million records categorized under eight different formats. These records represent a time span of 4,000 years and 370 languages. This has helped me since I have to deal with materials dating from several different centuries as well as written in various languages, including

French and Russian. To date, there has not been a record that I have been unable to find on OCLC.

In conclusion, OCLC has been very beneficial to the University of Missouri-Columbia Law Library because of its size and diversity. It has been especially helpful to me in my endeavor to accomplish the library's retrospective conversion project. Shared cataloging has come a long way since just a few decades ago. OCLC has been instrumental in the transformation of how cataloging is done. New challenges now face OCLC, but its main goal remains the same: to provide improved service to library patrons through shared cataloging.

## Sue Jackson
Carroll College
Helena, MT

"One cataloger's lament of chaos..."

In January 1995 the collection of our small college library was cataloged 1) in Dewey Decimal, with access provided by a card catalog, and 2) in Library of Congress, with access provided by an online public catalog. Books were shelved in two different arrangements, one area for Dewey materials, and another area for the LC items, making the physical access as schizophrenic as the intellectual access. And, please do not think for a moment that it was as simple as having all the literature collection in Dewey and all the science collection in LC. No, there were books in every classification field cataloged in both systems. Students, faculty and staff needed to search two access systems and two stack areas each and every time, for any and every topic.

It was no easier for the reference staff. The situation had created two groups of patrons: those who would never venture near the computer terminal because the card catalog provided such comfort, and those who would never go near anything as antiquated as a set of wooden drawers with cards to fumble through. It was the rare patron that could be persuaded to use both the old and the new to ensure a complete search of the library's holdings. And, with the collection physically split, it was not possible to have patrons browsing in an area with any confidence that they would find all relevant materials.

Enough doom and gloom. Now listen to what OCLC and a bit of grant money have been able to change. In the last fifteen months, one cataloger has been able to reclassify more than 15,000 Dewey Decimal classified volumes into the Library of Congress system. There remains only a small section of English literature in Dewey (the 820s) which will be completed during the summer. In addition, the MARC records exported from OCLC have been imported into the online catalog making it a more complete and valuable access tool. Patrons are learning to rely on the electronic access system more as the Dewey cards disappear from the card catalog.

It is only because of OCLC that this project could even be dreamed of, let alone accomplished. OCLC is incredibly comprehensive. Of all the titles needing to be reclassified, there were only a handful for which records could not be found in the database. In most cases, the records required only a minimum of alteration to fit our specific needs. The thousands of shelf list cards we ordered have been received in timely fashion and are in the format we require. OCLC is consistently reliable. During all the months of this project, the system was down only one day and that was due to severe flooding in Oregon. OCLC is economical. The fees for our project have been proclaimed economical even by the college's accountants. Comprehensive, reliable, economical—what more can be asked of a system?

What does OCLC mean to me? It means: Our Collection all in Library of Congress!

--------------------- ℐ ---------------------

## Grace Jackson-Brown
Indiana University
Bloomington, IN

As an undergraduate student almost twenty years ago, I found employment at the University of Kansas in Watson Library. I worked as a student library assistant with the Spanish, Portuguese, and Latin American Studies Department. One of my duties was to verify titles for purchase that were recommended by departmental faculty. The university was just beginning to use a wonderful new system known as OCLC which was still closely linked with the library consortium in Ohio. At the time, all I knew was that OCLC worked like magic. Just by entering a few letters of a formula based on the title of a requested book into an OCLC computer, full bibliographic information would instantly appear on the screen. Many of the titles that I searched for were in Spanish, and if I couldn't find them in OCLC I had to search for the titles in huge green-bound books from the Library of Congress Union Catalog. Each over-sized book seemed to weigh a ton when I pulled it off the shelf and onto a reading table. In 1996, 25 years after OCLC began, I discovered that Spanish is the fourth leading language of cataloging records that are a part of the OCLC Online Union Catalog.

My experience as an undergraduate student with the magic and awesome amounts of knowledge contained in OCLC was one of the things that led me to graduate school to study library science. OCLC's magnitude hinted to me the extent to which computers could be utilized to organize and access the knowledge present in libraries. I earned my master's of library science degree in 1984. Since then, I've served as a reference librarian in a public library and a university library. I'm now branch head librarian of a special collection library for African-American studies at Indiana University. In each of my positions, I continue to impress and dazzle library users with the magic of OCLC, and I don't see how librarians ever got along without it. OCLC keeps up with the times, by each year expanding its Online Union Catalog with millions of new bibliographic records in hundreds of languages. It has also broadened its circle of users to include novices from the general public, in addition to librarians and other information professionals. Services such as the WorldCat database, and combination searching using subjects provided through PRISM prove that OCLC is a "user-friendly" innovative use of technology that helps people keep ahead of the information explosion.

Happy 25th Birthday OCLC, and many happy returns!

———————————— ℳ ————————————

## Regina A. Jannink
Robert Morris College
Springfield, IL

Gateway to the world...

As a librarian, I am constantly faced with fulfilling the needs of my patrons. I am the director of a branch campus library. We house approximately 12,000 volumes in our collection. Our primary focus is business; however, because of our institution's growth, it has become necessary to expand our collection in other areas. Unfortunately, because of our limited space, it is necessary to be very selective in collection development. Therefore, we must rely on resource sharing to supplement the needs of our library patrons. We rely on a number of sources to fulfill these needs. When patrons need certain sources that are hard to come by, we rely on the OCLC Online Union Catalog, which is available through our regional library system, to help fulfill these needs. It is also a great cataloging tool for those hard-to-catalog library materials.

The OCLC Online Union Catalog is a valuable reference tool. Our students are required to complete a number of research projects in a limited amount of time. The depth of their research varies from superficial to very detailed. The topics they research are also many and various. Sometimes students will research unique topics that require an in-depth search in order to find the sources they require. When this happens, I first exhaust all of our resources, including regional and state. When this endeavor fails, I turn to the OCLC Online Union Catalog. With its vast resources, both national and international, I am sure to find the information that my patrons need. Plus I can get access to the materials through interlibrary loan.

In addition to fulfilling patron needs, the OCLC Online Union Catalog also fulfills catalogers' needs. Many of our materials come to us pre-processed from our main campus; however, I must catalog the remainder. I rely heavily on outside sources to catalog library materials in order to make them available to patrons in a timely fashion. There are times, however, when I cannot find in any regional online source to secure cataloging information. It is at times like this that I rely on the OCLC Online Union Catalog to provide that much-needed cataloging information.

The OCLC Online Union Catalog is, for all practical purposes, a portal to the universe of knowledge. With its vast resources, it can fulfill the needs of both the library user and the librarian. The library user can search as well as gain access to the resources offered by the catalog. The librarian also uses the catalog as a search tool for both reference and cataloging purposes. The world of information is in constant change. This constant flux of change demands that librarians keep up with what is available in the information world. They have many resources to accomplish this task. However, when they need ready access to a vast database of source material, they can always turn to the OCLC Online Union Catalog to fulfill not only their patrons' needs, but also their own needs.

## Elaine M. Jenkins
Smithfield High School
Esmond, RI

My library, Smithfield High School Library, has approximately 10,000 books, 23 periodicals and two newspapers. We have 760 students, grades 9–12. The OCLC Online Union Catalog has enabled us to keep up with technology because we have easy access to books and serials from other libraries in a fast, efficient manner. It has helped our students with term papers and our teachers with professional materials. So, you see, even though we are a small library, we have access to 35 million records and 560 million location listings. This year we were able to locate a hard to find government document from the Pell Marine Library, many books from out-of-state libraries including such a hard to find title as *My Life in Alcatraz.*

OCLC means to me seeing the smile on a student's face when I located three books on a bibliography about Jimmy Hoffa; the gratefulness of a student who is working on a paper on Al Capone and the Mafia and has no way of getting to another library; the teacher who is trying to help her class by finding more information for a special science project. A teacher even asked me to get seven copies of Hitler's *Mein Kampf* for her class of fifteen students. She wasn't able to buy them due to our high school's limited budget, but I was able to locate six from various libraries in Rhode Island and one from out-of-state. I know the teacher was very happy, but I can't vouch for the students.

OCLC has made my life more interesting and bridged the gap between my library and the world's libraries. I have the largest library in town. I may be small, but I am accomplishing big things. I just remembered... I still have to search for Mrs. Ritter's book.

## David Louis Jensen
Syracuse University
Syracuse, NY

(To the Tune of "BINGO")...
> O _ C _ L _ C _ oh!
> O _ C _ L _ C _ oh!
> O _ C _ L _ C _ oh!
> And RESOURCE is its game _ oh!

**Amy G. Job**
William Paterson College
Wayne, NJ

Books, maps, computer files, sound recordings—these and so much more make up a wonderful world of information resources. And to think that access to these can be brought right to our desks and to those of our library patrons!

More than just a dream, present reality finds all this possible through use of the OCLC Online Union Catalog. Using many different search strategies, users can find information presented in eight formats, 370 languages, and produced or published from 2000 B.C. up to the current year. In addition, access to these sources can be supplied via direct transmission, hook-up through dial-access, or even on the Internet!

We at the Sarah Byrd Askew Library of the William Paterson College of New Jersey have been helping our patrons locate information sources via the "OCLC system" since 1977. A medium-sized college library, we have found the OCLC Online Union Catalog to be an invaluable resource. Our students request materials from other libraries in order to complete their papers and projects, and our faculty search it as an aid for their research. Mention of the OCLC interlibrary loan service is a routine component of all our library bibliographic instruction programs and faculty orientation sessions.

To me personally, OCLC has been a ponderous tool to aid in my reference and cataloging duties. Having been on the staff at our library since 1968, I have seen many changes in the way in which we conduct our business. Moving from cataloging using Library of Congress cards, the *National Union Catalog*, and our own intuitive methods of original cataloging, to access via the OCLC system has been a great adventure. From the thrill of entering an original record into the database, to the satisfaction of locating an obscure record for a patron, OCLC has added immeasurably to the joy I feel for my occupation as a librarian.

The "OCLC system" is truly a doorway to the information world, and those who use it access resources that help them search the past and form the future. The OCLC Online Union Catalog provides more than 35 million information sources to all libraries and is accessible around the world. That is very impressive, to say the very least, and is one of the many reasons that OCLC is important to me!

**Dana Johnson**
Niles Public Library District
Niles, IL

When I applied for a cataloging position at the Niles Public Library in suburban Chicago two years ago, I noticed that one of the job requirements was foreign language expertise. After accepting the position, I discovered just which foreign languages I would be expected to handle, and that none of them were familiar to me. The OCLC Online Union Catalog has proven indispensable to me in dealing with my library's foreign language backlog.

In my first few months at Niles, I became both grateful for and dependent on the OCLC Online Union Catalog. Whenever I found a record for a book in Polish, Czech, Russian, or even Korean, I uttered a heartfelt "thank you" to the library that contributed the record. Sooner or later, I came to expect every foreign language book which my library owned to have a record in the OCLC Catalog. And for quite awhile, a "scan title," keyword or derived key search always produced the correct OCLC Catalog record.

My luck changed one day when I encountered what looked like a Polish astronomy book translated from the Latin. Neither a keyword, derived key or subject search yielded a record for the title we owned. After so many months of taking records from the OCLC Online Union Catalog, I would have to give something back to it.

Performing descriptive cataloging for this book proved less difficult than I feared, but doing subject analysis was another story. From examining the table of contents and the introduction, it appeared to be an analysis of copernican astronomy, and possibly of one of his works. Once again, I turned to the OCLC Catalog, entered the search "fin su copernicus and su astronomy" and began examining bibliographic records. Eventually I found one with what appeared to be the appropriate name-title subject heading. I compared my item to the bibliographic record, and after concluding the subject heading was correct, I edited the save file record and entered the update command. The OCLC Online Union Catalog had come to the rescue again!

Eventually I became more confident with creating original records for Polish, Czech and Russian items, and began to feel I was contributing at least a little to the uniqueness of the OCLC Catalog, particularly in relation to Polish and Czech. (The collection of fairy tales by Perrault in Polish was an especially rewarding new record.) And there is another opportunity for me to add more variety to the OCLC Catalog, since a box of one hundred Hindi books arrived several months ago.

Many books in Hindi remain to be cataloged. However, I know that, with over 38,000 records for Hindi materials, the OCLC Online Union Catalog will prove indispensable yet again. And I look forward to giving back, at least in small part, some of what I have taken from this great resource.

**Starla J. Johnson**
Casper College Library
Casper, WY

In a state where antelope outnumber automobiles, OCLC is Wyoming's connection to global information resources. OCLC is the electronic pony express of the library world, expanding horizons for our citizens by linking libraries and patrons over vast geographical areas. Research and information access for Wyomingites will never be the same. Buffalo Bill Cody, a Wyoming citizen committed to promoting the western way of life and the treasures of our state, would be impressed with the information available through OCLC. He would also enjoy searching for his name online!

As a community college library, we serve students from all across our state and the Rocky Mountain region. For a student coming to Casper College from Chugwater, Wyoming (population 282), our 80,000-volume library can be a scary place. Electronic tools help ease the technology terror our freshmen students experience when they are as friendly as OCLC. A timid freshman becomes a bold researcher when we say "Sure, we can get you current information on the latest physical therapy techniques. No, not in our library—but from a library at Florida A&M in Tallahassee." The OCLC Online Union Catalog means equal information access for each of our students.

At the Casper College Library, we serve the information needs of many community patrons and area businesses as well as the students from our campus. They depend on Casper College to provide current financial, medical and environmental data. The information resources available through OCLC encourage economic development in our city. Prospective corporations scouting our region to put down business roots look to us for training and retraining the local work force. We can step up to this challenge with the help of OCLC.

Not only does OCLC provide access to the world's resources for Wyoming library patrons, it also lets the world in on a formerly well-kept secret—the beauty, culture and history of our state. If you are standing in a library with access to OCLC, there is no excuse for the question, "Where is Chugwater, Wyoming?" Just do a scan title search on the word "Chugwater" and you'll get 13 hits! Maps, newspapers, city government documents, and a centennial history book are just a few of the resources available to OCLC libraries across the globe. You can find information on the famous "Chugwater Chili Cook-off" and if you are interested in the music of our state, simply request through OCLC interlibrary loan the musical scores and cassette recordings of the Chugwater Philharmonic String Quartet. OCLC is the gateway to sharing bibliographic information globally, and our patrons are ready to cross the threshold.

After working with OCLC for seven years, what a pleasure it is to celebrate this silver anniversary. In an information culture where few things are permanent, it is indeed important to recognize the stability of the OCLC Online Union Catalog.

## Felix Jung
Monroe County Public Library
Bloomington, IN

A life eating books: A brief OCLC retrospective...

OCLC is a strange organism. Born in Ohio on August 26, 1971, it began eating from the get-go. While many in Ohio were happy to see such a small creature with such a large zeal for books, every one of its 54 parent libraries were too busy trying to feed it to notice that it had suddenly grown much larger than they had expected. In fact, other libraries from outside Ohio began helping out, adding more books to try to satisfy OCLC's ever-growing hunger. Within the span of twenty-five years, it had grown to a monstrously terrifying, and yet strangely exhilarating, size. Funny thing is, it hasn't stopped.

It started small, as all things do, but had a voracious appetite. At first, its meals were comprised primarily of books. But then one day, someone got sloppy, and left a few Babylonian manuscripts lying around. It got its hands on a few parchments written in Sanskrit, a medieval scroll here and there, and that was the end of it. It has confessed to me that, with most texts dated before 1800, the thin layer of mold or dust add a flavor not unlike thyme or paprika. In addition, it has found a particular liking for Victorian pamphlets, Cyrillic love poems, Yiddish hymns, and Pre-Ming Dynasty literature on affairs of state.

While it was quite happy to partake of the delicacies of older writings, it did not take OCLC long to acquire a taste for the more modern. Vinyl recordings, from "Abba" to "Buckwheat Zydeco," were often a good aperitif; CDs added a bit of color to the meal; and to finish off its course, it felt that computer files were an excellent dessert. Surprisingly, despite the large amount it consumes on a daily basis, there is virtually no danger of cholesterol or fatty buildup. Books, it turns out, are 100% fat free.

Today, more than 63 countries lend their aid to this task, offering books and maps, serials and scores in over 370 languages. Its meals now span over 4,000 years, from works before the earliest translation of "Beowulf" to works that follow "Snoop Doggy Dogg." Its hunger does not discriminate.

And the best part of it all, is that OCLC keeps track of each portion of every meal it has ever had. All for the benefit of the librarian, the student, the scholar, and the patron. So that they too, may look over OCLC's impressive catalog of meals, find a particular item, and note its flavor and texture for themselves.

It is hoped, in the librarians' circle, that OCLC never devours enough to actually become full. There are secret rumors, whispered behind rows of stacked books, that the past 25 years have only whetted OCLC's palate, that it has only recently begun to truly eat. For now, it remains an organism of perpetual hunger, growing larger with each passing year. It remains an insatiable creature, which librarians are all too eager to feed.

## Jeannie Kamerman
University of West Florida
Pensacola, FL

Patrick Henry modestly asked, "Give me liberty or give me death." With no humility I ask, "Give me liberty to learn, give me an expansive and an ever-expanding quality cooperative database, give me a means to lighten my workload and increase my efficiency, but never give me word of the death of the OCLC Online Union Catalog."

OCLC gave me a ticket to ride into the age of technology, set my career path, and encouraged my pursuit of a career-enhancing degree.

In 1970 I was at Indiana University, working in the world of libraries before OCLC, where typists tapped out unit cards on IBM Selectrics. An old manual typewriter was used to add regulation, red subject headings to cards. From its inception, I believed fervently in the system as it was proposed and was astounded by the vision of the forefathers who were, in truth, mere mortals, although the resulting bibliographic control network belies that fact. When we began receiving card packets from OCLC/the OCLC Online Union Catalog, our red subject added entries were printed in black ink, in all capitals. This innovation alone was difficult to sell to some heads of technical services.

By geographical happenstance, I was a member of an outstanding regional network, The Indiana Cooperative Library Service Association (INCOLSA).

There librarians and support personnel were instilled with an understanding of the future capabilities of OCLC/the OCLC Online Catalog. We were willing to invest the time necessary to understand the MARC (Machine Readable Cataloging) format and we input only the highest quality records. Because of my knowledge of OCLC and MARC, I was offered an excellent position as the automation expert and trainer at the University of West Florida in Pensacola.

Soon after arriving, I was given responsibilities for the retrospective conversion project at my new library. Annually we were offered search enhancements, the ability to send full screens of editing instead of field by field, and as the hardware evolved we moved from terminals to personal computers. It seemed that I rewrote work-flows and processes annually to incorporate each year's enhancements and innovations.

As the system grew so did I. I realized my value would increase if I had a more fundamental understanding of systems science. I ultimately finished a degree in computer science so that I could do more informed planning for my institution.

In my capacity as trainer and searcher I have had coworkers who called me Christie, referring, I'm sure, to Agatha rather than Brinkley. I was so termed because of the quick and accurate responses I was able to get out of OCLC/the OCLC Catalog. Thanks to the quality and quantity of the system, I became the celebrated luminary.

Life in libraries, and in specific my life, is immeasurably better since OCLC/the OCLC Online Union Catalog was developed. "I know not what course others may take, but as for me" I would not "return to those golden days of yesteryear" if that means no OCLC Online Union Catalog.

## Laura Townsend Kane
University of South Carolina School of Medicine Library
Columbia, SC

What the OCLC Online Union Catalog means to me (and to Benjamin Franklin)…

Ben Franklin came to me in my dream. I looked up from my book and there he was, standing before me. Straightening from my comfortable but not-too-ergonomically-correct position on the sofa, I shut my book and smiled at him nervously.

"May I help you, sir?" I asked, ever the helpful librarian. It didn't occur to me to wonder why the ghost of an inventor/philosopher dead for 200 years should be paying me a visit.

He just stood there, staring, his spectacles slightly askew on his prominent nose. His silence was disconcerting, and I wondered if he disapproved of the book I was reading (a sultry romance with a flashy cover—shhh, don't tell!).

"Mr. Franklin?" I said. "Are you all right?"

At last he spoke softly. "Am I remembered?" he asked.

It was my turn to stare. Was he remembered?! Benjamin Franklin?! I realized that my mouth was gaping open rather unattractively, and I snapped it shut. I gulped, my mind racing.

Obviously his spirit was deeply troubled, and somehow it was up to me to put his fears to rest.

Sighing deeply, I rose from the warm couch and took Mr. Franklin's hand. "Come with me, sir. I have something to show you. "

The ten-minute car ride to my office was a most interesting experience. I practically had to blindfold poor Benjamin to prevent him from experiencing myocardial infarction and dying again. How would I explain that to the authorities? I sat him down in a chair next to my desk and switched on the computer.

He looked at it suspiciously. "What manner of box is this?" he asked.

"Well," I replied, "It's a storage box. Of information."

He cocked a gray eyebrow and leaned forward, staring intently at the flashing DOS commands. The computer beeped, and he jumped back as if he had been shot.

I decided it would take too long to explain the functionality of computers to him. I double-clicked on the "PRISM" icon on my Windows screen, and proceeded to log onto my faithful boon companion, the OCLC Online Union Catalog.

"Give me the title of one of your works," I commanded.

*"Poor Richard's Almanac," he replied.*

Click, click, click. "There are more than 36 printings of that work," I informed him. "Hundreds of libraries around the world own some version it. Another title."

"My *Autobiography*."

"This particular edition is held by 30 libraries. Another."

*"Experiments and Observations on Electricity,"* he said weakly.

"Seven holdings, five in the U.S. and two in Europe."

We continued like this through a long list of works, some common, some obscure. Every one was in the OCLC Catalog, and I explained to him how a person could get copies through interlibrary loan.

Mr. Franklin's expression gradually changed from confusion to wonder to awe to amazement.

"Well, it seems that you are remembered all right," I said finally. "What do you think?" I asked.

He looked at the computer screen and touched it delicately, a look of adoration on his features. "I have found it," he said softly.

"Found what?" I asked.

"The center of the universe."

******

The next morning, I went through my usual routine: falling out of bed, into the shower, jumping into clothes, and driving to work. I looked maliciously at the stacks of books in my office, but they refused to acknowledge my presence. Sighing resignedly, I logged onto the OCLC Online Union Catalog and began searching for records. In a flash, I remembered the dream. "You know, the man was right," I said to myself, smiling stupidly at the OCLC Catalog news screen. "In the world of libraries and information, the OCLC Online Union Catalog really is the center of the universe."

———————— *qV* ————————

**Mark Katzman**
University of Missouri–Kansas City
Kansas City, MO

The OCLC Online Union Catalog is an indispensable tool in my work as a Library Assistant. It's reassuring to know that such a vast and accurate storage house of information, spanning all of recorded history, actually exists.

The OCLC Online Union Catalog represents a knock-out punch of information power. It is, hands down, the premiere planetary node for professionals and paraprofessionals alike, aiding all of us in our quest for bibliographic excellence. To tell the truth, it's a miracle to me that such a thing exists. I'll bet there has probably been more human attention to detail in the formation of the OCLC Online Union Catalog than words can attest to.

Lord knows what new technological marvels the next 25 years will bring. We are living in the Information Age, and I'm sure new and profound ways of information interactivity will play a vital role in the continuing evolution of our young species. And I have no doubt that the OCLC Online Union Catalog will be right there, leading the way.

**Dr. Trishanjit Kaur**
Punjabi University
Punjab, India

How can I forget that day, it was 25th June of 1993 on the occasion of the 112th ALA Conference at New Orleans. I had my first experience with the OCLC Online Union Catalog here in the exhibit of OCLC. As long as I was in U.S.A. during the International Visitor Program everywhere we went the first thing I would check in each library would be the availability of OCLC Online Union Catalog. It was just incredible! While using it I felt as if the whole Pandora's box of information was being opened right in front of me on all possible subjects at all possible places. As a teacher I felt I could see anything available at so many libraries and make use of the information, the whole world looked so small because of the easy access to information.

Sitting here miles away in this university library (we do not have the Internet Connection as yet), I feel rather lost in the world of Info. Where to go? How to find out what's the latest? Why can't I have access to the OCLC Online Union Catalog again. I could also be one of the lucky ones to have a peep into the 35 million records. Maybe one day I will be able to do so. It is such a wonderful and an indispensable tool. No doubt it is the most frequently consulted database in the field of higher education. The beauty of this Union Catalog is not only the number of records but also the span of time period available. I believe the range of records is from 2000 B.C. till date. Tell me which other online union catalog can offer such a great deal? Wait a minute, it consists of records of all sorts NOT only in English language but in 370 languages of the world. I was fascinated by the location listings which are now 560 million. Boy! I could never count so many names in my dream too. It's so simple to know where lies what and you just have to click to get it. And mind you it's growing every year as new records are being added.

My brief encounter with the OCLC Catalog meant a great deal to me as it has changed my whole perspective of approaching to information. I bet users who are using it are hooked to it and why not, they cannot do without this Super Duper Wealth of Information.

It's there for anyone and everyone but not for me. Knock, knock Excuse me Librarian can't we have the facility of OCLC Online Union Catalog in our library, please?

Congratulations to OCLC on the Silver Anniversary of the OCLC Online Union Catalog.

## John C. Kazalia
Southwest Public Libraries
Columbus, OH

In this era of Internet hype and promotion of library interconnectivity, the term "virtual library" is regularly bandied throughout the professional literature as a completely new concept. While the push for interconnectivity, via the Internet or through other local or statewide networking initiatives, should prove an important development for all American libraries in an era of decreased budgets and increased expectations, it seems the library community has forgotten how the "virtual library" concept began with the creation of OCLC's Online Union Catalog.

Nearly every benefit the library profession anticipates to be achieved by the various networking initiatives of today has already been achieved by the Online Union Catalog. A review of professional library literature finds these anticipated benefits fall within the following categories:

1. *Equality of access.* American libraries have embraced the Internet and related networking projects because of their potential for providing the same level of access to information to every library user, regardless of physical location or local levels of library funding. The OCLC Online Union Catalog has provided equality of access for member libraries of all sizes to a growing pool of materials since its inception.

2. *Resource sharing.* Through shared database projects via Internet connections or state and local networking initiatives like OPLIN, libraries are hoping to cut costs by sharing access to databases and other information. The OCLC Online Union Catalog has fostered resource sharing by providing member libraries with the ability to locate and interlibrary loan materials of all formats, especially important for smaller libraries that could never hope to acquire these materials for their local collections.

3. *International perspective.* The Internet has been described as the "global marketplace" where people worldwide can share ideas on an equal footing, regardless of age, income, or other demographic factors. In an era where multiculturalism is becoming a standard theme in schools and libraries, such worldwide communication is often touted as the answer to

both American and international political and racial tensions. The OCLC Online Union Catalog serves as a pioneering presence in the move toward multiculturalism by providing worldwide access to materials produced in 370 languages.

4. *Information diversity*. Experts predict the Internet will allow information of all material types and formats to be shared globally via file transfer protocol (FTP) and other mechanisms. This prediction has become a reality with the ability to send audio files via the Internet. The experts seem to have forgotten how the OCLC Union Catalog provides access to a growing pool of over 33 million records representing every material type known to man.

The OCLC Online Union Catalog means that a professionally mediated "virtual library" containing nearly every material type and language in the world is available to librarians and library users worldwide at a reasonable cost. As stated in the announcement regarding this essay contest, the result is "a unique global resource" that is "the most frequently consulted database" by scholars and researchers in the academic world.

## Neville Keery
European Commission
Brussels, Belgium

You don't have to be a Dubliner to love the OCLC Online Union Catalog but it helps.

In Dublin, Ohio, the shining plate glass of today's OCLC headquarters is not just a monument to the achievement of an organization based on local college libraries, it is proof of the employment potential of the new information society. Online technology might have placed the world's foremost database of bibliographic information anywhere. Native intelligence and local enterprise has put it on the prairie rather than in a centre famous for its technology or culture.

My Dublin is in Ireland. It is known worldwide as a literary capital. Imagine this Dublin's literati cruising the Online Union Catalog in search of obscure editions or translations of its native writers such as Shaw, Swift, Wilde or Joyce among the more than 35 million OCLC records spanning 370 languages.

The Online Union Catalog and OCLC are not without their critics. I've heard allegations that quantity is more important than quality, that the catalog has not enough focus on collections, that the "not for profit" organization makes a lot of money. Is it true of all Dubliners that they never speak well of each other?

James Joyce claimed that a careful reading of his *Ulysses* could facilitate the reconstruction of Dublin should the city be destroyed. I am grateful that OCLC uses its "profit" to invest in library technology and conservation, particularly at a time when such things come very low on any public expenditure agenda. May my Dublin never be destroyed, may the plate glass of Dublin, Ohio never be ploughed under. But what comfort that—should it be required—a significant part of world culture might be re-constructed from the back-up and records of the Online Union Catalog carefully sent from Ohio to the salt-mine storage which is the safest we know.

## Latrina Keith
The New York Academy of Medicine
Bronx, NY

I am a technical assistant at a large medical library in New York City, in which our facilities are open to the general public. A major part of my profession is to catalog and update serial and monographic records for our large collection. In helping us to provide the very best of service to our patrons and to our subscribers, the OCLC Online Union Catalog plays a very vital role. In September 1994, our institution purchased the Cataloging MicroEnhancer Plus (CAT ME Plus) software. Our productivity increased by 30%, online searching took less time, and new materials were more rapidly available to our patrons.

In July 1995, our library was due to migrate from an older, antiquated local system to a new, more advanced system. Unfortunately, before the system migration was to begin, the older system "crashed" in February 1995. We were without a local area network for five months. During those five months, the OCLC system was a great help to our staff in enabling us to continuously provide prompt service. Thanks to OCLC, we were able to fill our patrons requests and to supply our subscribers with the materials they needed. To me, the OCLC Online Union Catalog means continued reliability and a continued commitment to the people we serve.

## Linda E. Kelley
U.S. Air Force
Bolling AFB, DC

The OCLC ONLINE UNION CATALOG is an essential tool that plays a very important part in the careers of the historians that work in the History Department at Bolling AFB in Washington, DC.

It means fast, easy, and convenient service on any history subject that our historians are interested in from their daily tasks to do their job better and efficiently. It's like the Bible... without it you can't do any harm in receiving the right answers for the outside public that have a particular question on any subject that has to do with history.

Whenever one of our historians is on reference that day and they receive a telephone call from the general public that has to do with a history question, the historians are delighted to plug in the information received from that individual on the OCLC ONLINE UNION CATALOG to hopefully receive the answer.

The OCLC ONLINE UNION CATALOG is a huge help to our historians especially when they receive a thank you note from a customer they had helped on a particular history question.

The OCLC ONLINE UNION CATALOG gives me a chance to catch up on my work and if they have any questions, or problems, I am always right there to help.

I just wish they had this OCLC ONLINE UNION CATLOG service earlier but now that we have it you can't beat the time it saves the researchers whenever they have a reference question in history.

Our historians at Bolling AFB in Washington, DC really appreciate the OCLC ONLINE UNION CATALOG. My hat's off to this wonderful creation.

## Majed Khader
Marshall University
Huntington, WV

As a librarian and specialist in Information Science, the OCLC Online Union Catalog means business to me and that I can do my work more efficiently. It has been and is for me a major problem solving tool. Most of all, OCLC Online Union Catalog means resource access and knowledge.

OCLC's various services, facilities, and databases are ideal sources of information and knowledge for librarians, and also for scholars, students, and researchers. Frequently, I help students and faculty with an inquiry about finding libraries around the country holding a given title, verifying a bibliographic citation, or finding a list of books written by a specific author. I still recall that moment, which is hard to explain in words, when a student came to me and asked how can I find other books by the same author without going through all of the printed sources? I asked him to give me a minute to search the OCLC Online Union Catalog for him. I proceeded to do a basic author search and printed the list of sources written by that particular author. The student was so elated and burst into "Thank you, thank you, this is perfect, I love it!" He wanted to know what this wonderful system was called. He planned to remember it and use it again for future inquires. This is just one example of the numerous occasions that I've used the OCLC Online Union Catalog to help patrons.

Whenever I need to verify a title or need a quick or complete bibliographic citation I always refer to the OCLC Online Union Catalog. The Catalog is my ultimate destination when I need to solve a problem related to an incomplete title, a misspelled author's name, a verification of publishing information, and many other bits and pieces of misspelled or misprinted information.

In my free time or when I feel tired with doing routine work, I take a break and start searching OCLC. This provides a refreshing break and I feel so excited when I find something interesting. Not only that, but I feel I have learned and gained new knowledge which makes me so ecstatic.

The OCLC Online Union Catalog with its various applications means business. It makes life easier for researchers, students, librarians, information specialists, businesses, and the general public by providing affordable access to the world's great library collections and records. If access to the world's millions of records added each year to the OCLC Online Union Catalog is not real business, then what should we call this huge, timely, valuable, and an affordable treasure house of information? It is a real business!

122

Finally, the OCLC Online Union Catalog is the ultimate resource tool. It is the Bible of knowledge, a bank of information, and a treasure house that should be acknowledged. If you need to search a topic, then OCLC is the solution. To verify a citation, OCLC is the tool! To check availability and locations of some given materials, OCLC is the answer! What else can I add to prove that OCLC is the ultimate in resources? The answer is in the literature and in the testimonies of the system users. It is the source of all information queries.

As we move toward the twenty-first century, OCLC is moving fast ahead of us. OCLC Online Union Catalog is my flag to the future of information dissemination.

———————————— ⚶ ————————————

## Tessa Killian
Mount Saint Mary College
Newburgh, NY

The OCLC Online Union Catalog is the only database I consistently use. When I search the OCLC Online Union Catalog or WorldCat, I know that I am using the largest bibliographic database in the world, which has the best records available. Librarians can rely on this database. The Online Union Catalog improves each year, retains what works well, while adding newer methods of searching, like scan title.

My first experience with the OCLC Online Union Catalog occurred the summer after my first year of college. I was working at the Buffalo and Erie County public library system as a senior page. I was assigned to a retrospective conversion team that was converting a neighboring library system. My job was to match shelf list cards with OCLC records. We used a dedicated terminal with an OCLC keyboard. All of our searching was derived. After three months of searching the Online Union Catalog, I was an excellent OCLC searcher. This was 1986, and, at the time, I did not know the value of the Catalog searching, or how it would affect my career. The Online Union Catalog helped me enter the field of librarianship with the knowledge of the best bibliographic database available. I cannot work without it. Since my summers as a senior page, I have used the cataloging subsystem, the serials subsystem, the ILL subsystem, and FirstSearch.

I work at Mount Saint Mary College in Newburgh, New York. Our library cannot afford the full range of services OCLC provides. We use the GAC for ILL and FirstSearch. I am well aware of the limitations of GAC use. Full membership allows for more effective use of the OCLC Online Union Catalog. We also use FirstSearch, where the WorldCat brings the OCLC Online Union Catalog directly to the public. Thanks to FirstSearch, our patrons have direct access to all of the reliable records and library holdings that librarians have used for years.

The reliability of the OCLC Online Union Catalog helps me provide the best bibliographic records to our patrons. Patrons do not necessarily care where the information comes from, but librarians do. To provide the best service possible to patrons, whether it be serials holdings or ILL transactions, I always know that patrons are receiving the best information available when using the OCLC Online Union Catalog.

The OCLC Catalog means the power of technology, the consistency of an excellent database, and the development of a resource.

## Carol Killough
Northeast Mississippi Community College
Booneville, MS

"You've come a long way, baby!" could be the motto for both OCLC and me. Both of us started our library careers in 1971, and technology throughout the library community has changed drastically since then. From manual typewriters to Pentium computers, library duties which once took hours can now be accomplished in minutes, at times even seconds with a single keystroke.

When asked what OCLC means to me, the first word that came to mind was "accuracy." When I recall developing a card catalog for my first school library in 1971, I remember walking into a library filled with about 6,000 volumes. The only catalog cards, including cards for books that were lost, discarded, or never ordered, were piled randomly in a box. When I tried to catalog, I retrieved my Sears and Dewey volumes, assigned applicable call numbers and subjects, and typed them, one card at a time, on a manual typewriter, trying to correct typing errors with an eraser. OCLC has changed all that, letting me secure accurate MARC records within minutes by dialing in to OCLC's database prepared by professional librarians. With a few keystrokes, the standard MARC record, with its precise typing and standard call numbers and subjects, can be downloaded into our catalog and instantaneously become available at twenty terminals.

"Cost-effectiveness" also describes what OCLC means. After years using hours of costly staff time trying to complete in-house cataloging and searching on expensive CD-ROM databases for titles not available, I agree with the statement made in a recent report by OCLC president and chief executive K. Wayne Smith: "From database size to number of transactions to financials, we (OCLC) set new standards of performance." Smith continued, "OCLC has an impressive record of responding to challenges with new, innovative, and cost-effective products and services." For me, in a rural college in northeast Mississippi, as well as for librarians in more than 560 million other locations, the OCLC database of more than 35 million records has made cataloging easier and less costly.

"Time-saving" is another word that explains what OCLC means to me. When I began my career, the average time between titles received and placed in patrons' hands was six months. In the intervening twenty-five years, processing time is more than twenty-five times faster. Our community college library's minimal staff has saved precious staff time due to OCLC's efficient processing and reduced editing work. OCLC continues to be on the cutting edge of methods for streamlining cataloging with services such as PromptCat, allowing fast copy cataloging with minimal staff intervention.

With the improvements made since 1971, I agree with K. Wayne Smith's report that OCLC will continue to provide timely and affordable information in the form needed. To quote Robert Browning, I want OCLC to "grow old along with me! The best is yet to be."

———————————— ✼ ————————————

**Sue Knoche**
East Tennessee State University
Johnson City, TN

What the OCLC Online Union Catalog means to me is accessibility to a vast database of bibliographic information for virtually every book that crosses my desk to catalog. I have the ability to search an 1865 title or older for our history of medicine collection, and literally retrieve a matching record. I commend OCLC on the information cooperation it must have required to initiate and continue to update the OCLC Online Union Catalog. The retrieval of information is essentially instantaneous and the turnaround time for cataloging is practically non-existent. Although our collection is primarily published in the English language, on occasion a German or other language publication is donated to our library. Due to the fact that OCLC has the cooperation of the international library community, there is no difficulty in locating a matching bibliographic record. The ability to export a record in MARC format in its entirety immediately to our local system saves time which can be directed to other projects.

The cliché "You've come a long way, baby" comes to mind when I remember struggling with the old "beehive" terminal. Thinking back, this marvel of machinery had blue function keys in all its splendor and the swiftness of a snail. Although it seemed sluggish at times, it was exciting to know I could generate cards through direct input that would assist users in locating the books they required. I recall the First System being very easy to understand, so when the PRISM system was introduced it seemed puzzling at first glance. Armed with a new PC-compatible computer that possessed the speed of lightening, in addition to a PASSPORT to a new system called PRISM, I was ready to go. It seems like only yesterday, although it was five years ago. The changes we have experienced brought new concepts to searching techniques, a broader database to search from, and a class to learn the basics with hands-on experience to maneuver through the PRISM. Like an old friend the standard search combinations were still in place, so the transition was not as perplexing as it could have been. In retrospect, I can't imagine returning to "the way it was." Current innovations allow me to cruise the Information Super Highway using the same terminology and search strategies, but at an accelerated rate, comparable to the blink of an eye. I am looking forward to opening the WINDOWS of new and exciting possibilities in the near future.

Congratulations on 25 years of service. The best just keeps on getting better.

———————————— ✼ ————————————

**Ted Kruse**
University of Baltimore
Baltimore, MD

The OCLC Online Union Catalog is a cost-effective, cooperative activity that benefits libraries both large and small.

As Head of Technical Services at a smaller academic library, access to the 33,000,000-plus records in the OCLC Online Union Catalog effectively increases the size of the collection available to our users by over 150-fold. Our interlibrary loan (ILL) usage patterns show the cooperative aspect of the OCLC Online Union Catalog. We borrow and lend to libraries much larger than ourselves and much smaller than ourselves. We use cataloging records from the Library of Congress and records from small, specialized libraries. Improvements in retrieval such as title scan and subject searching enables ILL to correctly fulfill requests with less-than-perfect bibliographic information. The ability of the OCLC Online Union Catalog to find the correct record from garbage input breaks the computer adage of "garbage in, garbage out." Elimination of duplicate cataloging records in the database has increased the chances of obtaining an item with less searching. IFM has reduced some of the bother and cost in processing payments for interlibrary loan charges making the 33,000,000-title collection available with less use of staff time.

Cataloging with a database as large as the OCLC Online Union Catalog limits expensive original cataloging to under 1% of our total cataloging. Despite changes in pricing, OCLC remains the most cost-effective method of providing quality with the option of title-by-title customizing of cataloging records. Even small libraries like ourselves can upgrade the union catalog by adding call numbers, reporting errors, adding original records to the online catalog without giving up the option of making cataloging adjustments to fit our library's needs. This cooperative aspect increases the quality of the OCLC Online Union Catalog as well as increasing the number of records available by 25,000,000 rather than just depending on Library of Congress cataloging records.

Quality records speed processing and get new materials in the hands of users faster. Some minor improvements in the OCLC Online Union Catalog have also increased accuracy and spend of processing. The capability to print spine labels directly from the cataloging records eliminates errors in spine label typing. The ability to use workforms for standardized types of original work such as theses also has increased the productivity and accuracy of cataloging. The ability of each library to program their own function keys improves library productivity for regular catalog and special cataloging projects.

The high-quality records in the OCLC Online Union Catalog save library staff time in quality control. Correct spelling, authority control of names, updating to new forms of subject headings and the ability of customizing cataloging records to meet our users' needs saves users time. This quality control of records is invisible to users but they certainly benefit from consistently accurate records.

The Online Catalog has helped our smaller academic library meet the big informational needs of our users.

———————— *gl* ————————

**Parvin Kujoory**
University of the District of Columbia
Wheaton, MD

"Just go 4,4" is not all...

My acquaintance with OCLC started in the mid-80s when, enrolled in the cataloging course, I, as well as my classmates, was assigned to retrieve bibliographic data of 100 Spanish books donated to the university. This assignment was meant to provide hands-on practice on OCLC and help the university cataloger who was overloaded with the new annual acquisitions.

The assignment created mixed emotions among students. "Oh, this is going to be fun!" exclaimed the younger students. "I don't think so..." grunted the more seasoned ones who, like me, were intimidated by any object with the shape of a computer screen. The professor instructed us "Go 3,2,2,1 for the title; 4,3,1 for the author; if no success in either, just go 4,4 for both." This was the extent of the guidance and information we received on OCLC. The professor had assumed we were already acquainted with the giant and it was time to challenge it! So we all received a two-hour-per-day schedule to search 100 books each on the two available terminals, without supervision. Well, I had not met the giant and little did I know of its awesome behavioral intricacies or its hideous idiosyncrasies. Nor did I (and still don't) read Spanish, for that matter. *Los* and *las* had as much right to start a title as any other word! Besides, I couldn't distinguish between the author and the publisher; that is, if I had identified the title by its different font type. Is a higher level of frustration possible?

The frustration, luckily, channeled in a positive direction. With a bunch of pink carnations in my shaking hand I approached the university cataloger who laughed and sarcastically dropped a pile of OCLC materials on my lap. "Here," she said, "Have fun with this stuff." I did have fun reading the well-organized informative "stuff" and applying the rules for my assignment. In fact, the more that OCLC technical bulletins and newsletters, modules and versions, rules and services have increased and improved, the more loyal yet shrewd I have become in deploying them. Case in point is the research I had to do for my recent book (*Black Slavery in America: An Annotated Mediagraphy*). Before approaching any other source for gathering my bibliography, I went "4,4" and exhausted OCLC's 520 field after Ms. Spies graciously granted me permission.

I chose OCLC over any other database because it is an internationally-recognized union catalog which offers modules for all major library services. OCLC is a unique, magnificent database to whose colossal size and extent, format variety and flexibility, effectiveness and accuracy dwarfs other databases. With efficiently introducing a host site for the Internet (OHIONET), thereby providing multi-faceted capabilities in communicating with the whole world, with conveniently transferring documents back and forth, with constantly upgrading its hard- and software, with instantly adding information, and with regularly publishing its informative bulletins and newsletters, this massive networking scheme is looked up to with awe and reverence. Yet, it is fun to use OCLC, whether one selects to "just go 4,4" or move the mouse.

———————————— *pk* ————————————

**Ross T. Labaugh**
University of Massachusetts, Dartmouth
North Dartmouth, MA

Mr. Porter...

I knew it was near closing time because I heard him shuffle in. His bags, always the same three, announced his entrance with a puffy, squishing sound as he struggled through the turnstile. Mr. Porter always arrived just before we closed. No matter when we closed. It was uncanny.

I looked up from the reference desk just as he rounded the corner past the elevator. I knew where he was headed and logged onto OCLC just as he got there.

"Oh thank you," he said still shuffling. "I just have a few things to check tonight." He spoke with a jack-o-lantern face, lowered his bony body to the chair, and released his bags like ballast.

"If you need anything just holler," I said glancing back to make sure he was okay.

He didn't answer... just made some sounds not meant to be words and began poking at the keyboard.

A few minutes later I heard the sound of rustling plastic again. I looked up and there he was... all smiles and baggage.

"Can you help me with OCLC? It stuck I think. I can't seem to get it to..." he grinned.

"No, problem... It happens all the time. The commands are a bit awkward, but when it works, it's great, don't you think?"

"Oh yes," he said. "It's mah-velous really. So much better than the old days." He spoke with the remains of an accent... slightly southern.

I rebooted the machine and as he repositioned himself, I pulled a chair next to him and the two of us sat waiting for OCLC to respond. He was quiet.

"What are you searching for tonight?" I asked, interrupting the silence.

There was a pause. "Oh... well... I am trying to verify some of these old citations on stochastic processes," slightly lifting the bags as evidence.

"Tough stuff. I'm not even sure what stochastic process is."

"Stochastic from the Greek. Random, you see. We were designing systems... dinosaurs really compared to this... we put components together not really sure what would happen. The Germans had done some work, you know after the war..." He was becoming animated.

I nodded as if I understood what he was talking about.

"Well much of the work is obscure, so tracking them down is difficult. And then I find all these wonderful things related to it. Marvelous, really."

He became quiet again.

"Oh good," he said as OCLC came back online. "I do want to get some of these done tonight and I know you close soon."

"Take your time. I'm staying a bit after closing and we can walk out together when you're ready."

He touched my arm slightly as I rose from the chair. "This is so wonderful... isn't it? I mean all this information right here at my fingertips. I really don't think I could finish my work without it. And it means so much." His word trailed.

"It is marvelous," I said, borrowing his word. "And you play that keyboard like a maestro!"

He laughed out loud. In the corner of his eye was a twinkle and a small tear.

### Cynde Bloom Lahey
New Canaan Library
New Canaan, CT

The OCLC Online Union Catalog is a dear friend and a valuable colleague most of the time. My relationship with the OCLC Online Union Catalog has evolved along with my changing positions within the Library. As a cataloger in a Library determined to automate, it became the center of my world. Bibliographic MARC records, authority control and retrospective conversion became the vocabulary within our Technical Services Department. We would gleefully locate titles we could export into our fast growing database and update with our holdings code for interlibrary loan purposes.

As the Technical Services Department Head my unguarded approval would temporarily waiver whenever we experienced technical difficulties and I would have to contact the Trouble desk. Of course with OCLC's superb technical support the problems would easily be resolved. Training staff and volunteers became easier with the use of PRISM.

My role also changed and now as Assistant Director, I value the OCLC Online Union Catalog. It is my first stop when I am searching for a title or the author of a book. It is also a primary tool when searching for audio-visual material. I have even used it to locate the name of a film's producer or director, an alternative title for a magazine, or an author's dates. It is definitely a primary resource for public services as well as technical services. My Library has two OCLC terminals. One terminal is located at the Information Desk and one in Technical Services. We often have staff members queue up for the first available terminal.

Using OCLC cataloging has enabled my Library to better expedite the availability of new material and provide excellence in Library service to our patrons. It is essential to our mission which states, "The New Canaan Library promotes and serves the individual's right to know and encourages personal pursuit of knowledge by providing free and convenient access to books and other resources for information, education, and the enrichment of life." The OCLC Online Union Catalog assists us in reaching our mission.

### Rebecca R. Laine
Longwood College Library
Farmville, VA

For those of us who became librarians before there *was* an OCLC, the Online Union Catalog has always seemed magical. As a beginning cataloger, I spent untold hours with heavy volumes of the *National Union Catalog,* checking entry forms, cross-references, call numbers, and elusive Library of Congress card numbers. After this daily body-building drill, I checked L.C. unit-card sets against newly-acquired books, writing instructions on the "process slip" for our typist, who made corrections on each printed card, added the call number, and over-typed secondary entries. Later I checked her typing, handed catalog cards and cross-references to student workers for alphabetizing, and gave shelflist cards to a clerk to arrange in classified order. Finally, I revised these workers' above-the-rod filing, "dropping" the cards in the trays. Every other library procedure was equally labor-intensive.

When I remember those pre-automated days and the drudgery of each operation, I marvel at the transformation in my workplace. In today's processing department, the workforce has progressed from routine clerical duties to high degrees of specialization and technical expertise. Staff members at all levels identify closely with their work and willingly devote precious hours to workshops, conferences, and staff development activities to keep pace with technological innovations. To think that, as a twenty-six-year-old newcomer to the library where I still work, I was awed that everyone in technical services had an electric typewriter!

I remember the apprehension we felt, when visiting another library, to see our first OCLC terminals. I recall how happy we were to see non-print records coming into the OCLC database and how the Minnesota OCLC trainers' manuals brought light to obscure areas of special-formats cataloging. And how we rejoiced when we could search sound recordings by record number!

Since then, we have become so accustomed to technological advances that our small staff no longer greets each as a minor miracle. The revolution which began with cataloging now extends to virtually every phase of library activity. Our materials budget recently doubled, but improved technology permitted us to process the flood of new materials—many in special formats—without additional staffing. We no longer worry that machines will take our jobs. For those willing to invest their best thought and effort, the OCLC database and related services have brought freedom from repetitive manual procedures and opportunity to upgrade technical skills and acquire valuable specialties. As we have learned and grown, we have discovered colleagues with similar skills and interests across the country and around the world. The old fear that computers would somehow dehumanize us was dispelled long ago by the realization that the OCLC Online Union Catalog links not just collections but those who build and utilize them.

OCLC Catalog...

It is March 1996. As I prepare for next week's SOLINET workshop, "Format Integration: Phase II," I recall many past workshops, all communicating understanding of then-new standards and system capabilities. Our shared goal remains the improvement of the resource upon which we all rely and for which we constitute a worldwide quality circle. The database is the creation of thousands, but we are *its* creatures also. Like other librarians of my generation, I am grateful for a system which brought us together and made us participants in the information revolution!

—————————— *⑨* ——————————

**Ruth Lamm**
The Cleveland Institute of Music
Cleveland, OH

As the manager of a music store located within a music school, I frequently receive requests for obscure works. Since I am always intrigued by searches involving uncommon questions and elusive answers, I welcomed our recent building-wide installation of fiber-optic cable bringing access via computer terminals to a variety of databases. Easily the largest and most far-reaching of these databases is the OCLC Online Union Catalog, with its 35 million worldwide bibliographic records ready to be disclosed at the touch of a finger. After an initial assist from the school's music librarian/computer specialist, I was soon charting my own course. I immediately recognized that no amount of printed music catalogs and library books, nor, indeed, any other accessible database, could match the enormous range and detail of the OCLC Catalog's informational entries. From the beginning, I have bypassed all other databases in favor of the OCLC Catalog exclusively.

Before the on-premises advent of the OCLC Online Union Catalog, the laborious process of locating rare material often took days, if not weeks. Sometimes no pertinent information whatsoever could be found. Now, through the OCLC Catalog, I almost invariably receive instantaneous answers to customers' inquiries. Moreover the OCLC Catalog has shown that over half the number of works presumed to be out-of-print, and thus lost to present and future generations, are in fact still available through new and different publishers. The ultimate satisfaction comes when I am able to continue onward via the music publishers supplied by the OCLC Catalog to the endpoint of obtaining and transmitting the actual desired items into customers' hands. Thus the OCLC Online Union Catalog contributes a real enrichment and broadening of musical horizons for my patrons—and myself as well. I must admit that the surprising ease of access and use for a computer novice like me makes the OCLC Catalog appealing for more routine look-ups as well. By now, I also feel practiced in the art of "directed surfing," often so invaluable to the successful outcome of specific searches.

Although small in size at 12-by-18 feet, the scope of the music store instantly expanded to global proportions upon the arrival of the OCLC Online Union Catalog. Among cognoscenti, it seems this is the place where "if they can't find it, nobody can." I have no doubt that the music store enterprise will continue to benefit immensely, and in as yet unexpected ways, from the power of the OCLC Online Union Catalog. It is difficult to imagine ever functioning at peak potential without it. I am sincerely grateful for the opportunities it presents and for the remarkable foresight of the 54 original cooperating Ohio librarians who initiated the project just 25 years ago.

**Holley R. Lange**
Colorado State University
Fort Collins, CO

OCLC, constant yet evolving...

I learned to love libraries long before the advent of the OCLC Online Union Catalog. I delighted in Jules Verne, adventured along with Horatio Hornblower, read about Madame Curie's life and cried as the chapters revealed her death. I learned to catalog before OCLC as well, beginning my coursework with the now antiquated *ALA Cataloging Rules*, and using the *National Union Catalog* as my first cooperative cataloging resource. My initial cataloging class held no hint of the revolution to come with OCLC. It was 1975, however, before I could complete my degree. By then OCLC was in place, but still little more than a whisper in my studies. We could "experience" OCLC if we wished, but it was not part of our coursework.

As a cataloger, researcher, and library user, OCLC is now an integral part of my life. I depend on it, and yet it challenges me as well. As a cataloger it has changed the nature of my work, broadening the resources I have at hand so that I and my co-workers process common materials quickly, unusual materials efficiently, and new materials correctly. Just as OCLC tugged catalogers and technical services departments into the computer age and the forefront of library automation years ago, it continues to demand our attention. As OCLC proposes, re-examines, and refines such products as PromptCat, it shakes up our professional world. It forces me to move beyond a more comfortable pace of change, and demands that I constantly re-examine my own and my library's workflows, procedures, and assumptions in a new light.

Although OCLC initially enhanced library service from the "back room," and was once under the purview of technical services departments and catalog librarians, its database is now open to the world. As a researcher, rather than cataloger, I can enjoy the benefits of OCLC's resource as it provides me with citations, and vital access to the materials themselves without time-consuming trips, letters or telephone calls to other institutions just to see if they might have the item I am seeking. I can then expand my knowledge base, my resources, and my universe from my home, at my convenience. In this way OCLC also challenges me as I write, encouraging me to seek the most appropriate resources for my work, and allowing me and a world of library users to share ideas and develop new ones through easy access to the printed word.

I marvel at how the numbers jump as I sit and produce original records, thinking of all the others around the world doing the same. Although I was first introduced to cataloging by a woman who knew the fine art of library hand, and while I have typed thousands of catalog cards on manual and then electric typewriters, I would not trade my OCLC terminal for pen nor typewriter even for old time's sake. OCLC works. It is constant yet evolving, and through its evolution and redefinition continues to serve me well.

**Fred Larimore**
University of Pennsylvania
Philadelphia, PA

Online catalogue looking complete...

From the germ of idea,
Starting small at the state,
Branching to the region,
Spreading to the country,
Asking the world to join.
Is the universe next?

Analyzing everyday mysteries,
Probing moral dilemmas,
Pondering life's decisions,
With information and knowledge,
Discovered with a probing, seeking search,

Online hunting,
Catalogue searching,
Looking, seeking,
Complete information.

OCLC, the quest, the hunt,
With strokes of keys,
Four - three - one;
Four - four;
Three - two - two - one.
The start, the stimulus, the hunt,
Begins with the stroking of keys.

In quest of questions,
Serious answers,
The scholar, the researcher,
The librarian, the seeker.
Lost in the woods,
Of problems dilemma,
Seeking a pebble,
To stir the quiet pond.

The quest of answers
Begins with the found pebble.
A kernel tossed upon the quiet pond.
The power of discovered information,
To mold and create knowledge,

Whose impact from the tossed pebble,
Ripples forth touching all the ponds shores,
Only to discover,
How small you really are,

And that in the end,
There are only more questions.
Online hunting,
Catalogue searching,
Looking, seeking,
Complete information.

**Wilita Larrison**
Phillips University
Enid, OK

The OCLC Online Union Catalog has helped me get through library school classes; given me help with my job (formerly interlibrary loan, now catalog/reference librarian); provided access to information regardless of where it is located; displayed bibliographic information for specific items; offered an awareness of global information; and provided a place to find out who owns what.

The Online Union Catalog has MARC records, tags and subfields, records of various information formats, linking of records, subject headings, name-address directory information, authority files. OCLC has established standard forms for inputting ISBD, ISSN, ISBN, and other publication numbers, physical description, GMD (general materials description), publication information (location, publisher, date), edition, audience, content notes, and classification numbers. This catalog is a place for sharing information through copy cataloging, interlibrary loan, and document delivery services.

Having access to the OCLC Online Union Catalog makes my job simpler by providing bibliographic records so that I do not have to do original cataloging on every item. It allows me to order catalog cards, print labels, and attach holdings to records. If someone else has classified an item, I can see what was used in that classification. I have the opportunity of doing original cataloging in a standardized form and sharing that cataloging with others. The OCLC Online Union Catalog serves as a backup to our shelflist.

WOW! The OCLC Online Union Catalog does all of this and more. It also provides a means of retrieving information through services such as EPIC and First Search's WorldCat.

## Kay Layten
Grizzell Middle School
Dublin, OH

WORKAHOLIC LIBRARIAN...

iso SYSCAT for fast accurate CATALOGING. Interested in long-term relationship with OCLC. Have PASSPORT and am anxious to EXPORT.

Using OCLC CATALOGING means I can have a personal life and still do a terrific job processing a multitude of media for our library patrons.

## Earl Lee
Pittsburg State University
Pittsburg, KS

Like many librarians, I wear a variety of hats. As a technical services librarian, who also does reference work in the evenings, I use the OCLC system for both cataloging and reference. More importantly, my first love is collection development, and it is here that the OCLC Online Union Catalog helps me decide what books to buy for our library.

In an age of diminishing resources, it is becoming more and more important to discover what resources other libraries have, both locally and regionally. Sometimes I can answer this question by going to the online catalog we share with our consortium partners and to other online library catalogs. But the best answer often comes from going to the source and consulting OCLC's Online Union Catalog. If I want to find out how many local libraries have copies of the latest business directories, I can find out in minutes. OCLC is especially valuable for locating both the newest reference sources and the oldest historical documents.

For cataloging, I enjoy the pleasure of sharing the labor with other librarians around the world. By creating new records for materials we have added to our collections, we all benefit from each others' efforts, saving time and creating a sense of common purpose and a strengthened commitment to our profession. Our library may have the only existing copy of a rare monograph or an obscure periodical, and making this information available to other librarians is extremely important. It contributes to the sum of human knowledge for everyone.

Finally, the OCLC Online Union Catalog provides organization and unity to information, creating standards and inspiring all of us to reach for new horizons. It challenges us to bring order to the chaos of new information sources.

## Leslie A. Lee, on behalf of the JBLL staff
George Washington University Law School
Washington, DC

Sung approximately to the tune of "My Favorite Things"...

Records in PRISM & catalogs on-line
Bright blinking cursors & phrases to combine
Titles & keywords all lined up in strings,

These are a few of my favorite things!

Double-oh-sixes & formats to master
Floppies & serials to catalog faster
F.I.-phase 2 has inspired me to sing
"These are a few of my favorite things!"

**Chorus**
OCLC !!
Someone help me !!
When I'm feeling lost
I simply remember the logoff command
And then I don't feel so cross!

Screens with no menus but mnemonic labels
Get me help soon with quick reference tables
Bib records organized by sub-sub-sub-fields
These are a few of my favorite yields!

**Chorus.**
3 2 2 1 ???!!!
L C C N ???!!!
When I'm in a lurch
I simply remember the logoff command
And then I call off the search!

| | |
|---|---|
| Lead-in Vocalists | Karen "Doe-ray-me-fah-sew-la-tee-doe" Douglas, Head of Acquisitions/Serials Leonard "Duke-duke-duke-duke-of-Earl" Klein, Legal Research Librarian |
| Finger snapper | Susan "Oompah-pah-oompah-pah" Chinoransky, Cataloging Librarian |
| Chorus of songbirds | Gail "Day-oh-daaaaaaaaay-oh" Bell, Circulation Supervisor Virginia "Shoop-shoop" Bryant, Head of Cataloging & Tech Services Coordinator Kate "Doo-wop" Ewing International/ Foreign Law Librarian Robert "Hi-dee-hi-dee-hi-dee-ho" Kim, Library Specialist Joseph "Boom-shack-a-lack-a-boom" Roushanfeker, Library Specialist Patty "Whoa-whoa-feeeeelings" Tobin, Reference/Government Contracts Librarian Michelle "Boop-boop-be-doop" Wu, Reference/Government Documents Librarian |

| Lyricist | Leslie "Sha-na-na-na-na-na-na-na-na-sha-na-na-na-na" Lee, Reference Librarian |

Views expressed herein do not necessarily reflect anything except random outbursts of merriment at JBLL.

**Sulan Lee**
Providence University
Taichung Hsien, Taiwan

My undergraduate major in Taiwan was in library science. In 1979, I went to the U.S. to study media education for my graduate degree. I made the big change because libraries here were poor and outdated, and librarians gained little professional respect in our society at that time.

I was astonished and impressed when I retrieved records from OCLC Online Union Catalog with the lists of library holdings which consists of libraries worldwide. It was amazing when I, as a student assistant, processed the interlibrary requests of OCLC ILL subsystem running on the Microenhancer workstation. I still can feel the emotional excitement while I held the antique-like book published in 1700, which arrived about 10 days after the ILL request was forwarded to the British Lending Library. Every publication of the 21,000 OCLC member libraries is accessible with the ILL subsystem. With that wonderful experience, I finally found my interest, and set up the goal of my career in the library and information science field which I almost gave up.

All the requests from other libraries, no matter whether in the U.S. or other countries, are printed out automatically before I, later being an ILL librarian in University of Alabama, get into the office every morning. We check for the materials locally. Within the same day, the lending materials are shipped out. Local patrons can know how their borrowing requests have been processed by other libraries. Has it been sent? Or is the charge more than what he is willing to pay? Every status of the whole transaction is well-controlled. ILL numbers are input in batch mode with a timer set up to update the records in the OCLC mainframe later to avoid the heavy traffic transmission hour. The whole process in the ILL office is streamlined. All of these are carried out under the infrastructure of OCLC Online Union Catalog.

Now, I work as a reference librarian and lecturer, teaching a "Library User Education" course, which is a one-unit course required by the freshmen in Providence University, Taiwan. I introduce how the OCLC Online Union Catalog was created and maintained by 21,000 libraries worldwide through cooperative teamwork. There are more than 35 million bibliographic records in more than 370 languages, and about 2 million records added annually into the database. It was a little difficult to introduce OCLC Online Union Catalog, the most comprehensive bibliographic record database, to our campus students without a demonstration. With the FirstSearch service, it makes students possibly feel the magnitude of the OCLC WorldCat database and the variety of bibliographic records. Also, the faculty can search any publications online to meet their needs without any interference from librarians. With the sharing of my experience with the OCLC system, the librarian's image, to our patrons, seems to become a high-tech profession.

The PRISM ILL will be operated in the library in the near future. Our patrons can have the same level of services as in the states, and they soon will. I have excitement as I did in the U.S. seventeen years ago. All I can say here is, "OCLC, you changed my personal life and escalated our patrons' knowledge. Thank you !"

## Linda C. Lewis
Jackson State University
Jackson, MS

Twenty-five years ago, few people could predict the impact of the OCLC Online Union Catalog on the genre of information science. From humble beginnings in 1971, the catalog has expanded at a phenomenal rate. It has also established and maintained OCLC's status as a leader in the field of automating the mostly repetitive processes that comprise the field of library and information services.

As libraries, we receive a proliferation of literature that is originated by "spin doctors" who seek to amaze and astonish us into believing that they have some magical control exerted upon the mechanisms of automation. These outlandish promises of online system capabilities are often nothing more than mere exaggerations by companies who either wish to self-aggrandize, or their direct aim is to carve out a share of the information services market for themselves using any means necessary. Fortunately for information specialists, and the various patron communities who are assisted through our direct efforts, OCLC has fulfilled every commitment that it has assumed on behalf of the rapid, orderly, systematic, affordable and accessible categorization, dissemination, and delivery of data. These responsibilities are accomplished daily through the support and services provided by OCLC to its member libraries.

I have developed a strong dependence upon the OCLC Online Union Catalog. The duties which I am required to perform necessitate access to accurate, fast, modern and progressive sources of information; OCLC provides that accessibility to me. As an employee of a university library, invariably patrons, especially students, wait until the last minute before attempting to complete the required semester's assignments, a lack of access to the online catalog would render the procurement of their requested resources a virtual impossibility, but access to the OCLC Online Union Catalog makes everyone employed by our library the benefactor of the positive publicity and goodwill that emanates when a task is completed to the satisfaction of the patron.

## Donna Valerie Liakas
Elgin Community College
Elgin, IL

Access, organization, and Willem Dafoe...

When I thought of how to describe what OCLC means to me, I settled on three basic topics: access, organization, and Willem Dafoe. It may not seem obvious why the latter springs to mind, but you'll probably find the explanation strikes a familiar chord.

Being an Interlibrary Loan Technician makes the access part of OCLC extremely crucial to my work. The increasing number of CD-ROM periodical indexes available to patrons, along with Internet access, has heightened the demand for more obscure items. Without access through OCLC to the larger universities and special libraries, I would be unable to meet that demand.

It's often miraculous to me that one system holds the key to obtaining an article on Thrombotic Thrombocytopenic Purpura (*Annals of Internal Medicine*, OCLC #1481385) as well as one of the great Jackie Chan movies, *Armour of God: Long Xiong Long Di* (#26947729). Not only can I discover these items exist, through FirstSearch, but I can then use the ILL database to obtain the items.

Of course what makes access like this so useful is that it is intelligibly organized, which is why I still go to OCLC before the Internet for a topic search. FirstSearch is extremely helpful in verifying skimpy citations I get from patrons, and for finding additional materials for their sometimes esoteric subjects. By utilizing the LIB command to check holdings, I can immediately get an idea about the turnaround time for that particular material.

Besides the obvious organization of all bibliographic records, union listings, and cataloging information, what I find incredibly useful is the Name Address Directory. When I look up that Jackie Chan movie for our anxious patron, I discover that WCM is a holding library. With just a few keystrokes I discover that WCM is in fact Williams College Library, and that the kind souls there lend A/V free of charge. Not having a budget for ILL costs, this information is *extremely* helpful to us *and* the patron, who has to absorb the costs if we can't find a free lender.

Now to Mr. Dafoe. Being an aspiring writer, I was very influenced by a dream I had which featured a stirring war scene starring none other that the aforementioned actor, and being a librarian, I was instantly driven to find every last bit of information that exists about Mr. Dafoe. With the help of OCLC, I collected articles from journals and newspapers from L.A. to New York. In my research I found references to an experimental performance art troupe the actor belongs to, and thus began my retrieval of items such as, from *Drama Review*, a layout of one of the hula dance numbers from the troupe's repertoire of performances. Not exactly the method of researching a novel that *Writer's Digest* speaks of, but it works for me.

That's what OCLC does. It provides a diligently organized, simple method of access to a wealth of materials for every subject of interest, whether it be medicine, martial arts, or Willem Dafoe.

**Gerald R. Lientz**
University of Virginia
Charlottesville, VA

For both library staff and library users, the data available through the OCLC Online Union Catalog is amazing. To have the resources of so many libraries cataloged together, and easily accessible, is one of the exciting developments of the computer age.

The amount of work saved cataloging departments is obvious. OCLC copy cuts the number of books any particular library has to catalog itself, as well as standardizing the way different libraries present the same material.

In addition, this massive amount of data makes the constantly increasing demands of the modern interlibrary loan system possible. OCLC makes it possible for interlibrary loan departments to locate material needed by their patrons, then makes the actual request much easier to send. In a period when tight budgets and high prices have increased the need for cooperation among libraries, this service is invaluable.

But while I can appreciate the help OCLC provides my colleagues in other library departments, I like it most because of the help it provides me as a book collector and constant reader.

OCLC greatly simplifies the problems in assembling complete lists of the works of favorite authors. The system is up-to-date, so that a user does not have to use multiple sources to hunt authors who continued writing after the completion of the data for the NUC pre-1956, or other printed sources. It also is easy to check for books published with more than one title, a common problem with writers published in both Britain and the United States in the first two-thirds of this century. Once a user finds his data, it is easy to print the information.

An even more fascinating use of OCLC for me is the discovery of books that I did not know existed. Keyword search is the tool for this esoteric effort. One area of books that I try to read and collect is "prequels" or sequels to Stevenson's *Treasure Island*, written by other authors. A keyword search of "Long John Silver" recently informed me of the book version of a movie, when I previously did not know that the book existed. A combination of "Treasure Island not Stevenson" also yielded several titles. Such searches were impossible with card catalogs, and tedious when I had to check individual libraries one by one.

To me, therefore, OCLC is a marvelous resource that makes life much easier for my colleagues in other departments, and also provides an amazing mine of information for library users.

**Stewart Lillard**
University of North Carolina
Charlotte, NC

I, searching the OCLC Online Union Catalog, have met old friends along the way, recalled forgotten names, reinforced forgotten titles, as a cat chasing its tail—a blur of dervish search formulas that unlock secret paths. Three-two-two-one, four-four, four-three-one, and do-si-do. I am back to back with titles reading right and reading left, from top to bottom and phrase by phrase—all "Romanized" to western aspirants. I aspire to fields of golden serials, to delimiters of subplots which demarcate scorecards of national libraries. I punctuate the records with flyspecks. My dance card is signed by member end lesser leveled contributors who play by different rules. I step sprightly now, but first I waltzed ever-so slowly. The music was new, the tempos challenging.

When I connect on a daily basis to the OCLC Online Union Catalog, I am astounded at the intensity of feeling generated by the response. I have unleashed a jinni who responds to my beck and call, my scan and produce commands. Headers and header codes mark the paths between mounds of space-age trash which in its discarded state contains gems of useful knowledge.

Twenty-five years is nothing to a life of commitment. I have joined onto a quest. The OCLC Online Union Catalog is my means for discovery, for instantaneous communications, for response and feedback. It is an anchor.

Pilloried before a green, or blue, or purple multicultural screen of movable, foreign images, I am flailed daily by millions of records, accentuated and marked as grave to acute character sets. I have spent a lifetime of collected experiences winking and wincing first at searches for theses, papyri, clay tablets, and then at prisms of bookish manuscripts, bound together over griddles of hot lead typeface.

In my stocks, my fetters, I (like Odysseus) row a stiff course between islands and countries seeking recorded knowledge shared digitally and located in millions of ports of call. My searches map a score of discs, motioning images larger than life and at decibels beyond the human mind.

Pilloried before a screen of movable images, I am a prisoner along with thousands of other cell-mates whose lives have been linked by a dedicated umbilical cord that gives oxygen to a profession once moribund like an scarecrow of straw cards flapping in the breeze of change.

The OCLC Online Union Catalog keeps me linked to the mother ship, moves me through lands of indolence, restrains my penchant for undisciplined adventures and unnecessary explorations; it calls me to yet uncharted courses as the ends of the earth are rounded into a dynamo, a sphere of atomic possibility.

Pilloried before a green, or blue, or purple multicultural screen of movable, foreign images, I experience daily the netted frenzy that celebrates twenty-five years of unbridled success. As when sailors sense the filling sails, I am ready for further voyages to distant lands.

## Martha Loeppky
Providence College and Theological Seminary
Otterburne, Manitoba, Canada

At our library we are mere babes in the OCLC Online Union Catalog as we have been on it for only six years of OCLC's twenty-five years. Without a doubt it has been the most efficient years of our library in terms of cataloguing and interlibrary loans. Life without it would be like re-entering the dark ages.

In the last six years our library catalogued more books than we did in the previous ten years. For some of that time (due to personal reasons) I was working part-time, yet we are more caught up now than when I began here fourteen years ago. The best thing about the OCLC Online Union Catalog is that with so many libraries inputting their data, virtually everything can be found on it that has been published. This is especially significant since we are a Canadian library cataloguing many items from small obscure Canadian publishers.

Interlibrary loans is another "miracle story." Before the OCLC Catalog I had to actively discourage students from requesting interlibrary loans as it took at least four to six weeks to obtain the item. Now almost everything is available within a fraction of the time. The difference is the OCLC Online Union Catalog. One could say, perhaps with tongue in cheek; It is the

> Only one of its kind; It is the
> Librarian's dream come true; It is
> Useful for so many things; Used with
> Confidence by librarians everywhere.

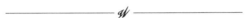

### Edythe E. Lord
Carmel Clay Schools
Carmel, IN

As an Information Services employee in charge of interlibrary loans, the OCLC Online Union Catalog makes me look good. The OCLC Online Union Catalog provides a library without walls, and therefore, few limitations. Almost every request made of me is fulfilled. Administrators, students, and fellow employees, think I have magical powers. Little do they know how easy it is to search the OCLC Online Union Catalog, thanks to the timely upgrades over the years. It is exciting to find that a prestigious school of higher learning or a large corporation wants to borrow from little old us. Although we loan more than we borrow, it is still worthwhile to share this wonderful communications network. After twenty-five years, it is still on the cutting edge, and it is a pleasure to have it at my service.

### Deixter A. Méndez Lorenzo
University of Puerto Rico
Mayagüez, Puerto Rico

I was a library assistant at the cataloging department of the University of Puerto Rico, Mayagüez Campus, when I was introduced to OCLC Online Union Catalog. It was 1985, and I just started graduate studies in Library and Information Sciences as a part-time student. I remember being assigned a paper on OCLC cataloging. I was pleased to find five books on our catalog under the OCLC subject. I was disappointed when looking at the shelves, I found none. I checked with the circulation desk to find none of the books had been checked out. I did some detective work. I talked to my supervisor about the assignment and the missing books. She hinted on whose desk the books could be found. At that time it was common to find unsigned journals or books on librarians' desks. Eventually, I got hold of the books. I found *OCLC: A National Library Network* to best describe the oncoming changes. I was eager to learn about it.

The OCLC topic became an ardent subject at the cataloging department. Our head of the department brought the news to the personnel that soon we would be using OCLC for cataloging. None of the library assistants knew exactly what she was talking about. The subject, though, I believe had been well discussed among the professional staff. I had read a few articles on the subject and knew the benefits it would bring to our library. The walls of the department were full of shelves stacked with years of backlogged books.

Whenever a professor came looking for a book, we went into a wild goose chase trying to find it. The books waiting to be cataloged were supposed to be shelved by title, but for some reason the title requested never appeared in the right place. Often, after the whole cataloging staff searched for "the most wanted book" it turned out the title given was wrong.

I don't remember who threw the joke first, but soon everyone was saying, "OCLC is coming." Someone from another department asked, "Who is that?" We laughed. We felt privileged, to be first for the big event. Finally we were connected to Mr. O. as we called it. We used the system from 7:00 a.m. to 4:30 p.m. We took shifts. I took the first shift for entering original cataloging at non-prime time. In the afternoon, I set the microenhancer to search at night. In the morning I read the reports and searched online those books that the program was unable to retrieve. All the cataloging staff participated in the search for records. Soon those shelves started to be emptied. Our statistics showed more than 90% hit rate on searches.

Proudly, I demonstrated how we cataloged using the OCLC database, and how to transfer records from OCLC to our database using DRA software. We did demonstrations to visiting librarians and to students from our Graduate School of Library and Information Science.

When I first came in contact with OCLC, the database had around 10 million records. That number had doubled by the time I received my degree in 1990. Our card catalog was closed, no more: filing of cards, typing, manual verification, backlogs of books, and wild goose chases. I can't conceive our library without OCLC just like my kitchen without the microwave oven. OCLC means higher productivity, cost effective cataloging, and a satisfied patron. It also frees librarians from routine procedures, allowing them to participate in other professional endeavors.

**Jean Lowerison**
San Diego City College
San Diego, CA

Melvil meets OCLC…

Unable to sleep, an exhausted Melvil resorted to his desperation technique of running through the Dewey Decimal system in his head. Somewhere past the 500s, he finally descended into the arms of Morpheus.

He looked up to find himself in an unfamiliar building, surrounded by what seemed to be new books waiting to be cataloged. He noted how different they looked from those he was used to—not maroon or brown leather bindings stamped with gold, but rather cheap-looking covers, though they seemed solid enough in a cheesy sort of way. Each one had a flashy paper cover announcing its contents. He picked one up. He was sure from the title, *Primary Colors*, that it belonged in the 700s, or perhaps the 370s. He opened the book, encountered a few salacious passages and slammed it shut, annoyed that it was not what it seemed.

A door opened and a gentleman dressed in most peculiar attire entered. He was not wearing a proper suit but rather a short-sleeved shirt and sporty-looking trousers. On his feet were strange-looking shoes which laced and seemed to be made of some sort of fabric—hardly the look Melvil would have expected of a professional.

Melvil hastened to get out of the way, but the man did not seem to see him at all. Picking up five of the books, he sat down before a strange machine that resembled a typewriter but had a sort of square glass picture frame on top. The man pushed a button somewhere and some sort of code appeared on the box. After typing a few letters, colors appeared on the screen; a few more and a message appeared that said something about OCLC. Melvil was flummoxed and fascinated.

The man picked up the vulgar *Primary Colors* and typed a few more letters. Like magic, the screen was filled with—was it?—a cataloging record for that book. Melvil gasped and leaned closer: the record was complete—call number, description, everything—and the man hadn't referred to a single manual! Melvil saw the man type a final line of information, hit a few more mysterious keys, and the screen cleared.

Melvil was marveling at this when the door opened and a woman entered. "Ken," she said, "I need to find a copy of the *Codex Nuttall* for a patron. Can you do an ILL search for me?"

"Sure, Karen," he said, and hit a few more keys. A few moments later he said, "We can get it from Indiana University."

"Thanks, Ken," Karen said. "Request it, will you?"

"Sure."

And with that she left. With a few more keystrokes, Ken finished the request, then picked up the next book in his stack.

Melvil woke with a start, mind reeling from his incredible experience. He dressed hurriedly and rushed off to work, anxious to describe his absurd dream to his colleagues.

## Jan Luksik
Reed Smith Shaw & McClay Law Library
Pittsburgh, PA

OCLC in short means Otherwise Chaotic and Laborious Compilations (without the OCLC Online Union Catalog).

As a user "trained under fire," the versatility of the OCLC system never ceases to amaze me. I am always discovering, by accident and otherwise, more ways that OCLC changes Chaos to Order in my Literary Universe.

It is my good fortune to work alongside an OCLC guru who, whenever I utter an "oops," is there to turn that "oops" into "aha." Many times, it is as simple as reorganizing a search or interpreting a line in a record, but each provides a broader awareness and promotes a fuller appreciation of the system. Even without my guru "crutch," I have been able to obtain materials I would have thought impossible to even identify, given the sketchy information sometimes provided by patrons.

Also amazing (and fortunate) is the relatively low cost of utilizing OCLC. In my position, placating patrons (a.k.a. attorneys) has become a major function in my professional life. "Get this for me now but I don't want to pay for it" has become the battle cry in the cost-effective war against the escalating price of document retrieval. Thanks (many times over) to the OCLC Online Union Catalog, I have been able to obtain the unobtainable in minimum time and at minimum (monetary and mental) cost.

The networking that occurs among the various resource centers across country and continents is yet another chaos-to-order offshoot of OCLC. It is interesting to discover the differences in usage, but more fascinating to observe the similarities in libraries from Anchorage to Miami. Everyone has the problem patron, the impossible research questions, and of course, not enough staff to handle the above. Rarely, however, have I encountered OCLC affiliates unwilling to at least attempt fulfillment of my requests.

Library service has come a long way from the ancient Greeks' attempts to create Order from Literary Chaos. Even the perennial card catalog has been overshadowed by the most significant development in recent history—the dawning of the database era.

Through its commitment to the assimilation and development of new information access technology, the directors and staff of the OCLC Online Union Catalog have provided libraries worldwide with an express lane on the often chaotic information highway with minimal toll booths!

From one of those drivers easing her way into this express lane, thanks, and happy anniversary!

———————————— ❧ ————————————

**Karen Lull**
Emory University
Atlanta, GA

There are many astounding statistics and facts that accompany the history of OCLC, but what it means to me and other library users is much more personal. It means Online Cruising of the Libraries of the Cosmos. It means that I, as a library staff person, can make library users happier than they were when they came into the library.

Users may never comprehend the incredible number of hours and decisions involved in the creation and maintenance of OCLC, but they are the very happy recipients of the results of that endeavor.

You already know the basic questions. Where can I find this book if you don't have it? Will the university in Iowa City have books by this author if I am there on sabbatical next semester? Do you know the earlier title of this book? What are the first works published by this author? Does anyone own those 14th century manuscripts? Our library's copy is missing; does anyone else in Atlanta have it? Is there a Japanese translation of this? Is there a new edition due out soon?

I love my job, and I love helping people find what they are seeking. OCLC helps me do that every day quickly and easily. My co-workers told me not to say this, but I shall anyhow: Where would I be sans OCLC? I would not be the happy library worker I am today.

———————————— ⅍ ————————————

## Shu Lan Ma

Naval Surface Warfare Center, Carderock Division Technical Information Center
Bethesda, MD.

Since 1974 I have been working professionally with OCLC on a daily basis. It has revolutionized my life from the very beginning when I was only a library technician. My job then was to input other catalogers' work into the database, but before I could do that, I was required to search whether the entry was already there so that we would not duplicate the work that others had already done. I was fascinated that in a split second I could find out whether someone, somewhere, had already done the work for us. This is, indeed, a revolution in communication. Now nobody needs to hide in his or her corner any longer saying he/she cannot do a job, when everybody is helping everyone else to save time, money, and effort—and when this can be done instantly.

As OCLC grew, so did my career! I progressed through copying cataloging to where I now do original cataloging. During each stage of my career, no matter for which library I worked, OCLC was always there to assist me in OCLC's faithful way, that is to help doing the work required at the lowest possible cost, at the highest quality, and in a timely fashion. My life has become intertwined with OCLC. I was ecstatic when I heard that OCLC had bought Information Dimensions, Inc., because it meant that OCLC was growing healthily and that I could remain a part of its vast global network.

Every morning when I log on my authorization number, I congratulate myself that I have this lucky number which enables me to tap into this wide and deep information ocean. The good fortune of having access to OCLC provides me with hope for my own future as a librarian in the information age.

———————— ๗ ————————

## Nancy K. Madigan

Albuquerque Academy Library
Albuquerque, NM

Well, since I work in a library, I have to ask:

What can OCLC do for you?
Here's an alphabetic clue...
Through its use you can be
accurate, bold and brave,
Helps makes the user
Clever, capable and suave.

It's a database, darlin'—
It makes you daring and discerning
Makes you Eager for that learning.
Depth of facts? It's reassuring
(Makes your thesis so enduring!)

It's a help, it's really great—

Makes you glad to gather knowledge,
    They'll say, "Hey! You went to college!"

Here's incentive, here's inducement
    to be informed (now there's no excusement!)
On your journey to find out
Go ahead, be a knock-out!
Use OCLC—don't be lame
Be so learn-èd; (think of
all that midnight oil
you've burn-èd.)
    Yes, do multiply your smarts some
With N-formation that's so heartsome.

OCLC, it's pretty clever,
    Communication quick and ever.
Recorded learning
    *That's its stuff*
In 63 countries! Hey, it is buff!

Now it's twenty-five years—the silver party,
First try the shelves, then, party hearty!

OCLC—umpteen figures
    and that many facts
OCLC equals lots of acts.
Very viable, very quick
(Could I get some info
on the limerick?)
(Or is it rap? Or should I
    make the form free?)
It's simply a winner
And easy as can be.
    Your biggest problem
is x and y and z.

———————————— *qv* ————————————

## Hjørdis Madsen
San Jose State University
San Jose, CA

OCLC everywhere...
    One morning, not too long ago, I was stopped at a signal light, waiting to turn in to the employee parking lot at San Jose State University, where I work in the university library's Interlibrary Loan Department. Out of the corner of my eye, I caught three initials on a city trash can and my first reaction was "Wow, they have our OCLC location symbol on that trash can." The initials were CSJ, which of

course in this case meant City of San Jose, not San Jose State University in OCLC location symbol language. However, as my working day is permeated by OCLC location symbols, I tend to see them even when they are not there.

Then, on a weekend, not too long after the above incident, I was sailing in the Oakland estuary, when on my starboard side I saw a large container ship with the initials OCLC prominently displayed on its hull. I turned to my husband in amazement with the comment "look at that, OCLC has its own ship." Again, this had nothing to do with OCLC, but the organization is such a large part of my life that anything that even remotely looks like OCLC gets a reaction.

Not only is OCLC a major part of my working life, but I have spoken about it enough to where it has become a part of my family's life as well, albeit not always accurately. Last winter, I was bemoaning the fact that my favorite author had not produced a book for a long time and my husband's immediate reaction was "well, when you go to work tomorrow, you should check your RCDC thing and find out if he has published anything recently." (We had just seen a Star Wars movie on TV and obviously R2D2 got mixed up with OCLC in the equation.)

So, OCLC is all around me, factually or not. Certainly, as an interlibrary loan type, I could not do my job with any speed and accuracy at all, if I did not have access to the OCLC ILL system. Because of OCLC, I can obtain material for patrons in an expeditious manner and also help them find out who might own any given item, in the event that they don't have time to wait for interlibrary loan. In fact, patrons are always amazed when I tell them how extensive the OCLC Online Union Catalog is and how many library holdings are reflected in the database. And this brings me back to the OCLC holdings symbols as patron, Professor B, looks at me in awe and says "you can tell, just from those symbols, that Harvard owns what I need?" I smile benignly and reply, "Yes, isn't it great," and then spend the rest of the day thinking, not Harvard, but HLS.

## Ingrid Maksirisombat
Virginia Mason Medical Center
Seattle, WA

OCLC means the Whole ABCs and more to our library and patrons:

| | | |
|---|---|---|
| A | — | Adam's apple, Adam, virtual man, Apple computer |
| B | — | Borrow |
| C | — | Cataloging |
| D | — | Downloading, downsizing |
| E | — | Eve, virtual woman |
| F | — | Friends, fields, fast |
| G | — | Good, Great |
| H | — | HELP! |
| I | — | ILL, ISSN, ISBN |
| J | — | Jumping for joy, juggling tasks |
| K | — | Kwik, keyword, keen |

| L | — | Link |
|---|---|---|
| M | — | Multi-focal, medical, multi-media |
| N | — | Network |
| O | — | OCLC—WHAT ELSE!! |
| P | — | Periodicals |
| Q | — | Quick response |
| R | — | Review, response time |
| S | — | Systematic, system |
| T | — | Timeliness, text |
| U | — | Ultralite |
| V | — | Vellum |
| W | — | WLN, World Wide Web |
| X | — | Xchange, Xerox |
| Y | — | Yesterday |
| Z | — | Zooper |

———————————— ⅍ ————————————

## Nannette Martin

U. S. Patent & Trademark Office
Arlington, VA

I have used OCLC almost from its inception. I have always taken it pretty much for granted and heartily missed it in libraries where I did not have it.

Most of my professional life, I have worked in specialized corporate libraries where I have had to be a one-person library.

MARC is MARC is MARC... OCLC has many competitors, but no one is quite like them. I can always count on finding my data in the shared cooperative environment: probably 97% of the time. This frees my time to devote to preservation, helping my boss with acquisitions, investigating new software, helping to promote our department. And, I can always comfortably count on not only the quantity of wonderful data to search through, but also on the quality of the contributors' work in all languages. This is especially reassuring and essential at the time when libraries are downsizing and staffs are shrinking.

It's an absolute godsend to be able to search function keys in the 33 million records plus to find new CD-ROMs, new books or new serials to buy. This is a wonderful boon to acquisitions and collection development because of the size and complexity of your database. I can even answer complicated cataloging questions by observing how other libraries have answered a cataloging problem: is it a serial, is it a book? I can even glance at other libraries overseas to see what the resolution was. This is particularly important because intelligent solutions help patrons, technical services staff and researchers who are trying to clarify a request.

I have constantly depended on OCLC's interlibrary loan system which has found books for me while I was stationed on every continent. It's user-friendly, instantly available and impresses customers (patrons) each and every time.

It's almost inconceivable to remember sitting in a law library, as a new librarian, with a telephone and a directory trying desperately to deliver services to an information-hungry environmental law group.

It's also great to be able to log on the OCLC over the Internet. This was especially helpful during a library move when our dedicated line was down. The technical staff at OCLC is always helpful whether it's helping a novice Internet user (like me) or responding to any other query.

People today talk about "intellectual property" and human memory and digitization and a lot of other techno buzz words I don't even understand. But OCLC, since I have used it since 1979, is like an old friend, a "Joy of Cataloging" that I can always return to.

OCLC is like a visit to a museum or a huge bookstore where tens of thousands of other librarians, information scientists and experts in fields from A to Zed have traveled. I love participating in that endeavor, to help that "bookstore" grow. OCLC is more than a web site, it's a web of human dreams, people, thoughts, subjects: a veritable wealth of information that, I trust, will exist far into the future bringing instruction and fun.

## LaVerne Laney McLaughlin
Georgia Southwestern College
Americus, GA

The OCLC Online Union Catalog is my step into the international world and the future. Through the world's largest library information network, it takes a simple logon message, authorization number and password to access the world's information at my fingertips. Through OCLC, I can view the cataloging of more than 23,000 libraries in the United States and in 63 other countries and territories.

Each day is a "new" day of discovery and learning for me. Through the use of the OCLC Online Union Catalog, I can travel in time to bibliographic records ranging from 2000 B.C. to 1 B.C., to the present day. It is indeed a wonder to be able to access books, serials, audiovisual media, maps, archive/manuscripts, sound recordings, scores, computer files, and so much more to come in the future.

I was introduced to the OCLC Online Union Catalog as I began my library career as a cataloger. And now, as head of technical services, I still maintain that hands-on contact! By being employed in a library which is a charter member of the Southeastern Library Network (SOLINET), I began utilizing the OCLC Online Union Catalog in 1975, just four years after the catalog began its operation. I have literally watched the information network grow by leaps and bounds. My slogan at work is, "just can't live or work in a library without the OCLC Online Union Catalog." It feels great to have played a part in helping to build the world's foremost bibliographic database. This great database contains more than 35 million records, and nearly 600 million location listings.

The Online Union Catalog spans over 4,000 years of recorded knowledge. It contains at least 370 languages. And, it is very rapidly growing by at least 38,000 records per week. I feel that the OCLC Online Union Catalog has grown right along with me. I started using the system at 23 years old. Therefore, it certainly has grown overwhelmingly, and I know the "best" of OCLC is yet to be!

It is quite exciting to have access to such a wealth of knowledge. I have used the OCLC Online Union Catalog as a librarian, library user, and faculty member. I have seen tremendous improvements in the system's response time, troubleshooting systems, and quality of cataloging. Without such access to speedy cataloging, libraries could not give ready access to library patrons. Now, in most libraries there is very little backlog of books to be processed. Through use of the OCLC Online Union Catalog, everything is processed so much more swiftly. The archive tape, which is created by cataloging via OCLC, makes possible so many more technological advances in the library workplace. Students now have access to many more reference services than ever before. To name a few, FirstSearch, EPIC, OCLC EJO, and many others.

The world's largest information network offers products and services that help libraries gain further access to information and reduce information cost. Through retrospective conversion, which is converting older cataloging records to machine readable form, the face of libraries has changed in the area of technological advances. Current cataloging with PRISM allows use of high-quality records and allows cataloging of any type of material, and an interlibrary loan service. This great interlibrary loan service means resource sharing. This service expands the information network while reducing operation costs. Communication and access through telecommunications provides Internet dial-up, multidrop or linking options for cataloging, resource sharing, and reference services. Where would libraries be without OCLC??? Libraries, we have much to celebrate... 25 years of library cooperation! Certainly, libraries, we have come a long, long way... but... the best is yet to be!!!!!

**Karen Meadows**
Rock Valley College
Rockford, IL

When the OCLC flyer came across my desk with the "What the OCLC Online Union Catalog Means to Me" contest, it started me thinking about grade school. More specifically, thinking about using the library in grade school. When you looked for information on a topic, you used materials that the school owned; most often books or sometimes a magazine article. You could go to your public library or the larger library in the next city, but your choices were usually limited. Over the years this stayed pretty much the same, slowly improving. But today with the OCLC Online Union Catalog, any person can easily find information simply by going to a library with OCLC access.

Currently, I work with interlibrary loan at a community college. I see many requests for materials on such varied topics that range from dissertations about education leaders to books on small lake management in Illinois. And whether a staff member needs bibliographic information for an in-house catalog of video tapes, or a student is looking for material on British comedy style, it is there to be found in the vast treasure chest that is the OCLC Online Union Catalog. The additions of EPIC and FirstSearch are the keys to subject searching on the Online Catalog. It is so convenient having the option of going to one source to find information that is beyond the range of our library. And the material can be readily obtained through interlibrary loan, regardless of the format. Imagine the size of the building if all the materials owned by every OCLC library were under one roof!

Just recently, I was looking for a book on the small figurines I collect. I did not know a title or author, just the topic. Having had no success in off-line searches, I proceeded to FirstSearch. I could have saved myself time and effort by going to the OCLC Online Union Catalog first, because, of course, there had been a book written about them. Just one book, but it was a very good one.

It has only been since mid-1989 that Rock Valley College's library joined OCLC, but what changes it has brought to all areas of our library. Access to a great range of materials for our library patrons; quicker and more accurate cataloging; improved interlibrary loan service; and, for myself, opportunities to learn and grow. I know the next 25 years will be just as amazing.

———————————— ℐ ————————————

**Max J. Merrell**
Veterans Affairs Medical Center
Walla Walla, WA

As I consider the marvelous changes which have occurred in the field of communications in the past generation, I am amazed at the capabilities of mankind, in developing wondrous technologies, inventions, work processes—many of which seem so commonplace in our busy lives today.

In the development of writing several thousand years ago, some early civilizations wrote on clay tablets, while some developed writing on cloth or parchment. Papyrus was used to write on and was stored in rolls. Referred to as "sticks," many of these formed libraries, even in those ancient times. Other ancient civilizations with an abundant supply of metals often used this to write on. Portions of the Old Testament were written on brass plates. Gold was molted into very thin sheets to write upon, and some have been found by archaeologists with the writings yet very distinguishable.

Unfortunately, in the case of many ancient manuscripts, we have not always been able to decipher what had been written by the "ancients." Until the discovery of the "Rosetta Stone," our knowledge of the ancient Egyptian empire had been lost. With the loss of the written word, and except for some "fabled" military histories, our knowledge of the those civilizations, their customs, beliefs, and abilities are lost.

Will this be our story to people of the 25th Century? Unless we destroy our civilization in the future, I would think the record for our posterity will be quite evident. The whole world is now linked together, culturally and intellectually, with universal communication. Only one generation ago, the *National Union Catalog* was begun, so scholars could find the locality of any published book in the world. Since that time, union catalogs have evolved into multiple subject databases—then hardly imagined, now becoming commonplace. Now that huge reference collection in the university library is contained on a small metal diskette in your home. Where the scholar had to peruse through many stacks of books or volumes of periodicals in a library, one can now simply dial up on a computer modem to obtain access to literature from all over the world.

## Lois K. Merry
Keene State College
Keene, NH

"May all your 'display-record-sends' be great!" wrote my supervisor on a good luck card as I left my job in a high school library to begin work as interlibrary loan supervisor at a local college. At the time I had no idea what he was talking about, but during my intense first week at the new job I found out quickly. The OCLC Online Union Catalog has been the underpinning of my working life ever since. OCLC's ILL subsystem has evolved so far since I first encountered it that that particular command now seems almost archaic. The OCLC Online Union Catalog remains the database with which I am most familiar and facile. Before access to WorldCat was available at our reference desk, I sorely wished for my OCLC terminal at hand. Even taking the long walk down the corridor to my office during a reference interview was worth the effort, rather than muddling through less successfully with an alternative.

Shared cataloging and its corollary, resource sharing, are what we librarians are in business to do. With the OCLC database I can procure materials for our library's patrons, or tell them where they can find that rare book or journal they need to use. Some astute patrons have taken to searching WorldCat independently now that it is available on FirstSearch. One of our interlibrary loan patrons often submits requests accompanied by helpful letters detailing the progress of his search for elusive local history materials. Having used WorldCat, he also includes the item's OCLC accession number.

The OCLC Online Catalog has given me a whole new language, known to us practitioners, esoteric to those we inadvertently confuse when we use it as shorthand. I think I will never again be able to drive past a college or university's sign on a highway without its three-letter OCLC code springing to my mind, and sometimes to my lips— "Oh, there's—!" Wading through the layers of the NAD, the Name-Address-Directory, can be challenging. Among holders of library materials, some may not lend them or some may charge fees to lend, but others provide scant clues to either possibility. Indeed, one of my job's greatest satisfactions is crafting an excellent online request with less-than-perfect information, either as submitted by the patron or as found in the OCLC database itself. The best bibliographic record occasionally hides among other less suitable ones. ILL people sometimes complain about needing to work within a system originally set up by catalogers which resulted in far too many duplicate records. Sorting them out can be frustrating, but finding the right one is as satisfying as solving a puzzle.

Certainly one of the best rewards of my job is obtaining an item on interlibrary loan for a patron who requests something rare, but the centerpiece of a research project. Only a database such as the OCLC Online Union Catalog could make that event as frequent as it is. "Would it be OK for me to do handsprings here in the library?" the aforementioned letter writer asked me recently in delighted response to my announcement that a particular roll of microfilm had come in. It had been located via OCLC and supplied by one of only a few libraries that indicated ownership in the entire country. That's the beauty of the OCLC Online Union Catalog!

―――――――――― ᚋ ――――――――――

## Arthur S. Meyers
Hammond Public Library
Hammond, IN

As a Library Director, I know the immense savings in time OCLC brings to our technical services staff, adding materials more quickly, and to our information services staff, promptly handling interlibrary loan requests.

The resource has a second, more personal meaning to me as an ILL user. In 1995, I was able to borrow microfilm copies of *The Papers of W. E. B. Du Bois*. As a result, I have uncovered major letters on a little-studied American movement, the Open Forum.

Begun in Boston in 1908, the lecture series made a significant impact on communities around the country. In 1924, when the Ku Klux Klan was powerful, Rabbi Max Bretton of Temple Beth-El started the Open Forum in Hammond, and among the speakers was William E. B. Du Bois of the NAACP. Du Bois' research refocused our understanding of American history and sociology, and his editing of *The Crisis* and laying the foundation for the Harlem Renaissance made him the most well-known African American spokesman in the 1920s.

Thankfully, Du Bois saved letters to him and copies of his responses. Archivists at the University of Massachusetts microfilmed the materials, and libraries purchased and added them to the OCLC Catalog. In this trove, I found handwritten letters from Hedwig Kuhn, a doctor and civic activist in Hammond.

"Those of us who know your work..." wrote Kuhn, "and are so warmly in back of it feel that it would mean a very great deal to have you come to this difficult industrial district." She described a "small nucleus of rare souls here on whom revolves the intellectual spiritual future of large groups of people. The famous Indiana Klan will undoubtedly discover us to be even more 'dangerous' than they do now." She had "several pitched battles with them and am only eager to reduce their ranks still more."

Following his 1926 lecture, Du Bois exchanged several letters with Kuhn. He "enjoyed tremendously" the experiences of Hammond, and was moved by the welcome and knowledge of his impact. She wrote about the "spiritual entity grown wider... like a blossom in fertile soil [that] will reach deeper and further into the far corners of thought and feeling." She thanked him for printing an article she had written. In her anonymously-written essay, she related in a personal way whether race prejudice is instinctive and incompatible, or acquired and artificial. She wrote an especially moving letter to him while recuperating from a Cesarean section.

Kuhn also expressed deep feelings about her children—"my proud hope [they] enrich themselves at the hearths of many nations and many races." "You have given me new strength and vision... the foundation is laid true and strong." She asked to contribute her energy and effort "to the great evolution."

Thanks to Du Bois, archivists, and OCLC, we have regained an important woman. Kuhn's and Du Bois' involvement in building a better world is before us. It is up to us to move forward.

## Patricia K. Michalowskij
Lawrence Law Library
Lawrence, MA

The front door to my library opened and closed, and she stood before me. Her raincoat was wrinkled and stained, and a pool of water began to collect around her as it dripped from her limp matted hair. A small child clung to her leg as though it were his entire universe. Although my law library is public and I am sadly accustomed to the diverse parade of patrons who pass through my portal in search of help, I was not prepared for this specter. There was an anguish and a fatigue in her eyes that spoke of monumental loss and pain. These were eyes that had not known joyful peace in many months, maybe years. Her slender fingers cupped the child's shoulder and gently pulled him closer. She looked at me and her lips parted but a moment, and then, as if frightened by the prospect of attracting attention, they closed again. She needed help, but I found myself strangely hesitant as well. I knew that neither she nor I would move beyond this paralyzing moment if I didn't approach her though. I realized too that she had had to summon every measure of courage to bring herself to this point, standing before a complete stranger hesitant with fear and timidity. It was only fair that I help her the rest of the way on this journey. I gently asked her how I could help her. She nervously gnawed to either side as if uncertain I had addressed her. When satisfied that she was the object of my attention, she moved closer to the reference desk and began her story. It was not a long story and she was surprisingly direct.

She told me that a friend had recommended she read a particular book on the subject of the role of mediation and counseling in cases of domestic violence. She asked me if my library owned the book. When she spoke the words "domestic violence," she looked away as though embarrassed and she cradled her son closer. I told her that I did not own the book, but that I was confident I could retrieve it for her through a national online catalog called OCLC. She nodded her head gratefully. I requested the book from several nearby libraries and told her I would call her in a few days when I had received it. She left me her telephone number and walked toward the door. I watched her. In the last few moments, she slowly turned and for the first time looked me directly in the eyes. The words that softly escaped from her lips were merely "thank you," but I sensed an unassuming gratitude that came from deep within. Then she disappeared as ghost-like as she had arrived, leaving behind only a pool of rainwater.

I couldn't help her to alleviate tomorrow's sorrow, nor could I help her to erase the memory of yesterday's pain and anguish. But I could help satisfy this one concern at this one particular point in time. And it was a start. It was one rung of the ladder in her journey out of the darkness. This is what OCLC means to me. It is a door to the world and a portal to the aggregate of human knowledge and wisdom. Sometimes that knowledge and wisdom has the power to heal.

———————————— ⅋ ————————————

## Daphne C. Miller
College of Mount St. Joseph
Cincinnati, OH

When I began using the OCLC Online Catalog, I never realized OCLC's importance to all people involved in libraries or using library services. After years of clerical library experience, part-time library school and cataloging work experience without OCLC, my passion for OCLC is summed up in one word—FRIENDSHIP.

In *Webster's Third New International Dictionary of the English Language Unabridged*, friendship has three related terms—AID, HELP, ASSISTANCE. I view sharing, cooperating and being dependable as the most important characteristics for a good friendship. Aren't all these qualities representative of what OCLC has and will continue to be?

The catalog database provides more than 35 million records that are shared by millions of users. Daily, catalogers use bibliographic records, contribute new records and assist in the database quality. I, personally, take pride in my cataloging work. OCLC provides a database and cataloging service I can trust. If OCLC did not exist today, I would not be a cataloger.

The OCLC Online Union Catalog provides the bibliographic records for Reference and Interlibrary loan librarians to obtain the correct items for the library users. The ILL system and the Union List of Serials are services that streamline and consolidate the processes involved with borrowing and lending materials between libraries. These services exemplify the nature of cooperation, sharing and assistance. Interlibrary loan continues to be more important and a necessary service provided by libraries. Knowing that there are others willing to help provide the requested information is a comfort, not only to me (supervising ILL operations), but to reference librarians that have helped find "that perfect piece of information."

Years ago, I had the position of Terminal operator. Most of my responsibilities involved working with OCLC. I remember the times I needed to use the Help Desk Line. Always helpful, always kind, and always there when I needed assistance. It was like talking with a friend, providing the answers to my problems and helping me through the difficulty.

I want to conclude with a quote that really summarizes my thoughts:

"Friendship is only a reciprocal conciliation of interests, and an exchange of good offices" (Duc de La Rochefoucauld Francis, *Maxim* 83).

———————————— ⅋ ————————————

**Mary Ann Miller**
Suffolk Community College, Eastern Campus
Riverhead, NY

What the OCLC Online Union Catalog means to the students and faculty of the Suffolk County Community College Eastern Campus Library...

*I'll be preparing several reports in clinical psychology and will need to consult classic texts and journal articles concerning strategies for questioning techniques. Most of the texts are out-of-print. Can the library help me?*

*My specialized research for science laboratory technology is ocean sunfish. The professor assigned me to read books and articles from a bibliography before beginning the experiment. I've checked the catalogs, and the library doesn't have these materials in the collections. What can I do?*

*Immigration patterns in Great Britain during the past one hundred years is the focus of my graduate thesis in world history. I don't have the time to visit major research libraries to consult these materials. Can the library locate and obtain these books?*

The answer to all of the above paraphrased student and faculty reference questions is YES. The SCCC Eastern Campus Library is able to successfully respond to very diverse types of requests for information and materials not available in the campus collections by accessing the extremely powerful and comprehensive resources of the OCLC Interlibrary Loan subsystem.

One of the three libraries of the SCCC Library system, the Eastern Campus library, established in 1977, maintains a collection of materials in order to meet the information needs for a comprehensive community college supporting 2500 full-time equivalent (FTE) students and 50 faculty with a book collection of 36,000 volumes and 300 current periodical titles. Although the three SCCC campus libraries actively share resources from a commonly-held OPAC and these pooled resources total 185,000 volumes and 1500 periodical titles, the divergent and complex research needs of the students and faculty from a small community college campus library frequently require access to much larger and more specialized collections. The OCLC Interlibrary Loan subsystem permits the SCCC Eastern Campus Library to go beyond the limitations of local materials to tap resources from literally around the world.

With success in obtaining materials through OCLC, attitudes and behaviors have changed. At first, students and faculty often appear to hesitate in asking for materials that are not listed in the catalogs. Next there is a degree of surprise and gratitude when books and periodical articles arrive. Our regular interlibrary loan clients now appear to challenge the system with more specialized and elusive citations. Certainly, the library staff feels a great deal of satisfaction in being able to complete these requests. Although there is no way to predict what the next series of requests will be, the OCLC Interlibrary Loan system will continue to help us to meet the information needs of the next generation by continuing to grow.

———————————— *qV* ————————————

**William Miller**
Florida Atlantic University
Boca Raton, FL

As a library administrator, I have a multiplicity of feelings about the OCLC Online Union Catalog, which over the years has provided many ways not only to save time and money, but also to avoid a wide variety of problems. For instance, the OCLC Online Union Catalog means *not* having to apologize to someone who has driven 50 miles for nothing, because the person thought that you had an issue of a periodical that you in fact don't have. Similarly, the Online Union Catalog means *not* having to type up and send out ALA interlibrary loan request forms blindly to other libraries, on the off-chance that they might have what you need; the corollary, of course, is that one also does *not* have to waste time responding to such requests from other libraries.

The OCLC Online Union Catalog means *not* needing a squadron of catalogers, which for our library is a good thing because we have only two catalogers at the moment; it means that we can accomplish most of our cataloging with paraprofessional staff and not need to let easily-catalogable materials languish for excessive amounts of time, blushing unseen, unknown and unused. The corollary is that the existence of the catalog enables one to brag to non-librarian bosses about saving money and staff by piggy-backing on the cataloging already created by others, which makes eminent good sense to these administrators.

The OCLC Online Union Catalog means being able to forego the purchase of expensive printed national bibliographies and other tools. I remember fondly rebuffing a salesman trying to sell me the *British Library Catalog* some years ago; he told me that his updated edition of this expensive tool was essential because it was something which I used every day; I informed him that, thanks to the OCLC Online Union Catalog, it was something which I used perhaps once or twice a year, and therefore it was hardly worth the price.

During my days as a reference librarian, the OCLC Online Union Catalog was a revolutionary tool which allowed me to bypass the whole morass of printed bibliographic apparatus, as well as use creative hunches, in the form of search keys, to ascertain quickly what the true title, author, publisher, or price of an item really was, the answer to which usually bore little resemblance to what the patron had stated.

The OCLC Online Union Catalog has come a long way from the days when I first used it surreptitiously in a small college library in Ohio, because the cataloger believed that the service contract would be invalidated if anyone other than her so much as touched the machine. The OCLC Online Union Catalog is now truly for everyone, and that means a lot to all of us.

———————————— *W* ————————————

**Marilyn Moore**
Prescott Public Library
Prescott, AZ

"O" is for the OVERWHELMING OCEAN of OPPORTUNITIES to OBTAIN ORGANIZED access to OPUSES from the world of recorded history from OEDIPUS to OTHELLO to OSCAR the Grouch.

"C" is for the CONSISTENT quality and COOPERATION of the CREATIVE CATALOGERS who CONTRIBUTE their talents for the sake of making a COMPLEX world a little less COMPLICATED, not to mention the COLOSSAL COST-REDUCING benefits of COPY CATALOGING, saving the world precious time and brain CELLS.

"L" is for the LIBRARY LOVERS who benefit from the LUSH growth of resources in the world's LARGEST bibliographic database, and for the almost LIMITLESS potential for LENDING by LIBRARIES from LOUISIANA to LITHUANIA.

And the final "C" is for the CULTURAL bridge that OCLC CREATES, bringing us all a little CLOSER—from CHINA to CZECHOSLOVAKIA to CHEEKTOWAGA. It means sharing resources on a planet-wide level, and gives us all a CATALOG in COMMON to CHERISH.

**Marianne D. Muha**
Jenkins Memorial Law Library
Philadelphia, PA

I was first introduced to OCLC in the fall of 1986, as a library school student at SUNY Buffalo. It's safe to say the love affair began then. As I was thinking about what I wanted to say in this essay, a colleague asked me if my feelings for OCLC were emotional or intellectual. I can honestly say it's a combination of both. Through my career as a librarian, I have used OCLC in various settings, including SUNY's Poetry/Rare Books Collection, their Central Technical Services, and in the law environment at Jenkins Memorial Law Library, my present job.

One of those jobs focused entirely on the authority file, which provided me with wonderful insights in that area. Recently I was given the task of introducing the authority file to a coworker, and I couldn't help thinking that for her, it's just the beginning. Once you learn to navigate, the search becomes a challenge, with bibliographic nirvana mere keystrokes away.

The most amazing thing to me about OCLC is its versatility. Through its myriad resources, I have been able to assist my brother in researching high school education theories for his master's thesis, kept track of the publishing efforts of poets and Ph.D. students who were once coworkers, and locate additional books by favorite authors I've found at the local public library. One time I actually looked to see what, if any, material OCLC had about forklift trucks for my husband. This was all in fun, but OCLC didn't disappoint.

I do a fair amount of original cataloging in my normal work routine, and this too never ceases to amaze me. For the multitude of materials which are found in OCLC, that the need for original cataloging exists still astounds me. I confess to a feeling of disbelief when I see the dreaded message "No matching records." I often wonder how this can be possible, then do an about-face and feel good that I can help contribute in a meaningful way to OCLC.

The local serials catalogers discussion group I belong to is comprised of people from numerous types of libraries. Those whose institutions do not use OCLC are often frankly jealous of those of us who do. They want to be able to take advantage of the strides that have been accomplished in capability and user-friendliness that the OCLC users utilize on a daily basis. I get the feeling they're just biding their time until they, too, can be proud members of the OCLC family.

OCLC has always embodied the pioneer spirit, from its early days right up to today's format integration. The implementation of this newest innovation can only help make our journey into the 21st century challenging and exhilarating. In closing, I'd just like to say that I look forward to working with OCLC for many years to come. It has enriched my career and always managed to keep life interesting.

**Betty Murgolo**
National Institutes of Health Library
Bethesda, MD

I am the lead technician in the interlibrary loan department of the National Institutes of Health Library in Bethesda, Maryland. It is my chief responsibility to see that the incoming requests submitted are filled in a timely manner. The NIH medical community is quite diverse, with many cultures of various medical and non-medical backgrounds represented. Because of this great diversity, a wide variety of disciplines are depicted in the ever-growing large volume of requests that come in each day. In order to meet the challenges of filling these requests, I rely a great deal on OCLC! I could not operate without it! OCLC, literally, is my window on the world. It lets me know what libraries and document services have what books, journals, dissertations, newspapers, audiovisuals, etc. It allows me superb searching capabilities so that I can find that sometimes obscure elusive document that is needed so badly for research by a very demanding scientist who, when he receives his material, leaves rather contentedly—purring like a kitten. OCLC to the rescue once again—one more tiger tamed!

Early in my library career, I worked at the Library of Congress as a cataloger for the *National Union Catalog*. I realized even then the tremendous need for a catalog that would bring all the world's resources together electronically under one roof for all to utilize. OCLC has superbly accomplished this task and I cannot imagine any library or research facility without it. Books and such were not meant to gather dust on a shelf, but rather to be used—knowledge passed on from one place and time to another.

OCLC allows me to communicate with places around the world. Its Name-Address Directory gives me needed information to let me get in touch with whomever and lets me know their lending policies. This capability has enabled me to develop a vast network of places that are willing to help me—sometimes at a moment's notice. This has enabled me on more than one occasion to satisfy emergency needs such as an urgent patient care request or information for an important ongoing experiment.

OCLC is the library's Internet—it enables me to locate a resource and lets me and my patrons know where they can get the materials they need. Its bibliographic record supplies me with information that I can then readily supply to our patrons who would like information such as who published it, edited it, languages it is in, editions, or even if it was published in something else.

OCLC brings the world to my fingertips and lets my fingers do the walking over this big wide world electronically. What else can I say, except that OCLC is the heart and soul of my interlibrary loan activities. I could not operate without it, and wouldn't even want to try. And to those who don't have it—they don't get it!

## Mary Ellen Murphy
Bozell Worldwide, Inc.
Chicago, IL

At the turn of the century, books and works of art resided in the private collections of wealthy individuals. The middle class purchased books at bookstores and the poor did without. The creation of libraries represented the access of information to all people. Materials became more widely disseminated, and everyone had an equal opportunity to examine and to learn from the body of knowledge that had been compiled over several decades. We could begin to build upon that knowledge and make discoveries and advancements of our own.

It is a concern, a valid one I think, that computers and the access to technology and information are becoming the province of the rich, as they were nearly one hundred years ago. Once again two classes of society will exist, one "information rich" and the other "information poor." Again libraries have come to the rescue in dealing with this problem, and OCLC is also part of the solution. Libraries, as much as schools, are a learning ground, an "incubator" if you will. Technologies such as online services, (including the Internet), and CD-ROMs are present. Librarians, like teachers in the classroom, instruct patrons how to use these materials.

However, no one library, no matter what its resources, can have everything its patrons need. But in this day and age, people should have the ability to have access to information in a timely manner. OCLC helps reference librarians to find materials the library does not own, and borrow them, through its vast network of sharing libraries. OCLC is an authoritative, exhaustive source to locate all the items written by a particular author, or about a specific topic, in all media and languages. OCLC also helps acquisition departments to identify items for purchase and confirm bibliographic information. OCLC helps to speed the pace of getting materials to the shelf through its cataloging operations, and to ensure that patrons can find the item in the card catalog. In addition, OCLC's system of regional networks helps library staff to keep up with advances in the system.

As we reach the millennium, we reflect upon our accomplishments as a human race. There have been numerous discoveries in science, advancements in technology and continued progress in literature and the arts. As a result of these developments, we have amassed an enormous body of knowledge. This information has been recorded and collected in books, journals and other media.

162

However, without the tools to access these materials, it is rendered useless. OCLC provides the key to unlocking our vast warehouses of information, for centuries and generations to come.

## Margaret Myers
Illinois State University
Bloomington, IL

Thanks for the memories…

Over my past seventeen years at Milner Library, Illinois State University, what I remember most about working with OCLC is the people. Each fellow employee—besides being an interesting, diverse individual—had something to teach me about cataloging and OCLC.

My first supervisor, Maxine, and her "second in command" Irma taught me the intricacies of OCLC editing at the terminal. I think they were amazed and amused at my youthful naiveté. With the advent of AACRII, Maxine used her background as a schoolteacher to patiently give us clerks a grounding in descriptive cataloging, machine-readable style.

Elspeth Moore was the mainstay of the card catalog until she retired. Coincidentally she and my aunt were college roommates, and she once took my mother and me to lunch before I had decided to attend Illinois State. Miss Moore moved so fast that even when she broke her ankle no one could keep up with her! I'm not sure to this day that anyone has been able to equal her enthusiasm or dedication.

My friend Mattie and I were partying buddies in my early years at Milner Library. Later on, I searched music for her and Melissa. By that time I was a little more settled and had acquired the patience such activity requires. When PRISM became a reality, it made our jobs that much easier. Now I wonder how we got along without it. (Kind of reminds me of cellular phones, air conditioning, personal computers, and yes, E-mail.)

When I was promoted to library technical assistant in the acquisitions department, I was privileged to search actual books on OCLC when they were received, in addition to ordering them. Judith and Bea were the champion searchers with the best detecting abilities around. They could "snoop out a dup" faster than anyone and they were my role models.

A few years ago, when online cataloging became a part of my job, I didn't think anything more could change. Now I know that life is change, and so is OCLC. No longer do we file at a card catalog, but instead make corrections to our online public access catalog. The differences between public services and technical services have become blurred. I note this every time I bar code a book as I catalog it at the terminal.

So what's in store for us folks who work with OCLC? I hear rumors of PromptCat in the future for our library. I know our jobs will change again, sooner than we know. That doesn't seem to stop us, though. We transform as life and circumstances require. By being such a talented, well-rounded group we are better able to meet the demands that continue to be made on us. I've been working with

OCLC for most of its first twenty-five years. I anxiously await the challenges of the next twenty-five.

**Note:** Names in this essay have been changed to protect the privacy of individuals mentioned.

## Susanne Nevin
St. Olaf College
Northfield, MN

Disbelief and shock. Pride and satisfaction. Such was my reaction when I read that OCLC is celebrating its 25th anniversary this year!

Disbelief and shock, because it means that I have been around libraries even longer than OCLC! Pride and satisfaction, because I know that I personally contributed to the ca. 35,000,000 records—including the thousands of foreign language titles—in the database.

In 1969, when I began working as a card-typing clerk at Miami University's library in Oxford, Ohio, OCLC was little more than a rumor in the catalog department, an acronym whispered with awe and fear. No more card-typing? Sharing our catalog records? No more duplication of effort? All our cataloging would be keyed directly into a C–O–M–P–U–T–E–R? Would we become expendable? Would they replace us with a machine? (Was it a coincidence that calls for unionization in academic libraries throughout Ohio sounded loudly and clearly, as implementation of OCLC began?)

When I left Ohio in late 1971 to work at the University of Minnesota's main library, I thought I had left OCLC behind as well. Wrong! The whispers and rumors had started here, too, and in 1977, the OCLC revolution swept across the most northern state of the midwest. In fact, it was here that the first "machine-readable" serials records were created from the Minnesota Union List of Serials, and would form the basis of the CONSER records at OCLC. Even if the few rudimentary MULS records remaining in the database annoy my "sophisticated" sensibilities today, I can still feel the reverberations of the triumph these records represented at the time of their creation.

OCLC has been a revolution which, unlike other revolutions, has never lost its momentum. An adventure working out of the Ohio State University library, OCLC has grown into a large international venture. Yet, while much has changed over the years—location, size, scope, and even the meaning of its acronym—the basic goals of OCLC have remained constant: library cooperation, shared cataloging, and creation of a large, high-quality bibliographic database.

Even after all these years, the OCLC Online Union Catalog remains a unique enterprise, thanks to the diversity of its membership; to its openness to participation by even the smallest library; and to its creative management and planning teams. Information and help are readily available, whether I choose to call my friendly regional network or click on "What's New at OCLC" at its World Wide Web site.

As someone who dates back to the days of keying records into the monstrous M100 computer, I feel proud to have been part of the OCLC revolution. It has not always been a smooth path, of course. There were many hours of downtime and training while migrating to a newer and better version of the catalog and the software driving it. But it was well worth it. As I sit at my slick Pentium PC and "click on stuff" using Passport in Windows today, and consult with my colleagues about how to catalog Internet resources, I know that we catalogers—thanks to OCLC—have been at the forefront of library technology ever since 1971!

**Angela Norell**
Minnesota Zoo
Apple Valley, MN

The Minnesota Zoo (MNZOO) has a professional staff who publish regularly and are deeply committed to conservation and quality animal care. The conservation director has developed an award-winning park program in Indonesia and is working cooperatively with Exxon for tiger preservation. MNZOO is headquarters for the Captive Breeding Specialist Group and the International Species Inventory System which develop global survival plans for critically endangered species. The collection of the MNZOO includes worldwide flora and fauna including marine mammals and a coral reef. MNZOO works with veterinary students on externships as well as interns from colleges. The staff, volunteers and students require a wide variety of information, often published in international books and journals. The zoo library is small, supporting a single, part-time librarian, and relies upon computer databases and interlibrary exchanges for many resources. The OCLC Union Catalog is a primary means of identifying materials and their locations such as journals whose titles mutate, and enables me to survive as a tiny minnow in this great ocean of libraries. Options to search by year, language and format make the huge database manageable. Unique videos on marine mammal diseases were located at a technical college in Virginia, who graciously made copies for us. We make friends throughout the U. S. with these exchanges, and feel connected by these exotic challenges.

In 1995, the zoo helped found the School of Environmental Studies, a high school unique in the United States. Zoo staff help teach at the school, and I have used OCLC to provide bibliographies of current material for their presentations, including high school-level resources. It enables me to say "yes" to many requests for information that previously were logistically impossible. With its ease and simplicity, you can seem to work magic in providing answers. The director's request for "someone named 'Popcorn' in marketing" was quickly answered.

OCLC can be an idea-generator as I assemble a mediography ranging from animal-related picture books to recent publications on population genetics. Zoo libraries are unique "beasts," even among special libraries, and as I scan subjects for collection-building, I am able to focus on zoo-specific purchases. It has greatly increased my productivity, a critical issue for librarians in a nonprofit field. After the small initial cost of a search, the ability to read and print results freely helps make the library economically supportable.

My second job is at a large public library in Hennepin County, Minnesota (HCL). OCLC has had a dramatic impact on service to people there as well. I have located a price guide for antique fishing rods, French genealogical materials in the midwest, and emu ranching organizations. It was OCLC descriptions that enabled me to find an autobiography by a wheelchair "cowboy" that was locally owned.

The documentation provided by OCLC is superb, and knowledgeable customer support is available whatever your facility size. Recently I was amazed to be personally notified that my OCLC access number had not been updated, as identified by a recent logon. I admire the excellence and foresight of OCLC as a model of bibliographic excellence and pioneering that brings credit to the entire profession.

## Carol G. Norman
Beverly Hills Public Library
Beverly Hills, CA

Every Tuesday, the supervisors of the various departments of our library meet to discuss mutual problems.

Recently, we had been going through a particularly trying budget preparation cycle. One day, immediately after yet another budget discussion, the head of reference brought up a new topic—he mentioned how impressed his staff had been with the name tags designed by a neighboring library. Instead of giving the staff member's personal name, these tags merely said "Librarian," "Clerk," "Page," etc. We could deal with the problem of turnover, and staff concerns about privacy, by merely ordering "x" number of generic tags for each position title. I piped up to ask him to order one for me labeled "Gibbering Idiot," since I felt that our bureaucratic maze had turned me into one. We all had a good laugh.

Towards the end of the meeting, our director passed out the announcement of OCLC's contest. I facetiously scribbled across the front of it, "The OCLC system is the only thing in this library and the only part of my job that has never turned me into a gibbering idiot," and passed it back to him.

However, upon reflection, I think that that is an excellent summation of the value of the OCLC system! How many times have I been aggravated by vendors who don't deliver what they advertise, whose documentation is sketchy, who get instructions garbled, who release new products that have not been thoroughly tested, who are hard to reach when I need help, who want me to buy something because it makes profits for them but don't care whether it meets any real need my library has? How many hours in my career have been spent troubleshooting errors on invoices, equipment failures, interpersonal conflicts, communication failures, missed deadlines, human ignorance? More than I can count; however, I cannot recall any instances where the guilty party was OCLC.

For more than 15 years, I have been impressed by OCLC's emphasis on thorough testing, careful planning and trying to anticipate libraries' future needs. I have noticed the precision and accuracy of both their documentation and their accounting. I have noticed immense efforts toward quality control, cost-effectiveness, user education and user support. OCLC has always delivered what it promised and continuously strives to perfect and expand its services. OCLC is the one thing that enables me to do my job, and my library to be as good as it is. In short, OCLC is the best preventative for "gibbering idiot-ism" that a librarian could have.

## Mary E. O'Donnell
Oklahoma State University
Stillwater, OK

In 1976, I was a paraprofessional at Iowa Wesleyan College, working in the catalog department to eke out my salary as a part-time instructor in art history. I had never heard of OCLC, and couldn't understand why my supervisor was so excited about the Kellogg grant that allowed the college to connect with OCLC. All I knew was that I was suddenly going to have to work with—A COMPUTER!

Of course I had heard vague rumors that someday libraries would be automated, but since I was not originally intending to make a career in librarianship, I was not overly concerned with how it would affect me. I was not comfortable with machines, and was not looking forward to having to deal with one which I might foul up with my ineptitude.

A few months later, I was pleasantly surprised to find that, not only would I not ruin the database by putting in the wrong tags, but having to work with OCLC was sharpening my amateur cataloging skills. Using defined areas for which only specific information was appropriate, I began to think more about why the cataloging rules were important to the library user and how information could be organized. Being exposed to other libraries' cataloging through OCLC, looking for "better" records to use, improved my judgment on my own in-house attempts and made me aware of how many other catalogers there must be out there providing this resource.

When I went on to library school a few years later, my computer phobia came back, fueled by an information science professor who spent more time on how computer memories worked than on how to find anything with them. At one point, only the assurances of a more experienced friend kept me from quitting. "You'll be using them the same way you use OCLC," she pointed out, to my relief. I knew OCLC; it was a friend.

As I became a professional, and began to enter my own records into the OCLC Online Union Catalog, it became even more important to me to do the best job I could; the way I cataloged something here in Oklahoma could affect the ability of someone in California or England to find that record and use it without editing. I also used OCLC as a resource to see how other libraries cataloged the more difficult works, such as non-print, foreign language, and conference proceeding items. Often I learned more about how to do a record (or, in some cases, how NOT to do it) from OCLC than I did from some of my cataloging tools!

With the advent of Passport for Windows, my cataloging skills and my computer skills are melding into an efficient whole. Some of the new formats, such as electronic journals, don't seem quite so frightening, because I know that I can study the work of experts through a search on OCLC. Working with the OCLC Online Union Catalog, I feel that I have been subtly prepared for the future.

## Erik S. Ohlander
University of Minnesota
Minneapolis, MN

The proliferation of new technologies and approaches towards these technologies has instituted what one can only deem a "paradigm shift" in the way we access, articulate, and use recorded knowledge. While the epistemological aspects of this shift cannot be so easily addressed in this format, the fact that the *way in which* we conceive of recorded knowledge has changed is in itself important. In the world of academia, the idea that an institution is only as strong as its libraries is an old one; but with the advent of new conceptual patterns in the methodology of research, this maxim is being challenged. In one way, the institution is no longer bound by its campus wall, but rather has been liberated in the sense that it is networked with its sister institutions. In the most fundamental sense, the core of the academy resides in its relationship to, and genesis in, the production and preservation of knowledge. This being the case, it is not too far a jump to consider the profound implications that a unified system of accessing information imparts to all academies.

Specifically, we are speaking of the idea that the goals of the global-academy can be furthered through a database system which gives each of its constituent parts, namely the college or university, access to the same data set. In having such access, the academy is able to act in tandem with the same dynamic present in other facets of the modern world; namely, the trend towards global integration we are experiencing on many fronts. Thus, the paradigm shift occurring in the world at large is being mirrored, (or led by?), the shift occurring in information access and manipulation. This same idea also functions on a micro-level, namely in the world of the individual member of the academy. It is important to stress that the ease of access provided by such bibliographic database systems not only opens up new doors, as it were, in the way one researches, but perhaps more importantly it enables one to reflect upon the amount, and depth, of our collective human intellectual legacy in a manner which not too long ago was virtually inconceivable.

On the surface this may seem like mere philosophical musing, but on closer inspection we realize that such an assertion holds profound implications. Procedurally, the use of a system such as OCLC is empowering in the simple fact that one has relatively easy access to vast amounts of recorded information. But on a deeper level, the empowerment engendered within one's conception of human knowledge is just as important. If we are to take the critical analysis of the modern world only being able to function best if its major components cooperate seriously, then we must (in realizing that the essential job of a scholar is service to humanity) also realize that it is our job to not disregard the value of academies cooperating through the modality of an online database. This essential dynamic is what the OCLC system represents to me, and I hope that in the future my colleagues come to similar conclusions.

**Nancy O'Neill**
Santa Monica Public Library
Santa Monica, CA

The "We'll See" catalog is what the Professor calls it. "The Professor" is what I call him, but I really don't know if he is. He comes in often, searching for material about 16th- and 17th-century mining in Wales and—although we're only a medium-sized library—we are almost always able to locate the items he needs.

When he first inquired if there were any possibility of us helping him with his research, I told him about the OCLC Online Union Catalog and how we could use it to locate materials all over the world, and ask libraries to lend them to us. That was exactly what he wanted to hear, so we went to work. The next time he came in he said, "I have some work for the We'll See Catalog."

I began to explain that the name was "OCLC" not "We'll See" but he stopped me. "No," he said, "It's like this. When I get to a place in my work where I need more books, I always think, 'We'll see if that big computer catalog at the library has these books.' So that's what I call it."

He knows what the OCLC Online Union Catalog means to him!

So far I've never had a chance to explain to the Professor that the Online Union Catalog means much more to us than simply locating books, although it's wonderful to be able to tell clients who urgently need an item our library does not have that it is available at another library nearby.

I'd like to tell him about the high cataloging standards promoted by OCLC, which mean that we can understand the information we locate and can rely on its accuracy. And that because we all use those same standards, we can more easily share resources by linking them electronically. And that sharing resources means that materials once restricted to those who could find them and afford to travel to them, can now be sent to local libraries for anyone to use and enjoy. And that our library's catalogers are able to make materials available more quickly to our community and to library users around the country, using OCLC Online Union Catalog tools. And that all this means extending the power of information beyond walls and catalogs and delivering it to students, amateur historians, family tree compilers, teachers, researchers.

But I think he may be right. The best thing we can say is, "Let's take a look at that 'We'll See Catalog' and we'll just see what it can do for us today."

## JoEllen Ostendorf
Georgia Department of Education
Atlanta, GA

Often, when I sit down at an OCLC terminal, I remember the first time I saw one. It was the mid-1970s and I was working as a student assistant at a large academic library while I went to library school. The personal computer had not yet arrived on the scene, and OCLC had just become the Online Computer Library Center rather than the Ohio College Library Center.

The catalogers were trying to the best of their abilities to tiptoe around the two squat, bulky machines sitting in the corner of the cavernous cataloging room. There was great trepidation about the changes this rumored "common catalog" would bring; some superiority about "our cataloging being better than their cataloging" (who in their right minds would use "their" cataloging anyway?); what in the world were MARC tags?; and, most importantly, what does this mean to our jobs?

In the spirit of cooperation, it was determined that my time would be sacrificed to enter records into this new system. Since I worked in the music library, the reasoning was that I would be a good test since all our records had uniform titles and other esoteric entries, which most folks manage to successfully avoid in the course of their cataloging careers. After the first week of struggling to remember the various tags without using a reference card, I sailed along. Catalogers started wandering over to peer over my shoulder and ask questions. The common view seemed to be, if I could do it, anyone could!

My stint as a guinea pig landed me my first professional job. OCLC was rapidly expanding outside of the university system, and other libraries were now going through the same fears and learning pangs the universities had experienced several years earlier. After a year as a cataloger, I received a promotion and, for the next ten years, worked with the talking-book program serving the handicapped, far away from the world of OCLC.

When I came to Georgia's state library nine years ago, I was given the task of finding an alternative to Georgia's manual interlibrary lending system. Interlibrary loan was now a major component of OCLC and, because of the substantial investment the state already had in the OCLC database, it was decided to use OCLC's group access capability for our automated interlibrary loan system and so, the Georgia Online Database (GOLD) was born.

Change is always painful, and GOLD was not established without much argument and controversy. After all, we had a perfectly good, if cumbersome, ILL system, so why change? As Georgia's libraries began using GOLD, the benefits became apparent. ILL was much faster, reporting much more accurate, and most of the paperwork had been eliminated. Plus, for the first time, the state had a union list of serials.

It was not, however, until a GOLD annual membership meeting several years later that the benefits of using OCLC were brought home to me and all of our member libraries. Proud and excited, a group of high school students from an extremely rural area of the state told us about their ILL experiences. Their high school library had only several hundred volumes and there was no bookstore or public library in town, yet, using the ILL system through their regional public library, they were able to obtain materials and resources to study for the national history day contest. They told us of the Christmas-like atmosphere when their packages of books and articles arrived. Not only did they win the state contest, but they went on to place third nationally!

OCLC had a major impact on the lives of those five high school students. It enabled them to compete on an equal footing with the largest schools in the country and gave them the confidence to achieve whatever goals they set for themselves. It also made them lifelong library advocates.

To me, my use of OCLC had come full circle. In the daily building and use of a system, we sometimes lose sight of the reason it was first created. What I had viewed from a technical viewpoint was finally brought home to me from the users' end. It reaffirmed my belief that we are stronger working together and sharing our resources than standing alone, and that all libraries have unique and valuable materials. GOLD has given us the solid framework upon which we have based our growth into a single statewide library, though the use of Internet and shared databases and, of course, OCLC.

## Erlinda G. Paguio
University of Louisville
Louisville, KY

The OCLC Online Union Catalog reminds me of my own immigrant experience to the United States which began in 1969. It has opened a variety of stimulating experiences for me.

Just as I had to adopt English as a second language, as an OCLC user, I had to use OCLC's MARC format to be able to adjust to searching and cataloging online. It took awhile before I became fully comfortable with many of the idiomatic expressions in English. It took a few years before I really felt fluent in the use of the MARC format. Its astounding impact is clearly shown by the fact that 31,126,380 records have been created in this format within the last 25 years! How awesome, too, is the 24,247,836 total participant-input throughout these years.

Coming from the Philippines, where we experienced only a dry and a wet climate, I had to be acclimated to the four seasons, especially the harsh winters in Chicago. The spring season was an altogether lovely experience. In the early 1970s, the climate of most libraries was apprehension for the new technology that OCLC made available to us. The arrival of the computers intimidated many of us who were computer illiterate. Gradually, however, we were initiated into using them by searching and calling up records online, updating various fields while cataloging and ordering catalog cards. It turned out to be a time-saving and a challenging experience and eventually the OCLC Online Union Catalog became an almost universal climate felt in 63 countries around the world. The database is indispensable to scholars, librarians, and researchers around the world.

Although I felt homesick in the new country that has become my new home, I have not regretted my decision to stay in the United States. In adopting the OCLC Online Union Catalog, some of us look back to those old days when we did all aspects of library work manually. For those of us who have discarded our public card catalog and other manual files, there is no turning back. We strive to become more acculturated to the system, and instruct others to it.

It is now 27 years since I first came to the United States. I feel much at home here. I feel at home, too, in using OCLC resources both as a library staff member and a researcher. By coming here, my cultural experiences have been much enriched. By using OCLC's Online Union Catalog, I have been introduced to its many capabilities to acquire and contribute to a vast network of information. It contains more than 35 million records and more than 560 million location listings in 370 languages! It covers 4,000 years of recorded knowledge. How overwhelming these may seem, it is for all of us one of the greatest contributions to this world!

## James C. Pakala
Covenant Theological Seminary
St. Louis, MO

A splendid necessity, lush survival, the consummate link: it is the OCLC Online Union Catalog. To me it has become the incomparable friend of libraries and all whom they serve.

A seminary library had called me as director. My mandate was to improve service and finish a retroconversion which had taken a decade to complete only halfway. I brought in a cataloger who knew both the first and the new PRISM system of the OCLC Online Union Catalog. She got us onto OCLC with the economical dial-access and CAT CD450 options, which together with her speed, acuity, and subject expertise enabled us to finish the retroconversion in eighteen months.

During the same time the services to our patrons increased dramatically but took much less time per transaction, thanks in large measure to the Online Union Catalog. Our faculty, students, and others have been elated. I not only met the mandated goals and stayed in the job, but significant recent budget increases testify to the library's accrued credibility with our administration.

As I reflect on what the Online Union Catalog means personally apart from the goals achieved, three things come to mind: vastness with intimacy, prudent cost-effectiveness, and superlative competence. Every time I look at an online record or discover a unique holding, I am reminded of the vast but close community which is the OCLC Online Union Catalog. Every budget I formulate makes me appreciate the fiscal prudence of OCLC. It's the best bargain we have. And lastly but most importantly, there is the sterling competence behind the OCLC Online Union Catalog. It stands out in everything from its total conception to the user-friendly execution of the last detail. It is as if they not only have us in mind, but are one with us!

## Irina A. Pakhomova

St. Petersburg Culture Academy—Rostov Campus
Postov-on-Don, Russia

OCLC for me is a magnificent optimal library cooperation, an evident and convincing example of what integration can offer in the creation of such a grandiose information resource as the electronic summary catalogue OCLC, and of such a powerful and reliable telecommunication network as the online system of OCLC. Today, no large library of the world can present its activities without OCLC, which provides them with services in collective use of resources. OCLC for me is a symbol of modern librarianship.

OCLC is a global center of research activities in the field of library and information science. Undertaken programs in scientific researches are organized in the interests of all present and future OCLC members and users. A convincing example is one of the recent projects, "Strategy of OCLC Connection: Internet and NREN," which provides access to major resources and systems of OCLC through the Internet. Thanks to this project, access to OCLC will become possible for my country—Russia—and for me personally.

But the particular importance of OCLC for me consists in the experience of the creation and development of OCLC in my dissertation, "Integration of Library and Information Resources in Creation of the Regional Network," as one of the models of library integration. I hope that the study of 25 years of OCLC development will help me to model the library network for the Rostov region.

OCLC for me is also a firm style, the main characteristic features of which are: efficiency, completeness, information quality and high technologies.

## Lisa D. Paland

Westmont College
Santa Barbara, CA

"You mean the world to me…"

I am intimately acquainted with OCLC, as I am a college student as well as a library cataloging assistant. There are numerous reasons why the OCLC Online Union Catalog is such a huge part of my life.

As a student I would never be able to take advantage of the vast resources our libraries hold. With over four million potential sources to choose from and over 370 languages to ponder the thoughts of others in, the OCLC catalog has helped me out many times, as I have spent hours bonding with the OCLC terminals.

As a cataloger I would be clueless without access to the OCLC Online Union Catalog. OCLC gives me the ability to complete my job efficiently and correctly. I can make the new books my library receives available to our public because of the OCLC Online Union Catalog. Being able to take the records, update the appropriate fields, and add them to our system offers the users easily accessible information.

The OCLC Online Union Catalog is my link to the world and all her resources. Without OCLC, I would be cut off from much of the awesome information available today.

## Susan Szasz Palmer
Cornell University
Ithaca, NY

OCLC: close encounters of the 3, 2, 2, 1 kind…

I still remember the first time I approached the sole OCLC terminal that resided in the center of technical services, a vast and forbidding department crammed with staff, book-trucks, kardex, shelf-lists, files, typewriters. And one computer terminal—OCLC. I was a reference librarian in the undergraduate library, now in training to work some hours at the graduate research library. "Verification" provided the mainstay of work at this reference desk, and we spent many hours pouring through the pages of reference bibles such as the *National Union Catalog Pre–1956 Imprints.*

I'd been searching for hours for an item, the title of which is long gone from my memory, when a more senior librarian suggested I search OCLC. I'd heard of OCLC, but confess I'd managed to graduate from library school without ever putting my hands on an OCLC keyboard. At that moment, I wished I had. My colleague sensed my hesitation, but nonetheless rattled off the "codes" for searching by title and by author: 3, 2, 2, 1… 4, 4. I repeated these numeric mnemonics in my head as I ventured into technical services. Writing them down would have made me look even more clueless.

Heads turned as I entered the room and approached the terminal, I assumed because I was a new face rather than because I was a reference librarian in cataloging territory. I can't remember how I searched first—3, 2, 2, 1… 4, 4—but I remember finding what I 'd been searching for all day on the first try! It was like magic, even if I didn't have a very good idea of what all those MARC tags meant. I hit the button marked print, thankful that it was labeled. I was ready to go back to reference and redeem my cluelessness. But the printer kept printing. And printing. And printing. I was too embarrassed to ask any of the unfamiliar faces around me for help, and not computer-savvy enough to try hitting Alt-something or Control-something. Hitting a key called "Break" was precisely what I didn't want to do! I turned the terminal off, tore out my printout, and slinked back to the reference desk.

Fifteen years have passed since my first encounter with OCLC—my first encounter as a reference librarian with technology on the job. We had no online public catalog. CD-ROM's were not yet on the horizon. Bibliographic database searching on utilities such as DIALOG and BRS was the "specialty" of another reference librarian.

How things have changed in a decade and a half: we've gone from one dedicated OCLC terminal, completely hidden from the public and remote from public services staff, to a "button" on all our public catalog terminals—giving it the prominence it has long deserved. But I still have trouble remembering what OCLC stands for when patrons ask. I usually smile and say, "Just think of it as One Colossal Library Collection!"

**Richard Palumbo**
Wagner College
Staten Island, NY

As Coordinator of Public Services in the Horrmann Library, Wagner College, Staten Island, N. Y., I have used the OCLC Online Union Catalog since 1982. I can truly say that I never stop marveling at its almost miraculous capabilities.

Before our Library joined OCLC, it was a labor intensive job to get a new book from Technical Services into the hands of our users. The process would begin with a manual search of the acquisition files and the public catalog to verify if the book was on order or already in the Library. Next, the book would have to be found in one of the multitudinous volumes of the Library of Congress's *National Union Catalog*. Then a stencil of the entry would be typed up and run off. Finally, the book would get cataloged and into the circulation stacks.

But now for more than 13 years this laborious process has been a thing of the past. Because of the OCLC Database thousands of libraries like ourselves are able to share cataloging information online. Now, within a matter of minutes, a new book gets cataloged and promptly into the hands of the student or professor who needs it. It goes without saying that this fantastic service works just as fast for our new non-print materials.

Another immense benefit the OCLC Online Union Catalog offers us is in an area with which I, as a reference librarian, am directly involved: Interlibrary loans. Obtaining an interlibrary loan, like cataloging a book, used to be a long, drawn out process. We would have to send a written request to our State Library in Albany. If they owned the book, they would in turn send it on to us, or, if not, attempt to find it for us at another N. Y. Library. Otherwise, we would have to check the Library of Congress's *Register of Additional Locations* volumes and then request the book by mail. Needless to say, neither procedure was expeditious.

At present, however, as soon as any library, our own included, catalogs a book, it immediately enters the ranks of OCLC's more than 560 million online location listings, accessible to libraries everywhere. This astounding resource allows libraries to locate and often borrow books anywhere in the country. For us it means we are able to tap the rich resources of the many outstanding libraries in the greater metropolitan New York City area as well as in the rest of the State and country, if need be.

Moreover, thanks to OCLC's Union List System, numerous union lists, such as NYME, our own New York Regional List of Serials are online. We are, therefore, able to locate and obtain articles from journals we do not own, but might be urgently needed for a student's or faculty's research paper. Multiply Wagner College Library by the countless other libraries across America, making use of the OCLC's Interlibrary Loan and Union List Systems, and you will readily perceive why the OCLC Database is so invaluable.

Although there are many other excellent advantages to the OCLC Online Union Catalog, if I did not mention one other one, I would certainly be amiss. A faculty member will often want to purchase a book for his class or personal use, but does not have complete bibliographic information. I cannot tell you how often, to the astonishment of the faculty member and my own satisfaction, I am able to find the book on the OCLC Database.

Who said the printed word and computers are incompatible? As OCLC celebrates its 25th anniversary it has proved beyond a shadow of a doubt that computer technology, far from being the enemy of the book, is, in reality, its greatest ally—its greatest ally, I believe, since the 15th century when the printing press was invented. The OCLC Database has in fact become the new Mercury, the swift-footed messenger god of the electronic age, bringing bibliographic data into libraries all over the world and allowing us to share resources in a manner never dreamed of a quarter of a century ago.

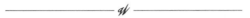

## Richard Pasichnyk
Arizona State University
Tempe, AZ

Making a world of difference...

Twenty-five years ago many experiences were shared by a myriad of Americans. The Apollo 15 crew took the first car ride on the Moon, *Look* magazine ceased publication after nearly 34 years, Walt Disney World opened, and "All in the Family" was the most popular show on TV. The favorite movies that year were "The French Connection," "The Last Picture Show," "Klute" and "A Clockwork Orange." That year, the 26th Amendment to the Constitution lowered the voting age to eighteen. Yet, behind the scenes there was a new frontier opening that generally went unnoticed, the beginning of the OCLC.

The OCLC continued to be one of the most important research tools in existence and has had an effect that goes beyond anything that occurred in 1971. From its meager beginnings, with only 54 academic libraries in the U.S., it has grown to the point of linking 23,000 libraries and 63 countries with 4,000 years of recorded knowledge in 370 languages. With its 560 million records, that grows by about two million each year, it is indispensable for finding rare and no longer published materials, or materials that are not at a local library. The most recent development is NetFirst, a catalog of Internet addresses to surf the World Wide Web. Because of these features, and a host of others, OCLC is the world's largest library information network.

There are an abundance of possible uses that make life easier for anyone who has ever used a library. When researching any subject, it is a vital medium for discovering the whereabouts of a source of information. Libraries are able to catalog and order books, journals, magazines and so forth with greater speed, so that someone who wants the latest information is more likely to get it quickly. With the various divisions, such as the Forest Press, Preservation Resources, Information Dimensions and others, libraries are able to integrate scores of services. This saves all of us money, either directly or through the use of our taxes.

For those who want an article or a book that is not at their institution, the OCLC can pinpoint a library that has it. With an electronic network of 5,500 libraries worldwide, a patron can request a source of information through interlibrary loan. In fact, the OCLC has a number of electronic journals and the full text of almost 300 books, and this grows each year. If a person has an incomplete citation for a book, or wants to know what an author has published, the OCLC makes it a simple task. Now, with NetFirst, an Internet browser, one can find a location for whatever subject he or she wishes.

Most people don't realize just how important the OCLC is in the scheme of everyday life. It is vital to academic institutions, the government, news media, television, radio, and just about any business that requires information sources. Aside from the invention of the computer, nothing is more important to unraveling the twists and turns of the information superhighway.

**Janet Perry**
Cerro Gordo CUSD 100
Cerro Gordo, IL

I am the library media specialist in a small rural district in central Illinois. The fact that our district is small and rural in no way indicates that our students' ideas are small or limited. Their need for knowledge and materials in a very wide variety of areas is just as great as those of students in the largest school district anywhere.

The OCLC Online Union Catalog, through our dial-access to ILLINET online and interlibrary loan, is invaluable in helping to meet this need. As library media specialist, it is my job to assist the students in gathering information needed for class projects. As library budgets decrease, while students' demand for unique subjects increases, the OCLC Online Union Catalog becomes more important than ever.

In the past, a student would have to fit his topic to those few general reference works the library could afford. Or the librarian would have to make a budget decision on whether or not there would be enough future demand to warrant purchase of these new materials. Today, the same money, invested in equipment, copy paper, and line charges, can allow a student access to the materials needed for his unique project.

To say that the OCLC Online Union Catalog provides our students a lifeline to the future would not be an understatement!

**Stephen P. Pilon**
Christendom College
Front Royal, VA

What the OCLC Online Union Catalog Means to Christendom College...

The first paragraph of the Christendom College Bulletin states that "the only rightful purpose of education is to learn the truth and live by it." Toward this goal, the college has always invested appropriate resources in the library and its collections. However, with a current base of only 180 students (and a projected maximum of only 450) it is not feasible for the library to gather all the materials necessary for such a pursuit of the truth. Therefore, although to some the costs seemed prohibitive for such a small institution, the board of directors approved membership in OCLC before the college was even ten years old.

OCLC membership has proven itself a valuable asset to such a small college. With access for both copy cataloging and interlibrary loan, the college is able to extend its available resources beyond that of its own holdings, yet remain within a reasonable budget.

An example of our use of interlibrary loan is in the work of our founder, a history professor. He has made frequent use of interlibrary loan in gathering sources for his projected seven-volume history of the church. Without ILL, he would be forced to spend much of his time simply locating books, time he now devotes to reading and studying them.

Due to restricted budgets, we are not able to purchase all the books we need. Therefore, we rely heavily on book donations—but donations are usually, of their very nature, older books. While these are very useful, filling an important place in our collection, we have little time and resources to devote to original cataloging.

With the OCLC Online Union Catalog, we are able to locate and copy over 95% of the records for the materials we produce each year. The remaining titles are cataloged here and added to the Online Union Catalog. In this respect, we feel that we are able to be true participants. If, out of 35 million records, we can add a few each year, we are reminded that each collection is unique.

While the most visible advantage of the OCLC Online Union Catalog is that many libraries can utilize the same record for multiple copies of the same book—thus eliminating the need to catalog each copy individually—by far the most astounding feature is that, though only one copy of a book (or other material) may exist, every other library in the system has access to it.

A small institution like Christendom College has everything to gain from participation in, and use of, the Online Union Catalog. Yet it is the very same type of institution that has a whole new world of knowledge to offer each and every time that it adds a new holding to that catalog. For O'Reilly Memorial Library, the OCLC Online Union Catalog represents a repository of the wisdom of the ages, and a fountain of knowledge. It holds for us the heritage entrusted to us by our predecessors, to be guarded and handed on to our descendants, for the edification and enrichment of the entire human race.

## Carol J. Pinson
North Suburban Library System
Wheeling, IL

The OCLC database impacts NSLS...

The OCLC Online Union Catalog is a wonderful tool which makes possible two major projects of the North Suburban Library System (NSLS) in Illinois. These are 1) a CD-ROM union catalog for books, videos, maps, etc. and 2) participation in a state-wide serials union catalog. Through OCLC, our system and its 600+ libraries are connected to tens of thousands of libraries throughout the United States and hundreds more in other parts of the world. In addition to more common materials, the easy-to-search database makes hard-to-find historical materials and materials on very specific subjects available to thousands of searchers.

Many of our libraries use OCLC catalog records as the basis for their automated systems. The 35 million records in the OCLC database save these libraries a considerable amount of cataloging time. Forty NSLS libraries have used MICROCON or TAPECON for retrospective conversions. Collecting and merging the MARC records of nearly 200 libraries for LIAison, the NSLS CD-ROM union catalog, is quite a project. A few libraries do their own cataloging, so we end up with some short records and some duplicates. Without the OCLC database, our union catalog would contain many more short or duplicate records. It would be more difficult to use and much more difficult to maintain.

Our second major project is participation in SILO, Serials of ILlinois Online. It is amazing how many serials records are already in the OCLC database. Attaching holdings to existing records is fairly easy. The earlier title and later title references in most OCLC serials records make the tedious job of tracing title runs much less time-consuming. Out of 19,000 different titles held by NSLS libraries, only 150 have required original cataloging. The cataloging program of OCLC is very helpful. It minimizes the time needed for entering a new record. Especially useful is the feature of basing a new record on an old one. The validation routine catches mistakes and helps keep the OCLC database uniform. NSLS mounts the SILO records of libraries in our system as a separate database on LIAison. Librarians appreciate having the information in electronic form as well as print form.

Out of twenty-six NSLS employees, six search the OCLC database and use the records in their work. More importantly, our projects involving the OCLC database enable resource sharing throughout the North Suburban Library System. We hope OCLC has a great 25th anniversary and continues strongly through the next 25 years (and more)!

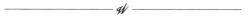

**Elissa Plank**
Eastman Kodak Company
Rochester, NY

Searching the OCLC database for bibliographic records has always seemed to me to be like hunting for buried treasure. I was first introduced to OCLC ten years ago, when I was working as an assistant to the cataloger of the rare books department of the university library where I was attending school. I had to search OCLC to see if the department's new acquisitions had previously been cataloged. If they had been, I printed out a copy of the existing OCLC record so that she could use it when actually cataloging the materials for the collection. Because the books and pamphlets were so old, most dating back to the seventeenth century, I found that it was quite challenging to find the right OCLC record. Sometimes I had to try a succession of the different derived title and author searches, the only tools available back then, before I could find exactly what I was looking for. This treasure hunt became the bright spot of my workday.

My knowledge of OCLC was the determining factor in my obtaining the present position as a library assistant in charge of the interlibrary loan department of a corporate library. When I was reintroduced to the OCLC database two years ago, I was pleased to see that now I had even more tools I could use to locate my treasure: "scan title" searches; author, title, and various other kinds of keyword searches (a tool I wished for ten years ago); and more. In the short time since I have been treasure hunting once again, I have seen even more refinements to OCLC, giving me even more tools with which to work. The OCLC training classes I have taken have sharpened my ability to use those tools aright. I still find, however, that sometimes the treasure is not easily yielded; the obscure nature of the reference may require trying two or three different tools, or kinds of searches, before I find the gem I am looking for. Thus, searching the OCLC database continues to be a challenge and a source of great intellectual satisfaction to me. May it always remain such!

Moreover, the OCLC database is both a treasure map and a treasure in itself. It's like a treasure map in that it allows me to pinpoint the location of books, journals, audio- and videocassettes, films, reports, dissertations, computer files, and all other types of library materials—the gemstones—and then allows me to request them from the holding libraries. The breadth and depth of its cataloging thus makes OCLC itself a treasure. Without it, I, along with other interlibrary loan librarians, would be unable to serve patrons as efficiently and as comprehensively. OCLC gives me access to information that, when used wisely, can improve lives. It is indeed an asset.

**Brenda Pollreisz**
University of Missouri–Columbia
Columbia, MO

In a matter of seconds…

An hour into a workday, creating one local data record after another, I had to do something to break the monotony. Enter: the Walkman.

"Time for the brain-buster trivia question. We all know her as Madonna. Question for today is: what's her real name? First person to answer correctly wins dinner for two at the Olive Garden," the local DJ hollered from my headphones.

Switching the search perimeters to "SET SELECT OLUC" I typed in an authority search, "mado,,." In a matter of seconds, I had the authority record stating her real name as Madonna Louise Ciccone, and consequently supper for that night.

Later in the day, I was reading the online news for serials title changes on the OCLC Online Union Catalog when one of the check-in assistants approached.

"I've searched every possible way in our database AND the serials card catalog for this thing," he said. "It ain't there."

"Let's see what OCLC has," I said, typing in a regular derived title search.

In a matter of seconds, a bibliographic record appeared on the screen. In the top left corner, a fixed field read, "Bib lvl: m."

"Well, there's the problem. It's a *monograph*."

At that, the assistant happily walked it and the Online Union Catalog bibliographic copy over to monographic acquisitions, where he was showered with gratefulness for having found their missing book.

By the afternoon, I was tired and ready to go home, when a person from the interlibrary loan department wandered into the office with a piece of paper in her hand and a disoriented look on her face, resembling a deer staring into the headlights of death.

"This is my first time down here. Could you tell me where Alan's desk is?" she inquired.

"Over there," I said, pointing toward the cataloging department. Alan overheard the conversation and put an arm up to flag her attention.

As she handed him the paper, I overheard the following conversation.

"Thought you might like to look at this request we just received," she said smiling. "It's from a library in Australia."

Alan glanced at the paper. "That record just went through a few seconds ago."

"I know. According to that library, we're the only people on the planet that own it. If you hadn't catalogued it on OCLC, they'd still be searching for it."

With that, I glanced up at the clock. It read five o'clock on the dot, so I grabbed my coat and walked home to get ready for my free dinner at the Olive Garden.

**Sharon Pratt**
IUPUI / Herron School of Art Library
Indianapolis, IN

Libraries revisited...

Why do I always wait until the last minute? It's not like I haven't known about this project since the beginning of the semester... it was announced the first day of class. I always do this—I bet there won't be a parking place. Maybe the library won't be open! That's it! I couldn't do my research because the library was closed and then they'll give me an extension.

Where is this place, anyway? I've been by it going to class... That must be it. How could I miss it with all those cars? I don't like libraries. I never know where anything is. I don't ask for help because I don't want those people to think I'm stupid. And those card files—what a pain. I always lose my place and I have to write everything down and then I have to walk all over the place trying to find stuff. And the things I need are never there. When I do find something, it's not what I want which means I just have to turn around and go somewhere else and start all over.

Okay, I'm here, now where is the card catalog? A couple of years ago it was over there where all those terminals are now. What's going on? Everybody seems to know what they're doing except me. Maybe if I read the screen, I can do this too. Hey! Something came up! I can't believe it. Look at all that information. There's everything I need to know—author, title, call number, location, and publisher. This is just like the card catalog but a lot better. I can look at the records and then print them out, instead of writing them down. This is going to make my bibliography a lot easier.

I can even do research on related topics based on the subject headings. I can search for information using many different terms and even combine key words for efficiency. Maybe I won't have to make any extra trips, because I can see right away if something is available here. I can even check the holdings of other libraries without losing my parking space.

I've been wrong about libraries. They are on the edge of computer technology and it's available to everyone, even me. Just by following the instructions on the screen, I can search for information across the city, within the state or around the world. Who knows what libraries will come up with next? Now if I could just get my parking ticket taken care of...

———————————— ✒ ————————————

**Zhou Qin**
Peking University Library
Beijing, People's Republic of China

From dream to hope...

I knew about OCLC for the first time in the university classroom ten years ago. The teacher told us that it is a database in which we can find a lot of bibliographical information. It is simply wonderful! Though I was excited, OCLC, at that hour, merely meant a dream for me. America is separated by vast oceans, so is OCLC.

After graduation, I have worked as an English cataloguer in Peking University Library. Never had I associated myself with OCLC until one day I came across a 1991 issue of *OCLC Newsletter* in the reading-room. The president's article, "The Best Is Yet to Come," carried on the first page caught my eyes. The telecommunication network had even linked more than 11,000 institutions in 41 countries! It occurred to me that I would be involved in this preeminent bibliographical database someday. Then came the Special Report which chronicled OCLC's 20 years online history. I sensed that OCLC database is a more useful one than I thought. From that time on, I have been reading almost every issue of *OCLC Newsletter*. I am told that cataloging by sharing records contributed by member libraries is certainly efficient and economical; I am convinced that besides cataloging and searching, we can do other things like researching and surveying with the OCLC Online Union Catalog; I am informed that Chinese materials can also be input into the Catalog. Encouraging! (I am a Chinese rare book cataloguer now.) How does it feel to travel among different files and records! And how does it feel to learn from which institution I can get a certain item in a flash! The imagination of using the OCLC Online Union Catalog always lays a hope ahead of me, e.g., the day we are connected to OCLC Network comes soon. This hope, thank goodness, is not unreachable. Internet helps!

If tomorrow is the day, what if I do not know how to perform but sit before the workstation at a loss? The very thought of being lagged behind often makes me feel uneasy. But I must face it. I survive if I have good language skills, computer knowledge and proper psychological preparation. Isn't that right?

If it will take some time for the day to come, we should let things take their natural course. Yet that does not mean that I just wait and dream away the hours.

In fact, there is no time to lose to accumulate records of high quality and introduce international standards into our records as far as possible.

From dream to hope, I realize that OCLC is drawing towards us. It will bring me a world full of not only imagination but also adventure. When the day comes, I will be part of it, and it will be part of me. Let us all pray for the day to come early.

———————————— ⅋ ————————————

**Helen Quigley**
Harvard University
Cambridge, MA

When my library first received the flyer heralding the essay contest sponsored by OCLC, everyone in the department read it with some amusement, made a few comments on how much fun it would be to write something, and passed the pamphlet on. I admit, that was my initial reaction. Why then am I now, one week later, sitting at my computer terminal writing an essay on what the OCLC Online Union Catalog means to me? Because I need to get a good night's sleep, that's why! Let me explain: I have found myself lying in bed these last few nights pondering this question, examining the ways in which I use OCLC in my daily tasks and considering the nature of my job and what it would mean to me if I did not have access to the OCLC Online Union Catalog.

As a cataloguing assistant in a major research library, I use OCLC daily in fulfilling my job responsibilities. In fact, logging into OCLC is virtually the first thing I do in the mornings when I arrive at work. Every monograph that has not been catalogued by the Library of Congress is searched in the OCLC database, either for a cataloguing record or for authority control, or both. Because we receive titles in a variety of languages, (Catalan, Finnish, Turkish and even African languages, to name just a few), finding cataloguing copy in OCLC simplifies my job immeasurably. The record can be downloaded into our local database for modification and we are able to take advantage of other libraries' expertise in foreign languages and subject scopes. In addition, finding a cataloguing record means the book is made available to patrons quickly. For a major research library which receives titles in lesser known languages and on esoteric subjects, it is wonderful that so many searches result in "hits." Conversely, all of the original cataloguing done in my department is taped out to the OCLC Online Union Catalog, enabling us to actively contribute to the resource sharing.

In addition to the daily uses of the OCLC Online Union Catalog, my department also utilized OCLC as a means to retroconvert our collection. In this age of Internet access, it is a distinct advantage to make a collection available online. Adding our bibliographic holdings to the Union Catalog means our collection can be accessed worldwide, thereby increasing its use via Interlibrary Loan and ensuring its availability to scholars and patrons.

The OCLC Online Union Catalog is an indispensable tool for any cataloguer. The immediate access to over 35 million records, the linguistic breadth of the database and the continual expansion of its membership worldwide make the OCLC Online Union Catalog a utility to be reckoned with!

## Ellen Raben
Saint Louis University
St. Louis, MO

OCLC means that the world is my public library. I work in interlibrary loan and am possibly my own "best" patron. Internet and the Web: I'm not impressed. The nets change every day, any self aggrandizing schmo can create a home page and represent himself as anything he wants: the Net has no authority file, you don't know who you're talking to or where anything is coming from.

Through keyword searching and FirstSearch I have resources to anything I need: when I got engaged, I borrowed *The Diamond Ring Buying Guide* by Renee Newman (OCLC 27682051) and when we bought our house, *Riches Under Your Roof: How You Can Make Your Home Worth Thousands More* by Jim Belliveau (OCLC 8708637), both from my local public library. I borrowed *Wisterias; A Comprehensive Guide* by Peter Valder (OCLC 32647814) from Minneapolis Public Library to take care of that unusual vine in our yard. When my old cat got sick an article from the *Journal of Veterinary Internal Medicine* (OCLC 14949161) came from VPI and then *Euthanasia in Veterinary Medicine* (OCLC 21213767) published by the Foundation of Thanatology came from the National Center for Death Education to help me justify and overcome a deep sadness over the loss of just a little animal.

It's not just my own problems for which I find solutions either. OCLC has improved my social life—I am the library resource to friends as well: *America's Neighborhood Bats* by Merlin Tuttle (OCLC 17806128) helped a neighbor change fear to welcome for our little visitors and a dissertation from University of Memphis: *Effects of a Waking Schedule on Primary Enuretic Children Treated with Full-spectrum Home Training* by James Wheelan (OCLC 20507283) quietly returned a little boy's dignity.

With OCLC keyword searching and FirstSearch I can find any information I want: I can solve problems, explore hobbies, learn how to do things, no intellectual or creative pursuit is closed to me. With OCLC I am not bound by how many volumes are in the academic library where I work with 1.2 million volumes, nor by the size of our public library with 1.7 million in holdings. No library is small if it has access to OCLC's 35 million records.

The world is my library: it is the catalog of human life. I own knowledge.

**Sulo Ravi**
Battelle Memorial Institute
Columbus, OH

Way back in the 1970s, in library school in India, I read about OCLC, then known as Ohio College Library Center. Later in my library career in the 1980s, I would come across articles about OCLC in library journals, and the wonderful things it did. Envying American librarians, I would return to my routine cataloging work, as America and OCLC seemed so far away and unreachable then.

In 1983, however, destiny brought me to America and that too very close to OCLC: Columbus, Ohio. I started looking for jobs in the library field, especially in cataloging. I was turned down many times because I did not have hands-on experience using OCLC. Luckily for me, Professor Prebble of Capital University Law School Library offered the opportunity of some voluntary work at his library. That was my first hands-on experience with OCLC. I felt right at home with OCLC and I felt as if I have known OCLC all along like a good friend.

In 1970, I had an opportunity to visit Dr. Ranganathan, father of library science in India, along with my classmates. I still remember the conversation we had with him. "Reference service is the most important function in the library, which serves as an important link between the patron and library collection/services and the most important tool to fulfill that function as well as other library functions is the library catalog," he emphasized. His message to us future librarians was to always keep the five laws of library science in mind for a successful library career. Looking back, what he said 25 years ago still holds. Ranganathan's Five Laws:

1   Books are for use.

2   Each reader his book.

3   Each book its reader.

4   Save the time of the reader.

5   A library is a growing organism.

Next to our own library's catalog, we depend on OCLC, which brings the universe of knowledge to our fingertips, in serving our patrons better, keeping the five laws in mind. There is not a day I do not utter the mantra 'OCLC.' OCLC, if I do not log on to you every day, I feel I missed something, that is how much you have become a part of my life. Like a good friend, you are always there for me! I just cannot imagine my library life without you!

You have come a long way, my dear friend, from good old *OCLC model 100* to *OCLC access through the Internet*, from *3,2,2,1* to *scan* and *find* command, from *produce cards* to *export* command; 4000 years of recorded knowledge in 370 languages, 560 million location listings, I just watch with awe for the next wonder to come. You are the best thing that has happened to the universe of libraries.

Thank you, Professor Ranganathan, for giving us the five laws and for instilling the importance of library catalogs in me. Thank you, Professor Prebble, for introducing me to OCLC, and thank you, Professor Kilgour, for giving us this wonderful gift, OCLC.

Happy 25th birthday OCLC, our OCLC, and many more to come!!!

## Keith Reagan
Keene State College
Keene, NH

The kid in the candy store...

One of the greatest tragedies of the ancient world was the destruction of the library at Alexandria. This was the storehouse of knowledge collected and passed down over hundreds, thousands of years. Alexandria was the greatest collection of knowledge on Earth, perhaps with secrets from the past, secrets now lost to us forever. Who built the Great Pyramid? How? Was there an Atlantis?

But the doors to the Alexandrian library were closed to all but the priestly class. Today, OCLC's virtual merging of so many hundreds and thousands of libraries of every type opens up those hallowed doors of information and knowledge to anyone with a mind, an imagination and a thirst for knowledge.

Only a short time ago, any sort of research was hampered or made outright impossible by time and money. Finding the location of materials was one thing. Traveling to them was out of the question for most people.

With OCLC's search modes and vast database, time and distance fade. 1 have borrowed books published during the Irish Famine and the Civil War. 1 have loaned items to Russia and to Hungary and to Czechoslovakia.

Through the marvels of prompt and efficient interlibrary loan and document delivery, millions of people are one step away from nearly any published or recorded work. The known and accepted knowledge of so many cultures—many times in conflict with contrasting beliefs in other cultures in this shrinking world—can be studied and better understood by anyone, anywhere.

As an ILL staffer, as a screenwriter and simply as a curious person, the information available to me is truly staggering. For work, research or that old curiosity, some facility with OCLC's software makes this all-important quest for knowledge successful and satisfying.

To me, the OCLC Online Union Catalog is simply no less than a window on the world—an open window. At Alexandria, information was lost, never to be recovered. Today's reliance on hard drives and networks and indeed electricity doesn't mean a similar loss will not occur again. But as far as published, "accepted," available information is concerned, never before in our history has so much been so available to so many. As one of the curious many, OCLC is to me an incredible tool and the map to a priceless treasure.

**Alice M. Reck**
Vigo County School Corporation
Terre Haute, IN

Having the OCLC Online Union Catalog available to the Vigo County School Corporation (VCSC) has opened the doorway to the shared expertise of the profession. It is like having a team of professionals assist in locating and cataloging of materials to serve the needs of all participating patrons. It has users with a common goal of providing information.

Vigo County Schools have subscribed to the OCLC Online Union Catalog since 1978. It has played a key role in providing timely processing of materials, has served as a model for local electronic networking, and has afforded the opportunity to become a collaborating team member. Being able to contribute to the community of professionals is a noteworthy experience.

The online catalog has served VCSC as a model to unify cataloging and classifying that eventually allowed it to electronically share information worldwide. It has been the vehicle for our entrance into global electronic networking.

Certainly for those entities unable to afford professional catalogers or those with limited staff such as VCSC, it has been a lifeline of hope. With the heavy demands and the limited resources and staff currently prevailing, the online catalog has impacted the quantity and quality of services provided in a very direct manner. While playing a behind the scene role, it has literally touched the lives of some 18,000 users each year.

Libraries are known for cooperating and collaborating to afford the best service possible. They are, in fact, leaders in the field of successfully sharing information. The online catalog has initiated a proactive role of libraries in facilitating the transmission of information worldwide in contrast to the old traditional image of being just a storehouse of information.

Traditionally, libraries have served to collect, organize and disseminate the annals of print. The online catalog has made possible the networking of the so called information "have and the have-nots" to become the common denominator for all geographic, social, economic or political affiliations of its users. It is gratifying to be a part of such a venture.

Never did VCSC envision the significant role that the OCLC Online Union Catalog would encompass in the corporation's endeavor to meet the demands of the "information age" of today and tomorrow. Being a participant has helped the students and staff in the Wabash Valley to become information literate. A special thanks to the visionaries who conceived and birthed the concept and paved the way for an "information bond" that links the past and present to the future around the world.

**Richard Reitsma**
Northwestern College
Orange City, IA

Minding the OCL Sea...

The OCLC is an incalculably vast ocean over which thousands of ships silently travel without so much as a wake in the water. Like millions of well-mannered fish, the bibliographic records fill that fluid universe with substance. Researchers and dabblers along with librarians and sportsmen reel in fiction, insight, froth and wisdom from the murky depths of that ocean.

But I am only one lonely fisherman at a distant outpost with my line in the water. As if it were yesterday, I still remember the first time that this ocean reached out for my bait. I thought that I had joined the ranks of the magicians who controlled the fish of the sea; with the touch of a key, a record was in my satchel.

At the time, I had not yet tangled with the seaweed which robs oxygen from some inlets of the ocean. I had yet to experience the fresh winds of change that blew in EPICs, PRISMs and the ever present FirstSearch. As a novice, I had not braced my feet against the tidal waves that would wash away the OXFORD and LINKS projects along with vast shorelines of strategic plans. During those distant decades, the M300 fishing rod was still a shiny new instrument in my hands.

Now, with the steady breeze of change in my face, those past OCL Sea tales seem as insignificant as stories of the distant journeys of the minute Pinta. But my past expeditions on that sea gave me new fishing and navigation skills. With a seasoned mind, I now survey the vast and increasingly turbulent universe of information. With a salty wind in my face, I steadily eye those troubled OCeans, Lakes and C's of data. I now know I am no magician, but am also aware that there is an antidote to the deluge.

**Donna R. R. Resetar**
Valparaiso University
Valparaiso, IN

Our university library is fortunate to have access to OCLC's FirstSearch WorldCat database, which is the lay person's version of the OCLC Online Union Catalog. When I explain this database to my students, I describe it as a catalog of resources owned by libraries all over the world. I show them how to find records using the various indexes and search features. Once they identify a useful resource, I show them how they can enter a request to borrow it from another library without getting up from their terminal.

What I don't tell students in a routine reference encounter, but often think about, is that many librarians and library staff members all over the world have worked long and hard to build this remarkable database, and make it accessible to them.

I think about the beginnings and the librarians who developed the cataloging rules. Like library patrons everywhere, our students assume that they can walk into any library and search a catalog by author, title, or subject. I want to tell them that it hasn't always been this simple. What they take for granted has really only existed for 120 years. This is not a very long time, if they consider the entire recorded history of human knowledge.

When students marvel at how they can limit their search by language or date in WorldCat or our local electronic catalog, I think about the librarians who made this all possible. I want to tell them how librarians worked out a way to code records so they could be easily and precisely retrieved in a computerized database. I want to tell them that librarians were thinking about their need to do this long before personal computers, floppy disks and the computer mouse were invented. I want to tell them how librarians have struggled to develop and maintain cataloging standards, so that library patrons everywhere could benefit from an easy-to-use global database of bibliographic records and holdings.

As I see students reap the rewards of this database, I think about my years as a cataloger, how I learned the code, the rules and the standards. I remember how I took pride in the records I copied from the union catalog to my local catalog, modifying them as needed to meet my patrons' needs. I remember some of the unique works for which I was privileged to contribute carefully crafted records to the union catalog. I like to think that someday, someone, somewhere, will find the resource they need quickly and easily because of my record.

I want to tell students that what they see on the screen is like a ballet. The ballerina makes it look so easy and elegant, but behind the performance is pain, sweat, the joy of hard work, and the satisfaction of a job well done.

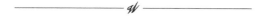

## Jean S. Riley
International Fertilizer Development Center
Muscle Shoals, AL

Only a quarter of a century in existence but a phenomenal information-dissemination revolution never before known to mankind—congratulations to OCLC on its 25th anniversary. The impact of OCLC on the lives of people in the developing countries may not be common knowledge. I have had 16 years of experience working with the international community in an information-dissemination capacity. I am most fortunate to have had the opportunity to converse with scientists of developing countries, learn of their projects, interests, and ideas, and then consult OCLC to obtain information geared to their specific needs. I have witnessed thousands of smiles and words of gratitude and praise for having placed information into hands that could not have otherwise obtained it.

The institution for which I work is the International Fertilizer Development Center (IFDC)—a public, international, nonprofit organization. Founded in 1974, the Center focuses on increasing and sustaining food and agricultural productivity in developing countries through the development and transfer of effective and environmentally sound plant nutrient technology and agribusiness expertise. Over the past 20 years, more than 12,000 technical visitors, trainees, and research scientists have visited IFDC from more than 170 developing countries of Asia, Africa, Latin America, and the newly emerging democracies of eastern and central Europe.

Not only have visitors benefited from OCLC but also IFDC has been able to pursue its mission because of the resources of OCLC. Due to budgetary constraints, the collection of the Travis P. Hignett Memorial Library is limited, but the work of IFDC's scientists and technical staff has never suffered from this limitation, thanks to OCLC. By applying innovative agricultural technologies in an agribusiness setting, IFDC's professional staff members have laid the groundwork for the alleviation of poverty in countries such as Albania, Bangladesh and Romania. A prime result of the Center's work in Bangladesh was that country's achievement of self-sufficiency in rice production in the early 1990s.

The keyword searching enhancement of the online catalog has enabled IFDC staff members to answer questions that are unrelated to their fields of expertise. For example, I was asked to locate information about the dispersal rate of liquid nutrients dropped into an ocean current; 15 pertinent references were found. Fish is the fifth most important agricultural commodity, and over one billion people in Asia alone rely on fish as the primary source of animal protein. To increase fish production, scientists must develop means of increasing the production of phytoplankton, which is the first link in the food chain for fish.

The technical and scientific information available to scientists through OCLC is helping to intensify agriculture and, thus, increase food production. Helping to feed the 700 million people in the developing world who do not have access to enough food to live healthy and productive lives, is the key to alleviating hunger and poverty. Out of the scientific, literary and educational disciplines has emerged an information highway with resource capabilities that should be correctly titled: OCLC—Eighth Wonder of the World.

### Katherine Jean Roberts

Oktibbeha County Library System
Starkville, MS

I have been using OCLC's Online Union Catalog for just a short time and have found it to be useful. When needing to find a book or magazine article that can't be found in-state, I turn to the OCLC Catalog. I usually find what I need at other libraries out-of-state.

The OCLC Catalog is fairly easy to access and search. The commands used can be confusing, especially not being able to use enter, but once used enough, it becomes fairly easy to use and can even be fun.

One feature I like is how much information is available. Looking in-state for something is somewhat limited to a few years, or as to whether the book is in large-print or regular print. OCLC offers a wide range of years and editions. You can find large-print books just as easily as regular print or audio/videos.

Another feature I like is the time frame for responses. I can be rather impatient at times, and waiting a few days for a response (especially if the requested book is for me) is sometimes not easy. When requesting books in-state, I have to wait at least three days to find out the response. When requesting books through OCLC, I can find out in just a few hours or the next day.

The OCLC Catalog is a source of information just waiting to be tapped into. Once you learn the basic commands of using it, you'll depend on it a lot.

### R. Bruce Robertson
Historical Society of Pennsylvania
Philadelphia, PA

Most gratifying in working with the OCLC database is contributing original records. I feel like, and identify with, those medieval stone masons who realized the great French and English Gothic cathedrals, carving away, stone by stone, all for the greater glory of civilization, and all done relatively anonymously, too. Already the world's premier database of surrogate records of human creativity, it will continue to grow.

Realists (particularly those of a theological bent) will insist that nothing natural can last forever, but can there be any reason not to expect that the OCLC database will be preserved through whatever metamorphoses future technologies will devise? The French have a saying—*il n'y a pas de sot métier*—to the effect that there is no such thing as honest work that is useless… to which might follow that "if it's worth doing, it's worth doing right." And all the more so with OCLC, for it is work not only for the decades, but the centuries and—why not?—the millennia as well. Exciting and humbling things to ponder, these, as one prepares to add yet another original record.

### Arthur J. Robinson
London Borough of Tower Hamlets
Prestatyn, Clwyd, Wales

In 1984 I was looking round the Online Exhibition in London when I stopped at the OCLC stand. I complained that it was difficult to find out details of some of the sound recordings and music scores we were asked for in our music library. "Why not join OCLC," answered the representative brightly.

So I did. Computer literacy had not penetrated very far into my library service so I joined as an individual with my very own library symbol, EQR. It cost me £50 initially and there was a cumbersome method for estimating use. Communication was via my own Apple IIe computer, logging on via the packet switch stream system and receiving data at 300 baud.

Next year I revisited the OCLC stand and reminded the rep. that I was an individual member. "Then you must be Mr. Robinson," He answered. He had lost none of his brightness. I asked him how he knew and he informed me that I was the only individual user in the system.

I was able to trace scores and sound recordings without having to wade through annual volumes of *British Catalogue of Music*, which, in any case, listed only scores published in UK. In the OCLC catalogue there were about 750,000 entries of interest to music librarians. Because I was searching library catalogues I could find publications which were hundreds of years old and not just those added since 1951. Locations were given and sound recordings could be retrieved from their makers' numbers. In our library, for instance, we collected a section of the Jazz alphabet as part of the Greater London Audio Specialisation scheme (GLASS) and I found that OCLC was useful for tracing American jazz artists.

In fact, it was so useful that I wrote an article about it which was published in the *Journal of IAML* UK—the music librarians' group.

It was not until later that the complete British Library Catalogue was digitised and put online and even then it didn't include scores or recordings.

In 1987 the British Library took over the distribution of OCLC data in the UK and in 1991 I acquired a PRISM password. I could still access PRISM from an ASCII terminal, though the logging-on procedure was messy.

But in 1993 charges for using the system rose dramatically and I reluctantly left it. They still send me the newsletter though.

By this time I had retired to Wales and acquired a Macintosh. I would still like to use the system for my own research and thought that, with the change in marketing and access from World Wide Web, I could join FirstSearch. But I found that searches must be purchased in batches of 500, enough to last the rest of my life. Why can't they be distributed by a wholesaler like cartons of canned soup which can be sold in smaller batches to individual users like myself?

### Judith S. Robinson
University of New York at Buffalo
Buffalo, NY

When books were rare
And citations few
There wasn't much for researchers to view.
But soon, finding a title became quite a chore
(*Mansell* volumes alone totaled 754)
Causing readers in search of knowledge to pore
Through many a creaky card catalog drawer
(Missing more than was found
Since collections renown
Were far from the poor reader's door).
And that wasn't all
Since knowledge did sprawl
Across language and centuries too
—Much more than a reader could ever review.
Until OCLC made its debut.

The initial blow to the status quo
Was a database launched in Dublin, Ohio.
What began as a trickle
Today is a stream,
As accessible in Podunk
As in academe.

Full MARC record, with holdings,
The world's knowledge in bytes
In millions and millions of electronic cites.
Whether written or spoken or acted or sung
No matter the format, the time frame, or tongue.
It bows to no boundaries of time nor of place
To document records from the whole human race.

Snowbound in my office
Far from the crowd
My fingers keep typing
I'm skillful and proud.
I tap into novels,
Then books by John Donne.
And—if I want to—a 3,2,2,1.
It's the tool of my trade, my reference, my key
My on-ramp into the next century.
That's what OCLC means to me.

---

**Kevin M. Roddy**
University of Hawai'i at Hilo
Hilo, HI

Picture an island chain where geologists monitor a volcano that has erupted continuously for 13 years. Atop Mauna Kea, an extinct volcano rising some 31,000 feet above the seafloor, astronomers huddle in groups to gaze through the largest telescopes on earth. In fields and valleys cooled by trade winds and heavy rains, agriculture specialists conduct tests to improve crop yields and battle invasive insects. In rain forests, biologists study the bizarre results of evolution in isolation, while archaeologists are kept busy at prehistoric digs that seem to be just about everywhere. Welcome to the Island of Hawai'i and to the University of Hawai'i. Though we are the most geographically remote of any islands in the world, our faculty and students thrive because of our ability to rapidly access information. Through the magic of T1, ethernet, fiber optics and personal computers, the vast resources of the OCLC Online Union Catalog are brought to our windswept shores.

Supplying information to a wide variety of research interests is no easy task. No library can acquire and house everything. But services like FirstSearch make linking users to information easy. OCLC Online Union Catalog has helped me win many a round of the age-old, good-natured game of "stump the reference desk!" Before OCLC Online Union Catalog's arrival at the reference desk, I secretly dreaded this game, a favorite of faculty everywhere. Now, armed with my Online Union Catalog talisman, I rise to the challenge and play along.

Recently, a professor asked me to locate an obscure title on hex sign artistry she remembered seeing in a county library in rural Pennsylvania. She was accompanied by another professor who was looking for a copy of a musical score originally written in Ladino, and published in Zagreb in 1939. In seconds, I was online with WorldCat through OCLC's new web service. My fingers flew over the keyboard as the two chatted. In less than two minutes, I informed one that Jane Zook's *Pennsylvania Dutch Hex Signs* at the Lancaster County library was the book she remembered. Turning to her companion, I asked if he wanted the *Romanized* Ladino version of the score with Croatian and French translations. Playful smirks faded. Though happy, they were dismayed that I won the round so easily. With printouts in hand, they nodded and left. I also used the web's E-mail feature to send the citations to them, just in case they misplaced their printouts. We know how absent-minded professors can get.

What does the OCLC Online Union Catalog mean to me? It has leveled the playing field for librarians in far-flung places. Whether you work in middle of the Pacific or in the middle of Manhattan, verifying and locating items is easy AND affordable. The OCLC Online Union Catalog has come a long way from "3-2-2-1," "message not clear" and my personal favorite, "request impossible!" I thank all of you at OCLC who have worked so hard to deliver a product that makes my work easier, more satisfying and just plain fun.

———————————— *9/* ————————————

## Kristen Roland
U.S. EPA Library Services
Research Triangle Park, NC

*You don't realize what you have until it's gone...*

These nine words characterize our experience last fall at the U.S. Environmental Protection Agency (EPA) Library in Research Triangle Park, North Carolina. The library staff, researchers, and patron community endured two government shutdowns and long stretches of time during which budget uncertainty prevented us from using OCLC. Most of the staff is too young to remember library procedures before the creation of the OCLC Online Union Catalog; its absence forced us to recognize its importance in the day-to-day operation of the library. To us, the Online Union Catalog means many things that we measure in different ways.

As a single source of bibliographic information that spans a wide range of subjects, formats, and years, the OCLC Catalog eliminates the "needle in a haystack" approach of searching for needed material. Forced to do the latter during the government furloughs, the library became much less efficient; access to the Catalog enables us to double productivity.

The OCLC Online Union Catalog makes our library part of an international research community. When the same symbols repeatedly appear in OCLC holdings data, we know that there are people in other settings collecting and working with the same type of information that we do. Without the OCLC Catalog, the EPA library, and thus EPA researchers, virtually are cut off from accessing research being done by colleagues around the globe.

As a federal agency, the EPA has an obligation to supply government information to the public, and the OCLC Online Union Catalog provides a means for doing so. Using the cataloging application, we add original titles to the database; this process records items that only may be available from our library and otherwise might become "fugitive" documents. Existence of the Online Union

Catalog also means that the EPA library network can have its own online library catalog. From records that are part of the Catalog, the EPA uploads tape files to create what serves both as an electronic card catalog and as an index to virtually all of the documents that have been published by the Agency over the years. These vital public services are interrupted when access to the Catalog is unavailable.

Use of the OCLC Catalog means that library staff members, comprised primarily of master's student interns from the School of Information and Library Science at the University of North Carolina at Chapel Hill under contract with the EPA, have the opportunity to work at a professional level. The cataloging intern does original cataloging which is added to the Catalog; interlibrary loan interns download, fill, and update ILL requests made through the Catalog. There are very few instances in which students are able to acquire professional experience before earning an advanced degree; the Catalog facilitates such training.

The meaning of the OCLC Online Union Catalog is measured by the EPA library in several ways; all were affected when our access to the database was restricted. While life before the OCLC Online Union Catalog is foreign to much of the staff, it will take a while to forget our recent experience *without* it.

**Betty Lee Ronayne**
California State University–Sacramento
Sacramento, CA

In the jargon-filled lexicon of librarianship, one acronym will always resonate with particular meaning for me. OCLC played a unique role in my mid-life career decision.

In 1974, I was a re-entry student completing a long-delayed bachelor's degree and working part-time at San Diego Public Library as a bibliographic searcher. A demonstration of the OCLC database so dazzled me with the possibilities for relatively instantaneous bibliographic verification that I... but wait; let me fill in some background context.

At that time, San Diego Public, under a progressive new director, had finally accepted the concept of cooperation and agreed to join a regional consortium of multi-type libraries—a dramatic departure from decades of catering to a narrowly defined geographic constituency and charging stiff fees to those beyond the boundaries. Thus, the Serra Regional Library System of Southern California came to be and, due largely to OCLC, came to flourish.

Free sharing of resources among the various types of libraries that belonged to the Serra System was enabled by the OCLC Online Union Catalog. Users of small public libraries in the remote desert towns of Imperial Valley had access to materials at the University of California San Diego by virtue of membership in the Serra System. And UCSD students had access to materials in special libraries belonging to the consortium. That this is by now a familiar scenario is itself a tribute to OCLC's enduring significance.

The momentum engendered by OCLC's remarkable example, and its burgeoning database, stimulated similar cooperative ventures throughout North America and eventually spanned the seas to encompass the globe. Today such cooperative endeavors are commonplace. But at the time, this transformation of closely-held collections into barrier-free borrowing and lending was an intellectual glasnost of inspiring proportions, a model of multi-national collaboration.

To return to my personal transformation: OCLC inspired me to become a reference librarian. Yes, I know it's hokey, but it's true. I wanted to teach as many library users as possible about the vast store of knowledge made accessible by the shared database that was linking libraries worldwide.

I first saw OCLC demonstrated at the University of California San Diego, and naturally enough assumed that it originated at that institution. When I learned that the OCLC enterprise was developed in Ohio—a state I knew almost nothing about—I determined to go to library school in Ohio. And so I did. Thank you, OCLC, for helping me to make a career choice I have never regretted in 22 years.

**Laura Rose**
National Sporting Library
Middleburg, VA

This is the story of a girl and a database.

When the OCLC Online Union Catalog was born in 1971, I myself was just a babe in the cradle. How both of us have grown—the OCLC database into the largest bibliographic database of its kind, and I myself into a graduate student in library science. Was it pure fate that brought us together at a SOLINET training workshop four years ago? Perhaps, though I'd like to think that parallels in our development may also have been a factor.

For starters, we were both developed with nurturing care. Both the database and I were gifted to be the products of people who respected and passed on the rich traditions that preceded them. Looking back, I can see the influential wisdom of my parents and the many teachers who guided me to this day. In the same way, one can see the hands of librarians, computer scientists and others who thoughtfully shaped the growth of the OCLC database.

Under such care, we were both bound to blossom. We were carefully programmed with high standards that would allow us to perform at our peak, communicate well with others, and explore new horizons the world over. Of course, when it comes to foreign languages, the OCLC database—with 370 under its belt—has my basic French and Italian beat!

As we grew, we both developed many tools to help us do what we do best—link people with information. We incorporated skills that would allow us to entertain our reverence for history, and to sniff out information in all its guises—from ancient texts to breaking news online. As time goes by, we continue to recognize and appreciate the changes in the world of information, and in the populations served by it.

Of course, though we were both programmed for growth, we've had our share of ups and downs as we continually adapt to an era of rapid change. We'll try anything if we think it will help someone—and do it efficiently. But if that "anything"—a new technological tool, for example—doesn't work, we don't stop. We learn from our experiences, and continue moving toward the future.

And our future is an exciting one. We don't see the information superhighway as a "roadblock" but an "on-ramp" and we're ready to ride it to new challenges and possibilities. We are confident that we will reach amazing heights that those who have nurtured us in our early days would never have thought possible. In addition, we are learning how to effectively join forces with an increasingly diverse information community in order to provide a higher and higher level of service for our users.

Library philosopher Jesse Shera said that the librarian's goal should be to "maximize the social utility of graphic records for the benefit of humanity." As we move toward the next millennium, the OCLC Online Union Catalog and I can continue to work toward Shera's goal and make the world a better place—together.

———————————— ⅋ ————————————

**Lutishoor Salisbury**
University of Arkansas
Fayetteville, AR

A researcher's perspective...

I have in recent years had the opportunity to search and experiment with many databases. However, when the OCLC Online Union Catalog became available as WorldCat in 1992, I was amazed at the range of questions that I could answer while using this database with ease and confidence. This experience left me boasting to friends and colleagues that "I have access to the greatest database in the world, which is truly multi-national, multi-disciplinary, current, comprehensive, accessible from remote locations, supports interlibrary lending and allows full end-user searching."

As a researcher, I need to be able to locate quickly, the information I perceive as being important to me, through comprehensive and current sources with the least amount of frustrations and cost. Thus being able to access WorldCat has saved me a substantial amount of time and effort rather than trying to search individual libraries on the Internet with limited success and many disappointments. Through WorldCat, true end-user searching potential has finally been realized. In fact, WorldCat can lay claim to being the mother of end-user searching capability which the information world and end-users welcome with open arms. This database has also forced me to alter drastically the ways in which I seek information and introduced me to the technologies of the twenty-first century.

If this Online Union Catalog were not widely available to end-users, many of the valuable resources listed therein would have been lost to researchers, scholars and practitioners or would have otherwise been very difficult to locate at substantial costs.

But now I can consult the WorldCat database at my convenience, whether I am writing my bibliography and feel the need to verify or check on the accuracy of a citation, or starting a research project and am looking for leads to follow, or trying to identify researchers in the field, or look for dissertations that have been written on my subject, or if trying to locate institutions that are in the forefront of research in a specific area. The Online Union Catalog has consolidated all this information for me in a gold mine of resources. I can also keep my colleagues current by E-mailing them any relevant citations which might be useful.

I have also come to cherish the capability of being able to identify on my own, libraries that may have an item I need within my state and to be able to request electronically both single as well as analytic items from our interlibrary loan department through this database.

This access and empowerment of the user is what the Internet should be about. It is through access to content-based systems like this union catalog that I feel that the "Information Superhighway" is serving its purpose. I applaud OCLC for providing end-user access to the world's most comprehensive, multi-disciplinary, multi-national and current database in the online environment of the World Wide Web at an affordable price.

**Katharine Samuel**
University of Canterbury
Christchurch, New Zealand

OCLC enables me to do miracles...

In 1989, shortly after I had become Interloan Librarian at the Central Library, University of Canterbury, (Christchurch, New Zealand) we took the first tentative steps along the information technology highway when we joined New Zealand Bibliographic Network (NZBN) Interloan, and electronic interloan request service linked to the national database. It is vital however that bibliographic searching tools keep abreast of an electronic interloan service and until *OCLC* became available there was a gap.

Many books published before 1980 can be found only on the New Zealand Union Catalog (NZUC) on microfiche and only under the main entry (which may not be provided by the borrower). Incorrect or insufficient information made many items impossible to trace. Now that I have access to WorldCat on OCLC's FirstSearch I have been able to locate books not only held overseas but which are actually held in New Zealand and occasionally even in our own library!

One of these was called *The Psychology of Reproduction* by Warren Miller. When I traced this on FirstSearch and found that it was an official (NICHD) report, I sent the request to our Parliamentary Library which is a depository library for official publications. The borrower was delighted when it arrived on microfiche.

When *The military papers of Sir Claude Auchinleck* was requested, I was at a loss to find this until I searched on *FirstSearch* and discovered under the series note that it had been published in the *Bulletin of the John Rylands University Library.* Guess where this was held! Yes, in our own library.

Another challenging request which presented few problems for FirstSearch was one in which the one word title given by the borrower was incorrect and the author's name James MacGregor Burns was jumbled. Despite being held in New Zealand, without FirstSearch this book would have been unavailable.

It is often the case that using FirstSearch as the first port of call saves much fruitless searching on NZBN and NZUC. Recently a librarian rang about an old book which her borrower thought our library held. As my colleague was vainly searching NZUC with the few details given, I was able to find it on FirstSearch and supply her with the correct author and title for her to search successfully.

Sometimes I overreact to a difficult sounding request. When an academic staff member requested *A Survey of Palestine* which was prepared in 1945/1946 and which sounded like a report which had never seen the light of day here, I headed straight for FirstSearch and printed screens of records only to discover later that it was a two volume work which was on NZBN and held in New Zealand!

Nevertheless the knowledge that I have FirstSearch has prevented many anxiety attacks and FirstSearch has enabled me to demonstrate to academic staff members (many of whom are overseas) that the latest information technology is available here. In fact the wonders of FirstSearch have also surprised our Deputy Librarian.

Thanks to *OCLC Online Union Catalog* I can indeed do miracles!

## Marian Sanko
Hartford Hospital
Hartford, CT

"Like all men of the Library, I have traveled in my youth; I have wandered in search of a book…"*

Jorge Luis Borges' simple line has always struck me as achingly poignant as a definition of learning. For me, travel and books were always the source of achieving knowledge. Travel was encouraged by my father, but my affair with books seems to have been innate. In my childhood I spent many an hour wandering through the book stacks of the local library, sometimes in search of a specific title, other times sifting aimlessly through bookshelf after bookshelf hoping to discover some exciting new treasure. There seemed to be no end in sight for a reader like myself. I'd come home laden down with adventures like *Black Beauty, The Lion, the Witch, and the Wardrobe,* or the latest Nancy Drew or Hardy Boys saga. And while other kids would be outside running around and doing who knows what, I would lie reading on my parents' bed and travel to faraway lands.

With my background, it seems inevitable that I'd find myself working in a library as a book cataloger. Though my educational career precluded any training in library sciences, I say it was truly a stroke of good fortune that led me to my current position. In 1986 I was feeling burnt-out and needing/wanting to learn a new job in the library when the cataloging position opened up. I expressed interest and Dr. Gertrude Lamb, who was the director of Hartford Hospitals' Health Science Libraries at the time, happened to believe in my ability to catalog. We held numerous meetings at which she discussed the intellectual aspects of cataloging, all the while noting her ideas on post-its which she scattered over the tabletop. I listened and asked questions, over and over again, until one day "the light bulb" went off. The little yellow papers made sense!

The next step was to immerse myself in the countless "tools"—the *OCLC Cataloging Manual,* the *OCLC MARC Tape Record Manual,* all the *Formats and Standards Manuals,* the *Cataloging Micro Enhancer User Guide.* Pretty boring stuff to a non-manual kind of reader? So I at first thought, but fairly quickly got caught up in learning all the tiny details of a MARC record. Then the fun stuff began.

People talk about surfing the Internet…I surf the OCLC Online Union Catalog. Almost every day I come across something really interesting. Just today it was "An essay on the recovery of the apparently dead" by Charles Kite, 1788, published by C. Dilly in the Poultry, London. Some day I am sure this bit of information will come in handy. I could go on and on, and sometimes do, about my "finds," but I've begun to realize that the things that excite catalogers are unique to them.

I guess you could say that I'm a chip off the old block—my father used to tell us children that everyday, as we approached the entrance door to school we were supposed to say to ourselves "today I will learn something."

Everyday, as I logon to the OCLC Online Union Catalog, I wonder to myself where my travels will take me and what will I learn!

*The Library of Babel.* Jorge Luis Borges

## James L. Sauer
Eastern College
St. Davids, PA

| | | | |
|---|---|---|---|
| > | 1 | 000 | WORD |
| > | 2 | 001 | In |
| > | 3 | 002 | the |
| > | 4 | 003 | beginning |
| > | 5 | 004 | was |
| > | 6 | 005 | the |
| > | 7 | 006 | Word: |
| > | 8 | 007 | Sabbath |
| > | 9 | 008 | Pro/creation//Re/creation//Co/creation: |
| > | 10 | 010 | 96-00000// r1 |
| > | 11 | 040 | DLC ‡c DCL‡d OCL |
| > | 12 | 019 00 | My not-quite-so-sincere |
| > | 13 | 019 01 | apologies to: |
| > | 14 | 019 02 | ain't I a kick in the proverbials( |
| > | 15 | 019.03 | e. |
| > | 16 | 019.04 | e. |
| > | 17 | 019.05 | C |

umm
ing                  s )poet

| | | | |
|---|---|---|---|
| > | 18 | 020 | ISSN:777777777  : =c $0.02 |
| > | 19 | 041 | Language code: Anglo-satiric |
| > | 20 | 044 | US |
| > | 21 | 049 | OCLC |
| > | 22 | 050 | A 1 ‡b .AOk |
| > | 23 | 082 | 000.0001 2 20 |
| > | 24 | 100 | Sauer, James L. |
| > | 25 | 101 | Format, MARC |
| > | 26 | 130 | Uniform Title: Fatigues |
| > | 27 | 211 | Short Title: What! |
| > | 28 | 212 | Variant Title: !tahW |
| > | 29 | 222 | Key Title: Skeleton |
| > | 30 | 241 | Romanized Title: OCLC SPQR |
| > | 31 | 243 | Collective Title: OCLC R Us |
| > | 32 | 245 | What the OCLC Online Union Catalog means to |

me/

‡c James L. Sauer and Marc Format

| | | | |
|---|---|---|---|
| > | 33 | 250 | Late City; 1st ed; Last ed. |
| > | 34 | 260 | St Davids, PA: ‡b Bitterman Publishers, ‡c c1996 |
| > | 35 | 300 | 2 p. ; =c 28 cm |
| > | 36 | 400 | Series: World |
| > | 37 | 500 | General Note: George Patton wore suspenders. |
| > | 38 | 501 | With Note: "With" |
| > | 39 | 502 | Dissertation Note: Roast Pig |
| > | 40 | 503 | History Note: Washington used wooden dentures. |
| > | 41 | 504 | Bibliography Note: Books are fun! |
| > | 42 | 505 | Contents Note: Read side of box. |
| > | 43 | 506 | Credits: I'd like to thank my Mom for making all this possible. |
| > | 45 | 520 | Abstract: The Authors tell us in 500 words or Less what the OCLC Online Union Catalog means to them, their library, and their library users. |
| > | 46 | 521 | Audience Note: Librarians and Info Nerds Unite! |
| > | 47 | 527 | Censorship Note: F(r)ee Access to Information |
| > | 48 | 533 | Reproduction Note: Birds do it, bees do it. Even educated bibliographic systems do it. |
| > | 49 | 545 | Biographical Note: I catalog, therefore I am. |
| > | 50 | 546 | Languages: Catalan, Urdu, Serbo, Vietnamese, Yiddish, Persian (carpets), Finnish, (please do) Romanian, Hindi, Ukrainian, Thai (paisley), Bulgarian, Croatian, Greek, Turkish (delight), Norwegian (Wood), Hungarian (goulash), Czech (in the mail) Indonesian, Danish (with cream cheese), Korean, Swedish (meatballs), Polish, Arabic (numerals), Hebrew, Dutch (treat), Portuguese, Latin, Japanese, Chinese (checkers), Italian, Russian (where angels fear to tread), Spanish, German, French (kiss), English, Pig Latin. |
| > | 51 | 567 | Methodology Note: Start at start; end at end. |
| > | 52 | 583 | Action Note: Keep reading. |
| > | 53 | 586 | Awards Note: [To be announced by OCLC] |
| > | 54 | 596 | Held by: 21,000+ libraries |
| > | 55 | 650 | Cataloging, Cooperative—Data processing |
| > | 56 | 650 | OCLC Cataloging Subsystem |
| > | 57 | 650 | OCLC PRISM (Information retrieval system) |
| > | 58 | 650 | OCLC Interlibrary Loan Subsystem |
| > | 59 | 650 | OCLC Serials Control Subsystem |
| > | 60 | 650 | OCLC FirstSearch |
| > | 61 | 650 | Information Storage and retrieval system |
| > | 62 | 650 | Format integration |
| > | 63 | 655 | Non-Epic Literature |
| > | 64 | 690 | Bibliographic Fun |
| > | 65 | 752 | Hierarchical Place: Heaven |

| > | 66 | 754 | Taxonomic Name: Onlinus Computerus Librarius Centerius, Inc-ius |
|---|----|-----|----------------------------------------------------------------|
| > | 67 | 767 | Translation Note: atalogers-cay ove-lay ooks-bay (edia-may oo-tay) |
| > | 68 | 780 | Earlier Title: Ohio College Library Center |
| > | 69 | 850 | Bib holdings: Infants only |
| > | 70 | 856 | Electronic Holdings: Yes |
| > | 71 | 998 | Redundant entry: Sauer, James L. ‡What the OCLC Online Catalog means to me. |
| > | 72 | 999 | Holdings: Word |

———————————— ⁊ ————————————

## Linda Loos Scarth
Mount Mercy College
Cedar Rapids, IA

"What is yours is mine, and all mine is yours." Plautus, the Roman comic dramatist, wrote that over 2000 years ago. This statement is humorously altered in the Toddler's Creed on the wall of a nearby child care center. It probably should be on the wall of every library in the world, but especially those who use and are a part of OCLC.

"There must be a book on it!" How many times have reference librarians heard that or said it themselves? I often do. While we will thoroughly search our book holdings, those of nearby libraries accessible over the Internet, and Books in Print, I know that the OCLC Online Union Catalog is the likely authority on the existence of books our users are seeking.

The times OCLC has come to the rescue, by having bibliographic records, has done more than make the seeker happy—it has been a chance to demonstrate the resources of this library. That is because we regard all the resources we use as "ours." *What is yours is mine!* Of course, the second clause also applies.

Just as our print and electronic in-house sources are integrated and have equal status, so do the remote telnet, gopher and World Wide Web resources. It matters not that the OCLC database is 700 miles away and the book may be owned by a more distant library. Our users access the information here in *this* library with our assistance. The computer is here and because it is, so is OCLC.

The OCLC Online Union Catalog is ours because we, like other libraries, use it for cataloging, interlibrary loan, collection development and reference. It is both an extension of us and a vast contributor to our collection and activities. We use it in the manner predicted by Vannevar Bush some 50 years ago, as part of a scholar's workstation. He did not imagine computers and telecommunication as the storage and retrieval mechanisms but the outcome he anticipated is in the process of becoming. The access to other remotely-stored information is increased beyond the OCLC Online Union Catalog because of its connection to OCLC's FirstSearch.

It is ours because we are committed to customer service and to collaborative effort in teaching, research and service, just as OCLC is. It is ours and yours because our holdings are also part of other libraries' resources. As part of the wider library community, we both find and provide resources in an ever widening circle. OCLC allows us, as a small college, to contribute to satisfying the needs of our users whether they are across the desk or across the country.

## Virginia Scheschy
University of Nevada
Reno, NV

OCLC and the Online Union Catalog have been a part of my professional life since December, 1977, when I began my library career as a cataloger. On my first day of work, I remember being ushered into the "terminal room" where several staff sat at a cluster of beehive terminals. While OCLC facilitated the production of catalog cards, I knew that in the future these machine-readable records would be the foundation for an online public catalog. Therefore the first thing that the OCLC Online Union Catalog meant to me was the use of technology to serve libraries.

As I looked at the books waiting to be cataloged, I was told that this represented only a fraction of the backlog that had existed prior to joining OCLC. The previous system had involved typing cards from LC proof slips and using photocopy technology to produce card sets. With OCLC, the library was able to reduce its backlog and increase turnaround time on cataloging new materials for the collection, all at a cost savings over the previous manual system. So another thing that the OCLC Online Union Catalog meant, and still means, to me is efficiency.

I was impressed by the model of cooperation and sharing that OCLC represented. Each library took what it could from the system in terms of cataloging records, then contributed unique records for the original cataloging that was done. An interlibrary loan module was developed that permitted the sharing of physical items, by using the location symbols that were attached to the bibliographic records prepared and used by catalogers. Another thing that the OCLC Online Union Catalog means to me is cooperation.

As OCLC membership grew, the number of records in the system began to increase rapidly. Soon reference librarians and scholars discovered the value of this extensive database as a research tool. Public OCLC terminals started appearing in some libraries. With the advent of FirstSearch, my library and others now provide OCLC access to patrons through WorldCat. The addition of subject searching and a user-friendly search interface expanded the meaning of the OCLC Online Union Catalog to include end-user information.

One of the challenges catalogers must contend with is the wide variety of languages represented by the materials they catalog. OCLC continues to increase the number of national libraries that contribute records to the Online Union Catalog. Recently, publishers and vendors from various countries also started contributing records. With an OCLC presence in over 60 countries around the world, the OCLC Online Union Catalog now has a decidedly international meaning for me and others.

Despite a number of new initiatives which OCLC has undertaken over the years, the heart of OCLC, and its most valued asset, continues to be the Online

Union Catalog. What this catalog means to me is the use of information technology on an international scale, to permit my library to carry out its mission as efficiently and cost-effectively as possible. While improving and expanding over the years, the OCLC Online Union Catalog has continued to represent consistency and reliability to me and to the library profession as a whole.

## Cecilia M. Schmitz
Auburn University Libraries
Auburn, AL

Ever since my cataloging professor warned me of dire consequences if I even contemplated updating the fictitious information she was giving me to type into the save file, OCLC has influenced my life. OCLC has affected my decision to be a cataloger, my career as a cataloger, and my philosophy both as a cataloger and as a bibliographer.

OCLC influenced my decision to be a cataloger by making it possible to enter high-quality records quickly and easily without being haunted by a typewriter. Whereas I am an agile user of a computer, sprinting along effortlessly; I plod along with a typewriter, stumbling often over errors. If I had been required to create records manually, I would have perceived cataloging as a stressful and frustrating career.

OCLC has also influenced my career as a cataloger. After graduating, I became Microforms Cataloger at Texas A&M University. During this time, I cataloged a major microfilm set, the *Goldsmiths'-Kress Library of Economic Literature*. The idea of providing access to rare, hard to obtain information via a national database appealed to me so greatly that I applied for and obtained a temporary grant-funded position at Auburn University cataloging the *Confederate Imprints, 1861–1865*, another microfilm set. While I was cataloging this set, OCLC provided the necessary equipment and assistance when that equipment crashed. One kind soul at SOLINET even saved the 300 plus records in my save file while my equipment was being moved to the new library addition. The experience I gained from these two cataloging projects led to my obtaining a permanent position at Auburn.

Finally, OCLC has made it possible to fulfill my career goal both as a cataloger and as a bibliographer—to make quality information available to people quickly and easily. As a cataloger, I can download information from OCLC to NOTIS and make it available to people here in Auburn as well as to people utilizing the Internet. I can add records to OCLC making them accessible to people all over the world. In this manner, current information as well as information which is rare, outdated, or hard to obtain due to its format (i.e., information on microform) is made available to anyone.

This goal also extends to my life as a bibliographer. My bibliographies assist researchers by providing a literature review of the subject in question, such as smoking and organ donation. Often I obtain this information by searching OCLC. I ascertain whether a citation is relevant by analyzing both the holdings information and the record itself. I obtain much information through interlibrary loan. The book-length bibliographies I have done have bibliographic records in OCLC, making the information I have produced available to millions.

All and all, if the information that I have made available either through cataloging or through my bibliographies effects a person's life positively, then I have accomplished something in my life. OCLC has played a major role and deserves much of the credit.

———————————— ✒ ————————————

## Brenda Searcy
Clear Creek Baptist Bible College
Pineville, KY

There is no doubt that the OCLC Online Union Catalog means many different things to different people in different situations. I am sure, as a matter of fact, that I am not even aware of many of the benefits that others use on a regular basis. I must even admit to the fact that I have been spoiled by a CD database system made available by our state library association, making bibliographic searching and interlibrary loans within the state very simple and inexpensive. With that system becoming obsolete, however, I have been forced to use the OCLC Online Union Catalog on a more regular basis. In other words, I am a beginner on this system. It is, however, already of great benefit to me and my situation, and I look forward to learning more and more about it.

I am the assistant librarian in a small Bible college in the mountains of Kentucky. To many of you, that is the equivalent to the middle of nowhere! While our library holdings are good for who we are and what we do, there are many areas that are not well covered in our library, nor anywhere nearby. For this reason, we rely on bibliographic searches and interlibrary loans to supplement in these areas. The OCLC Online Union Catalog is becoming a best friend. I have been able to go into the catalog and nearly always find what I am looking for, due to the vastness of the database. I can find the listing, the record and easily do an interlibrary loan from there. It has expanded our possibilities, not only from within our college, but from within our state. There have been several instances where a requested item was not available anywhere within our state, but I was able to find it through the OCLC Online Union Catalog and request it from other states. This makes our library patrons happy, which makes our library look good; and is very gratifying to me to be able to help someone find what they are looking for. That is why I am doing what I do and the OCLC Online Union Catalog helps me better do that. Congratulations OCLC Online Union Catalog for 25 years of getting better and better, and for making me, and librarians around the country, better at what we do.

———————————— ✒ ————————————

**Cindy Sears**
Elbert Ivey Memorial Library
Hickory, NC

My library's selective membership in the OCLC Online Union Catalog has helped me to turn a part-time, basically dead-end job into a full time, ever-expanding window of opportunity.

I was pushed into the computer age when, as the assistant interlibrary loan clerk, I was sent to Raleigh, North Carolina to be trained to use the Passport software for interlibrary borrowing instead of the old way of calling our state library for locations and then sending out hard-copy request forms to one library at a time. Despite no previous computer experience, I literally sailed through the OCLC Passport training. It was so easy to learn! I became the interlibrary loan expert, instead of just an assistant. The biggest advantage of the new system was the time that it saved me since I could request from up to five locations by preparing only one request form, already partially filled out, and immediately send it on its way. Patrons could have the item in days or a report about unavailability which, with the new system, doesn't happen as often as before.

So, despite a growing number of interlibrary loan requests, I had extra time on my hands that I used for self-training in other computer programs, including word processing, database and eventually a publishing program, all of which I now use to prepare promotional handouts, bibliographies and displays to promote our library's fiction collection. Because of my efficient handling of the interlibrary loan services in the library and the other activities I have voluntarily taken on, I am now a full-time information services assistant.

The database and searching experience that I have gained over the last few years using the OCLC Online Union Catalog placed me "ahead of the pack" when our library recently automated its catalog and circulation system and the staff had to learn a whole new way of doing things. Another result of the automation is that some of our library's holdings have been listed in the OCLC Online Union Catalog, and I now process requests for loans as well as our own customers' borrowing requests. But despite the increased activity created by the lending requests, with all the new features in the Passport software—such as constant data records, custom holdings macros, and new search methods, I can still keep up with the demands of interlibrary loan and continue to add and complete other tasks (which in a constantly understaffed public library is a great asset).

Here's a BIG THANKS to the OCLC Online Union Catalog and the people who helped create and manage it. I couldn't have done it without you.

**Janet Seibert**
Florida State University
Tallahassee, FL

I am impressed with the OCLC Online Union Catalog! It greatly assists me in finding bibliographic records for extremely old books, for foreign books, and for microfiche. It is a real time-saver when I find bibliographic records or series authority records, because that means that I don't have to do an original record. I am continually and pleasantly surprised with the number of bibliographic records and authority records that are available to me as a cataloger.

I participated in a special project that dealt with cataloging Asian books online in our library. This project challenged me to retrieve bibliographic records from OCLC. I had a shelf list card to aid me as I searched for these bibliographic records, but I soon realized that numerous Asian titles, authors, and series may differ by only one or two Chinese words. Searching became fun when I realized I could play detective when searching for these Asian books by using searching qualifiers. Though they had helped me beyond my own imagination of their usefulness, sometimes I couldn't find the Asian books by using search qualifiers. I began to explore again, and my mind began ticking like a clock. Hey! Why not use the title phrase index? What do you know, I was loving every minute when I found bibliographic records that I needed.

Now I am working on a project that deals with our manual series authority shelf list cards. Believe me, I consult OCLC immediately to see if OCLC has a series already established. Again, playing detective, I use the search methods that are available to me through OCLC to help me find that particular series. If I don't find that series established in OCLC, I further investigate by searching for other bibliographic records with that series or find a series similar to the one I am working on.

It's exciting to utilize all the possible ways that are available to me for searching for bibliographic records and authority records. Not only can I use OCLC to retrieve bibliographic records and authority records, but I can use it to help verify a call number for a particular book. There are many things that I do with OCLC Online Union Catalog, and it is a pleasure to take advantage of what it offers me as a cataloger.

## Gary K. Shepherd
Southern Illinois University
Carbondale, IL

Few librarians or library workers couldn't give some account of the impact OCLC has had on their work. As a paraprofessional specializing in government documents (boy, that sounds impressive, doesn't it?) I have my own particular "take" on that impact.

In government documents, OCLC is particularly useful for solving classification problems—and those familiar with government documents know that there are a *lot* of problems. The GPO's Superintendent of Documents classification system, affectionately known as Sudoc, is, to put it mildly, somewhat confusing at first. After that, it becomes even more confusing. The multitude of different numbering systems within the Sudoc system makes it difficult, if not impossible, to figure out what the class number of a particular item should be.

More importantly, the class numbers are often changed, duplicate numbers are often assigned to totally different documents issued at different times, and documents are issued with typographical errors on the shipping lists. Combined, these glitches can lead to problems of near nightmarish proportions. In these cases,

OCLC can be a lifesaver; so much so that the lack of an 086 field (which contains the Sudoc number) is enough to cause panic.

Since government documents' titles are often similar or even identical, the scan title feature and the search by government documents number allowed in PRISM come in very handy. Our library computer system does not allow for searches by government document number.

Unfortunately there are problems with our computer system. Often changes in Sudoc number that appear in the OCLC's 086 don't make it into our "ILLINET Online" records. Since the OCLC 086 lists numbers with the most recent number first, it can give us a clue when we have an "IO" record that says one thing, and a piece that has an older (or even a newer) number on it.

In one case an item was issued with one Sudoc number, changed to a second number, changed back to the first number, and then changed again to the second number. The 086 line faithfully recorded these changes, clearing up what would have been a great deal of confusion (except, of course, for our confusion as to why they kept changing it in the first place).

Since we have so many government documents that were issued before the days of computers, a great many of them were entered into the computer catalog by hand. Needless to say, a goodly number were botched in one way or another. Since our cataloging department is too short-handed to retrospectively convert those records, we're stuck with them. At least when glaring errors become evident, we can use OCLC to correct them one at a time.

Recently we received an unexpected present from our administration: they purchased Passport to OCLC for individual employee terminals. Until then, we had been sharing one dedicated terminal with the rest of the social studies department (where we are hidden away) who use it mainly for Interlibrary Loan. This occasionally causes some congestion, though we usually manage to avoid gridlock. With Passport there's no need to wrestle anyone for a free terminal.

The current plan (one is tempted to say plot) to convert as many government documents as possible to electronic format, will mean even more problems that we are going to have to deal with, especially the issue of how these electronic documents will be handled when, a few years down the road, they become obsolete too. My colleagues and I back in government documents are grateful that we will have OCLC to stand by with us to stave off the onslaught of constant change.

**Mary Sidwell**
Bob Jones University
Greenville, SC

In those lazy hazy days of my childhood, my conscientious father used to scratch his head and mutter, "There must be a book about that somewhere," whenever I asked one of those wide-eyed, innocent-child questions that had no handy adult answer. These were questions such as "Why do people get chicken pox?" or "What is a black hole?"

My father, having no reasonable method of either identifying such books or of obtaining them from our trusty county bookmobile and our dear Miss Yarnell, was usually forced to answer either "I don't know," or to use the standard parent line, "Because," to such questions.

That was then, of course, but in the grown-up now-and-now, I find myself muttering, "There must be a book about that somewhere," to the questions of the students and faculty in my academic library. The difference, however, is that I have access to a reasonable, cost-effective method of finding the right information for the right question at the right time. In my little college library, operating on a bookmobile-sized acquisitions budget, instead of answering, "Sorry, we don't have anything" on (plasma physics, early Montana history, etc., etc.), I can search and identify books and journals on OCLC, request some interlibrary loans, and deliver the information to my questioner. This small miracle happens on a daily basis because OCLC has had the vision, the leadership and the cooperativeness to link the holdings of most of the nation's libraries and even some of those beyond our borders. They have also managed to make these holdings approachable for the person of average intelligence, no small feat in the murky land of Technobabble.

Perhaps the first years of the transcontinental railroads evoked similar feelings of appreciation from users making the long trek coast to coast behind the great steam engines, and eventually the same sense of wonder, "How had people ever *managed* before?"

———————————— ℐ ————————————

**Lynn Smeal**
Southwest Texas State University
San Marcos, TX

Me & the OCLC Online Union Catalog...

Who am I, that OCLC should mean something to me? For eight years, I have worked as a library assistant for Southwest Texas State University, at what is now called the Albert B. Alkek Library in San Marcos, Texas. My duties have, of course, changed over these eight years, varying from Stacks Assistant to Reserve and now Serials Assistant, including serving as a Security Attendant for the first six months of my employment. I must admit, until I started working in serials cataloging, OCLC meant nothing to me. OCLC was just another anonymous acronym, and then it turned into something else. It became a tool, and if I learned to use it, OCLC meant job enrichment.

My employers somehow recognized my potential—it is still unclear to me how this happened—but they gave me the opportunity to make the transition from reserve to serials cataloging, introducing me to OCLC, the Online Computer Library Center and the Online Union Catalog. I suppose my skills with computer technology, having had college course work toward a computer science degree, and my few years of experience working at reserve, with all material types from audio-visual to periodical, as well as learning the hierarchy of our library, afforded me my advancement. Because I had yet to knowingly step into the world of OCLC.

In retrospect, as a student, every time I fingered my way through a card catalog or keyed an online catalog system, OCLC sprang into action. Meaning, as OCLC has informed us, that "thousands of libraries" from "63 countries" have cooperated to bring to the world a bibliographic database which is a catalog of

"4,000 years of recorded knowledge in 370 languages." An accomplishment which has taken only 25 years. The achievement is truly astounding. Consider, if only 370 people, each knowing a different language, came into agreement on how to catalog one piece of information; in this world, what communication barriers could not be overcome?

This brings us to what OCLC means to me. I view the Online Union Catalog as a way for people to communicate with each other, by sharing access to "35 million" pieces of recorded information from over "560 million" corners of the world. This level of communication having been achieved, gives hope that even world peace is attainable.

It is most definitely time to take a moment to celebrate, for from 2000 B.C. until now that is all this is: but a moment. Congratulations are due to the 54 Ohio libraries who took the "first steps" that lead OCLC to where it is today, at the forefront of the information highway. Happy 25th anniversary to OCLC and the many participants who have collectively built this "unique global resource" valued by not only scholars and researchers, but every unsuspecting library user and worker.

By continuing to use and support OCLC, we not only help others but help ourselves, to provide the best possible means of communication of knowledge and information transfer to users worldwide, as well as to promote education in all subject areas from A to Z, using a variety of forms of media. Books, recordings, computer files, along with other formats, have all been cataloged. With advancements in technology, only time will tell what is to come. OCLC is truly a collaboration on the grandest of scales, a historical monument whose future is boundaryless.

---

## Deatra Smith
Crawfordsville District Public Library
Crawfordsville, IN

When we got our first OCLC terminal in October, 1982, I knew almost nothing about computers and thought I'd never be able to learn to use one without ruining something. A few lessons and some practice soon let me know that I could actually work with a computer and understand the manuals that were provided. I was assured that I couldn't ruin any records and that any mistake could be fixed eventually.

Our network, via OCLC, keeps us informed of changes and offers classes or special help that we need, but just using the records regularly allows me to become familiar with any changes that are taking place, especially in subject headings. I can find almost any record I need, and there is someone (OCLC, our network and other librarians who use the system) just a phone call away to help me with problems that arise.

Using OCLC is like having a personal assistant since the work goes so quickly. It means that I can sit down with my books and catalogue approximately sixty titles within three hours, have cards within a week and the books ready to use the day after that.

It is fairly easy to add an original record since I can usually find a similar example to use.

Libraries without OCLC are often envious. That makes me appreciate even more that my library chose to participate in the best database there is and that I can do my part by adding our records.

Our patrons are pleased when we can tell them the location of materials that we don't own but that they'd like to use. Other libraries have asked to borrow books I've catalogued even before the cards arrive since our symbol is attached to the record immediately.

Vendors we've talked to concerning their automation systems know that they must be able to use our OCLC records in their system. Most of all, having all of our records on OCLC means that we will be ready for automation.

In 1982 it was hard to imagine needing an online system for cataloguing, but now it's even harder to imagine trying to live without OCLC.

## Tammy Smith
Clark County Public Library
Springfield, OH

Advanced cataloging class was my first experience with the OCLC Online Union Catalog, and what an impact it made! We were assigned to read the PRISM manual and each class member would demonstrate a specific nonbook cataloging method on OCLC. Connecting with other librarians was a privilege given to me by working with OCLC. Since I had studied the PRISM manual and could catalog on a limited mode, directors at Wittenberg and Urbana Universities allowed me to use their OCLC workstations to complete my homework assignments. The library I was working in had no access to OCLC at that time, and my only other option was to travel to the school lab, an hour trip each way. OCLC let me contact other librarians and to experience librarianship in the real world.

"How do you live without OCLC?" was a comment I often heard at school and at conferences. A simple reference question that could easily be answered using OCLC could take hours of searching Cumulative Book Index. When I took an online reference class at OCLC, I asked my instructor how I might convince our library to connect to OCLC. With contact by a salesperson from OCLC and a knowledgeable technical services supervisor, we are now connected to OCLC. Satisfaction in answering questions, finding books nobody has ever heard of, and satisfaction in cataloging are now an everyday occurrence. Since my advanced cataloging class, I am comfortable using OCLC for reference and cataloging. It is a special feeling when I get a hit for a book for which someone tells me they have been searching for years. Or, if I am having trouble cataloging a book, I can get one or more hits and see what other catalogers have done with that item.

Customer satisfaction is my main goal in librarianship, and through the use of OCLC, I see it more and more. When we can get an elusive book for someone quickly, they are thrilled and we are the recipients of their satisfaction. My supervisor said to me once, "If it's out there, I'll find it." She has this confidence because she has used OCLC for years and has obtained continual satisfaction.

Now catalogers and reference librarians at our library are saying, "How did we ever live without OCLC?" We feel more connected to other librarians, catalog more quickly and confidently, and see satisfied customers every day! Connections, personal satisfaction and customer satisfaction is what the OCLC Online Union Catalog means to me.

## Paul G. Smithson
Kalamazoo College
Kalamazoo, MI

EMPOWERMENT! OCLC Online Union Catalog means EMPOWERMENT! for library staff and patrons.

In that magical moment seventeen years ago when an OCLC terminal was first installed, we were EMPOWERED with cataloging shared among all members. Suddenly, catalog cards could be ordered at the push of a button—cards which arrived ready to be filed! No more photocopying, typing, proofing, erasing, correcting card sets. EMPOWERMENT!

The OCLC Online Union Catalog EMPOWERED us and other OCLC members with information of other institutions' collections. Gone was the guessing as to who might own a needed text. No longer was it necessary to direct requests only to the research libraries in the hope that they might own (and loan) a title. We were EMPOWERED with the ability to find obscure titles. One faculty member enthused, "OCLC's Online Union Catalog eliminates any disadvantage of not being at a research institution. This is fantastic!" A title for which he had been searching had just been put into his hands—a title located and borrowed through the OCLC Online Union Catalog. At the same time, the rest of the world could now tell which titles were available in our collection. Within the first year of membership, we became a net lender. Today, OCLC interlibrary loan activities, occurring at the rate of almost one million a month, EMPOWER students and faculty doing research by speeding transactions, and by reducing or eliminating delivery uncertainties. EMPOWERMENT!

The OCLC Online Union Catalog's rich resources EMPOWERED the library to make a smooth transition to local automated services. Technical Services staff undertook the special project of creating the core bibliographic file for the online catalog through the OCLC Online Union Catalog. Over 200,000 titles were converted to electronic form, one card at a time, while simultaneously identifying to the rest of the world titles available at Kalamazoo College. EMPOWERMENT!

The online catalog's union lists of serials EMPOWERS us by indicating not only who owns a needed title, but by revealing the specific volumes held by each participant.

FirstSearch has further EMPOWERED patrons by opening up the resources of the online union catalog without requiring staff intervention, and with search strategies not otherwise available.

One need experience only a minor interruption in OCLC service to appreciate our dependence on the online union catalog. Whenever it is unavailable, work grinds to a halt as we face, time and time again, a need to search the database. It was a grim picture when, years ago, a backhoe operator severed the lines connecting half the country to OCLC, forcing hundreds of us to face life without OCLC for days on end.

In 25 short years, OCLC has grown from a dream and an experiment in inter-institutional cooperation as the Ohio College Library Center to become the largest bibliographic database of its kind in the world. The OCLC network spans the globe and the entire range of mankind's knowledge. The beauty of all this, for librarians and for all our constituencies, is information EMPOWERMENT!

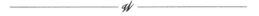

### Jody Snyder
Hayward Public Library
Hayward, CA

Having the OCLC Online Union Catalog means that our patrons will never have to feel that they live in a "small town," even though they choose to. The world is now open to them, and the opportunities for all manner of materials and experiences are there, as though they resided in a metropolis.

It is heartening to know that, in these days of budget cuts and library closures, there is still a way for people to obtain needed materials, even if their own library cannot afford it. With a tool like the OCLC Online Union Catalog, no one need feel like a "second-class citizen" with an inferior library, or "intellectually deprived" by the constraints of regional resources. One's vistas may be widened and their curiosity sated by OCLC's miles of library shelves.

### Dania Vergez Soriano
Miami–Dade Community College
Miami, FL

In the early 1980s, I worked in different libraries—all of them small—except for Universidad Central del Este in the Dominican Republic. In 1988, when I was attending my last semester in business management, I decided to work in this new field and discontinue my position as library technician.

In 1992, I emigrated to this great country and eventually I returned to work in libraries. It was a great change for me. In the Dominican Republic, we used to do everything manually, and here routine tasks are performed by computers.

For me, the most difficult and tedious work is cataloging. But having direct access to *OCLC* has made everything easier, faster and simpler. The records have all the information about a particular library resource, no matter what country it is from. Since *OCLC* supplies its services internationally, it provides the different cataloging and classification systems those countries use. Therefore, all that is required is to search the appropriate record, and export it to our statewide database, LINCC, and it is as quick as that: the item has been cataloged in the twinkling of an eye, without wasting time searching the appropriate subject headings or entering the Dewey labyrinth.

For me this is truly amazing, maybe because I've not been using it for a long time. In the Dominican Republic, I remember how happy I was any time I cataloged a book that had the Library of Congress in-Publication Data: that saved me a half-hour or more of my time. And now I have that and much more at the reach of my fingers, thanks to *OCLC*.

I cannot wait for the Dominican Republic to obtain the economical resources for integrating *OCLC* services. I will be very proud when the Dominican Republic's flag appears in the lobby of *OCLC* headquarters as a proof of our efforts for modernizing and internationalizing education. Meanwhile, thanks, *OCLC*, for being the link that connects over 23,000 libraries in 63 countries around the world, and for saving valuable time for the staff and patrons of those libraries.

## Mary Stanco
Cleveland State University
Cleveland, OH

OCLC: The key to my career...

OCLC has been, and is, one of the most valuable resources in my professional education and development. In 1992, as a library science graduate student, I discovered that the key to my future was to be proficient in searching OCLC. The rewards of knowing how to effectively search opened the door to my career in technical services.

Once I could master searching OCLC, I was soon delighted with the ability to contribute full cataloging records to a bibliographic utility that will be accessed by millions of users. My world as a catalog librarian expands as I feel a responsibility in being able to contribute records that will be accessed by OCLC users who may consider my record worthwhile for their online database, or to place a request from my library through interlibrary loan. With my record exported and edited into another library's online database, more users will use it to search by subject or assist in their access of materials through the dynamic world of the Internet. It was a rite of passage into the collaborative efforts of catalogers to contribute my first original cataloging record and check it weeks later to discover that more library holding symbols had been added. It is an induction into a private club where skill in searching online and cataloging knowledge of AACR2 and MARC formats is the key to being considered a contributor to the success of OCLC.

OCLC has given me the environment to use my knowledge of AACR2 and MARC tags and delimiters, which is the framework I use to make accessible and searchable the records that I select and create for my library's OPAC. The concept of using a CIP or pre-published bibliographic record is not only beneficial for copy cataloging, but allows libraries to consider new ways to streamline and run more effectively online. This could only be done through the coordination of OCLC, Library of Congress and other contributing bodies, along with a catalog librarian's understanding of the matrix of rules and standards needed to allow publishers and libraries to share resources.

OCLC is one of the essential professional development resources that I use in order to succeed in my field. I consider OCLC to be a major provider of the best possible services and products for libraries. The exciting projects that OCLC supports, such as cataloging the Internet, answers the concerns of catalogers establishing standards for new interfaces such as the World Wide Web.

OCLC has supported the continuing education of catalogers through regional library networks. The history of OCLC and its dedication to finding ways to renovate MARC format as it adapts to new electronic storage and retrieval systems, moves technical services into this dynamic information age. There is so much more that OCLC offers in services and products that I have yet to encounter, and I hope OCLC continues to set trends for libraries as it has for the past 25 years.

------------------------------ *❧* ------------------------------

### Andrew M. Stauffer
University of Virginia
Charlottesville, VA

Cataloging greatness…

Now that the virtues of networked information resources have become so apparent to everyone, we turn around and realize that the OCLC Online Union Catalog has been there all along. For 25 years, the OCLC Online Union Catalog has served as a definitive example of institutional cooperation combining with computer technology to produce powerful research tools. OCLC editors, bibliographers, and programmers have set the standard for such tools, by ensuring the accurate records, logical organization, and easy accessibility that have earned our appreciation and respect. For librarians, researchers, and teachers, the OCLC Online Union Catalog has become a favorite resource, at once indispensable and enjoyable to use.

I'm speaking from experience. As a graduate student of English Literature and a part-time reference assistant in our main library, I wear these various hats from day to day. I use OCLC when answering a patron's reference questions, when conducting my own research, and when working with my undergraduate students. For each of these activities, I typically want to draw on one of the OCLC Online Union Catalog's specific strengths.

When I use OCLC at the reference desk, I am usually looking for a specific piece of accurate information: where is the nearest copy of a book located? Who published a given title and when? In these cases, OCLC's rapid and reliable ability to fetch the desired bit of data is invaluable. I never know what I'll be looking for next, and the Online Catalog always responds with agility.

As a researcher, I more often turn to OCLC for its comprehensiveness, in order to survey records for all editions of a given work, or to discover what books were issued by a publisher in a particular year. Without OCLC, these research tasks would either undo me, or simply go undone.

Finally, as a teacher, I draw upon a third aspect of the Online Catalog: its ability to evoke a sense of bibliographical "history" for my students. Too often, I feel that my undergraduates have a limited conception of the past, and of the books that contain records of it. So I turn them loose on OCLC, asking them to produce extensive bibliographies of literary or historical works. They come back, eyes opened by the astonishing wealth of information in the Catalog, with a better awareness of the depth and breadth of the written past.

In this sense, for all of its hypnotic shimmer, the flat computer screen that presents the OCLC Online Union Catalog belies the enormous spaces behind it.

Perform a search on OCLC, and you are drawing on the largest accumulation of bibliographical knowledge in the world. You range through thousands of quiet, dusty bookshelves at superhuman speed, thumbing through millions of catalog cards in seconds, visiting libraries in 64 countries around the world—and all of this while seated before that smoothly glowing screen. For a librarian, a researcher, and a teacher (and his students), that experience has been, for 25 years now, a great cause for celebration.

## Stephanie Stavinsky
Massachusetts Institute of Technology
Cambridge, MA

Universal bibliographic control and cooperation…

When I was a child spending hours in the children's department of Haddonfield Public Library, I had no concept of cataloging or of cooperation among libraries. But there, I learned how to use a card catalog and to find the information I needed. I decided I wanted to be a librarian when I was eleven. I made my own library on the porch of my house, cataloging and labeling each volume and fining those who dared to dog-ear and doodle on pages. I interviewed the town library's head of reference and envied him selecting books and answering questions. I still had no real idea about the framework necessary to hold these things together: bibliographic control.

As my library career progressed through college work-study jobs in microforms/current periodicals and special collections, I gained a vague understanding of the backbone supporting the card catalog and eventually the OPAC. But it wasn't until my first "real" library job doing serials checking that I discovered the need for bibliographic utilities. As my work evolved and I began dealing with the complexities of government documents, the efforts of catalogers around the world made my job easier. When I held only one piece of a puzzle, others often held the surrounding pieces. Today, as a CONSER copy cataloger working on OCLC, I am adding my knowledge to the cumulative efforts of others worldwide. All of the institutions who use and maintain records on OCLC contribute to the goal of universal bibliographic control.

Advances in technology are increasing the speed with which information is produced and made available; and new formats of information delivery are challenging all libraries. Yet the fundamental mission of all libraries—providing access—has not changed. In order to provide access to all materials, libraries must continue to cooperate in a global sense. For twenty-five years, OCLC has been a functional and inspirational forum for this cooperation. With thousands of libraries in sixty-three countries participating, the goal of providing universal bibliographic control and access is more of a reality now than ever before.

What will the next twenty-five years of OCLC bring? Further cooperative efforts by even more libraries. Attempts at cataloging new types of information resources and making them available in innovative ways. Continued quality control of the world's largest bibliographic database. And, in turn, the chance for young users in small town libraries to discover a wealth of knowledge.

## Douglas M. Stehle
Pittsburg State University
Pittsburg, KS

One can appreciate the hermeneutic subtlety of Nietzsche's perspectivism when confronted with a topic such as the meaning of the OCLC database. There are so many *me's* that the question itself seems to invite randomness or instability. Surely we can find a general sense of the meaning of OCLC above the hum of personal stories. Critical theory, however, has given little support lately to notions of essence or the metanarratives that produce them. Given the postmodern picture, one is apt to ignore meaning altogether and concentrate on these *me's* and partake in the politics of identity. This political vision offers us endless alternative voices representing various possible vantage points, none of which possess access to an ultimate ground from which to propose the authority of their position over the others. Thus power constructs knowledge in the humid night of epistemic relativity. Can OCLC be seen as part of this postmodern quagmire? OCLC as a prominent actor in this political situation and a cultural tool that serves Foucault's world of knowledge/power? A silly question begs a silly answer!

OCLC, through its delivery of the largest bibliographic list, serves both modernity's logic of unity and, to the degree of its success in this project, becomes an epiphany in the theater of textual absurdity via postmodern logic. Far from being a database of knowledge, the OCLC database stands as the best empirical proof of the claim that all is text, just text, marks and noises with no hidden intention or innate wisdom evident to the general logos we all once shared. *A huge bibliographic listing of text which conveys little significance beyond its own internal linguistic practice of description and passing reference to the locations of ever expanding textual units* sums up a vision of OCLC that is not so much a vantage point from within librarianship but is instead a move to see OCLC as a part of the larger culture and as a player in the production of knowledge.

OCLC, for all its good intentions, may look fairly pathetic in another hundred years given the ever escalating rate of publication and subsequent inclusion in the database of text revealed by the statistics. Possibly users are rushing to the Internet and are over enthused about the World Wide Web precisely because it is not a bibliographic listing of text that conveys only that, just text. OCLC is the shimmering example of our commitment to information in and of itself. Such a commitment, as it unfolds in this final decade of the twentieth century, may be our undoing.

**Gordon Stein**
Center for Inquiry
Amherst, NY

From the perspective of a reference librarian and bibliographer, the OCLC Online Union Catalog means a lot to me. It means that I now have a quick and accurate way to determine what the correct citation to a book is, or to fill in that missing date of publication, place of publication or publisher for a complete citation. It means that I can quickly tell a patron what the correct title (or author) is of the item for which he or she is searching. It means that I can tell patrons which nearby library (if any) has the item they want, if our library doesn't have it. It also means that I can tell the patron to use interlibrary loan when no nearby library has the item wanted.

But the OCLC Online Union Catalog has many uses for me that go beyond anything that the vast majority of patrons would need. The Catalog allows me to get the Library of Congress call number for a particular item that our library does not have. I can then go to a nearby, much larger, library, even if it doesn't have the item I want, and do a "serendipitous" search among other items on that exact subject. The number of times that this tactic has paid off is beyond easy counting. The Catalog has allowed me to compile an instant bibliography on a subject by using the "fin su" command. The use of "fin ti" has allowed me to find that congress, symposium or conference item, when nearly every word in the title was "generic."

When dealing with the periodical literature, the OCLC Union Catalog has its limits and yet its uses. While the titles of individual articles or their authors' names are not accessible in this system, one can still find out which libraries have which journals, and even (in the interlibrary loan mode) which volumes each library has. The birth dates of obscure authors can be found, their birth names identified; their pseudonyms revealed. Foreign language translations (or English versions of foreign language books) can be identified. It is easy to tell whether volume 2 of a supposed 2-volume book ever was published (many times it wasn't). I am certain that there are still more tricks to be learned by me that will give me new uses for the OCLC Online Union Catalog. I look forward to learning them.

**Michael Steinmacher**
Jewish Hospital
Louisville, KY

When considering the question "What the OCLC Online Union Catalog Means To Me," I immediately realize that the system plays an integral role in the life of our library. In my position as coordinator of interlibrary loan, I find myself consulting the massive database on an almost hourly basis. Whether it is to request a particular item, confirm a serial or book title, or perform a search for material, I find the thorough OCLC Catalog to be an invaluable tool.

As someone who spends the majority of his day processing patron requests for materials, I find great comfort in having OCLC as a resource. Oftentimes, I am presented with an incomplete or incorrect citation, which reduces my effectiveness. With OCLC, I have an expansive network at my disposal. The many ways of searching OCLC make it quite likely that I will locate the item in question in a prompt and expedient way. The different ways of searching OCLC are also a great strength of the database, as the variety of search forms allows me to be sure that I can find the appropriate item.

The OCLC database's expansive range also makes it vital in locating items or confirming references. As someone who works with the physician in a hands-on capacity, I find it reassuring that I can be confident that I can meet their needs, no matter how esoteric the request. Many of the physicians regard me as a magician, as they think I can pull obscure books and serial articles out of thin air. What few realize is that the "magic" behind me is OCLC. Without it, I would be severely limited in my effectiveness and the services which I provide.

OCLC is by far my favorite database. As a library that also uses the National Library of Medicine's MEDLINE database, I find myself shying away from the NLM system because it is much more limited in terms of resources and scope. As NLM's identified references are limited to 1966, I seldom use their system other than to request mundane, commonplace items. In actuality, I could do without that system entirely, as the breadth of material available through the OCLC catalog makes other databases pale in comparison.

I truly enjoy working in libraries and OCLC has made my life a lot easier. The depth of the Online Union Catalog's holdings has not only proven to be a gold mine of resources to both me and my patrons, but a database with which I feel both comfortable and confident.

**Ion Stoica**
The Central University Library
Bucharest, Romania

We never know how many roles we actually play in our lives. Often, with some surprise, we only discover ourselves actors of the most varied situations, sometimes contradictory, called up by the deep and multifarious senses of life.

Thinking of the OCLC Online Union Catalog as a screen play—and without doubt it is a scenario, very special and complex, but however a scenario—I asked myself many times what role I could act on this great stage of information movement in the contemporary world. And I discovered with amazement not only that the scenario contains all the possible professional roles, but that I was able to play them all with the same dedication.

Returning to the unforgettable empire of student-days memories, I played the role of the young man I used to be, thirsty of knowledge, ready to run with every thought through the thirty-five million records of the treasure from thousands of libraries in sixty-three countries as if they would have been gathered in a magical mirror just for me.

Wearing the everyday clothes of a large-library user, I stated my case on the issue out of loneliness. Then, I have convinced myself and the others that I, the unknown, suddenly found myself in the middle of a circle with its vectors orientated in my direction, bringing with them the 360 degrees of the world voices which surrounded me.

With the golden gown of a specialist teacher called to teach others the secrets of knowledge, I played the role of that one who, with great confidence, found milestones in a universe of messages, fuller now than ever before of form and color.

Then I remembered that, first and foremost, I am the most skillful of the illusionists, the librarian—Cicero, the necessary guide in a world of shadows and light, who holds in his hand the miraculous wand which can open the doors to reveal the treasure named OCLC Online Union Catalog.

I played all roles with a great passion. The spectators were overjoyed, awarding me with great applause. And, as at every premiere, an enlightened public cried, "Author! Author!" I raised the curtain, inviting up on the stage the maestro, in his prime youth, at twenty-five: OCLC, Dublin, Ohio, United States of America.

With the modesty of all great creators, the maestro came close to me and with a superb wide gesture, reached up to the skyways, he said, "Your applause is not only for me, but for those thousands of librarians who have worked alongside me."

The OCLC Online Union Catalogue is a monument on the grandest scale of any collective work yet created.

## Mark Stover
Phillips Graduate Institute
Encino, CA

When I think of the OCLC Online Union Catalog, I immediately think of the four A's that are fundamental to my work.

First, I think of "authentic." The OCLC Online Union Catalog provides me with a measure of authenticity or legitimacy that I cannot find anywhere else. When I search the OCLC Online Union Catalog I can be sure that the results of my search will contain accurate and trustworthy bibliographical information. I never have to worry that the citations will in any way be inaccurate or corrupt.

Second, I think of "authoritative." The subject headings and author files in the OCLC Online Union Catalog carry with them the combined expertise of thousands of catalogers throughout the world. These headings perform two primary tasks. They provide a richness of access to the many students, researchers, and scholars who search this database each day. Simply put, these headings allow searchers to find what they are looking for. They also make it possible for small and less-specialized libraries to utilize the work of others when cataloging and classifying esoteric or more remote materials. The subject and author headings of the OCLC Online Union Catalog are authoritative in every sense of the word: strong, reliable, well-researched, and well-maintained.

Third, I think of "all-encompassing." The broad scope of the OCLC Online Union Catalog is sometimes difficult to fathom. It is a huge database, filled with books and other media in many different languages and covering many centuries of recorded knowledge. The vast size of the Catalog makes it all the more likely that the searcher's quest for information will be rewarded. In my case, the OCLC Catalog has helped me on numerous occasions track down difficult citations that I could not find anywhere else.

Fourth, I think of "available." The OCLC Online Union Catalog is not just a sterile compendium of data, but a living organism that attaches meaning to each catalog record by informing the user where the material can be found. The library holdings symbols that are attached to each record have given me direction and guidance when I needed to find an actual location of a bibliographic entity.

The OCLC Online Union Catalog is a magnificent structure, built over many years by diligent and capable librarians. It will stand for years to come as a monument to cooperation, precision, and hard work. I am proud to be a contributor to and user of this great database.

## Naomi Curtis Sturtevant
Smith College
Northampton, MA

I love books and I love people—in that order. So it follows that I also love OCLC. Every day when I come to work, turn on the 546 Quantum Fireball and log on to OCLC, I am in love.

OCLC never ceases to amaze and delight me. Searching for the material requested by our interlibrary loan patrons is a joy and never-ending pleasure because of the Online Computer Library Catalog. The OCLC bibliographic database contains more than 35 million records and more than 560 million location listings. And it grows every day. Ever since I began working in the interlibrary loan section in the Neilson Library at Smith College, I have looked forward to each day of work. My supervisor, Victoria Hart, showed me how to use basic searches and then gradually introduced me to another new technique as soon as I became comfortable with the previous one. She advised me to follow a set sequence of searches until I found exactly what the patron needed.

Sometimes the patron is not exactly sure what it is they are looking for, because they have only heard about the material from another colleague's friend of a friend. This is fun on OCLC. I find the material even when the patron has written the wrong author and title on the request card. Can you believe it? OCLC has it all. I can look for the material using only the date and place of publication. I learn new things about all kinds of published material with each search. I love OCLC.

One of our patrons said that our interlibrary loan section is the best on the east coast, which is probably a slight exaggeration but with the capabilities of OCLC at our command, he could be right. OCLC makes it possible for us to find needles in haystacks. It was not surprising to me to learn that it is the most frequently consulted database in higher education.

Because of my love for books, I delight in the enormous collection of authors and titles familiar to me that pop up on the screen. I am learning all the time from my co-coordinator, Christina Ryan, just how to logically proceed with the searches. She helps me by using her considerable talents to make connections between the dates when certain subjects would have been likely to have been published, which narrows the number of searches required. OCLC does the rest.

The wealth of information available through OCLC boggles the mind. The capabilities for creative use of this huge treasure-trove of information on publications of all kinds delights me. And OCLC makes me look good, too. I just love to be able to find what the patron is looking for so they will be pleased, too. With a few keystrokes, "custom holdings" supplies locations. I hit the F12 key to produce the request and in a few days the requested material arrives at Smith. I just love OCLC.

## Qin Tang

Loyola University of Chicago
Chicago, IL

When I came to the United States in 1991, My English was so poor that I could not understand what other people were saying and could not express what I wanted to say in English. I spent my first two years at home. For me, it was like a life of the deaf and the dumb.

Due to my strong desire to learn, to master the English language and to know this new country, I started to go to the Library School at the University of Wisconsin—Madison, first as a special student. For me there was no better place in the world than the library that could lead me to the knowledge and information I needed to better survive in this new world. Studying library science would give me the skills and abilities to learn how to learn on my own and how to find my way around in this information world. I knew I could benefit from it all my life long. Besides, I liked the idea of working in the library and dealing with people and books every day. Yet I had never heard about OCLC when I entered the library school.

I still remember the first time I was introduced to the OCLC Online Union Catalog. How amazed and unbelievable I felt! I did not know that cataloging, which many people said was too technical and boring, could also be so interesting. The usefulness of OCLC was at first hard to image for me.

After I learned how to use OCLC, the first book I wanted to search was the book that included an article of mine: *Fremd Unter Deutschen: Auslandische Studenten Berichten*. What was more exciting than to find out if there were any libraries in the United States that had this book published in a foreign country? To my surprise, the book was right there where I was, in the University of Wisconsin—Madison Memorial Library. Before I knew OCLC, I never came to the idea of searching this book in the university's own online system.

The power and magic of OCLC overwhelmed me. I immediately thought of my landlord in Germany who was a sociology professor and published many books during his more than 30-year teaching career. When I asked him once how many books he had published, he said he did not keep track of it. So I did a search under his name, Helmut Klages, and got more than forty entries. Later, I sent him the printed list of his publications and he was very happy. His wife told me that he took the list to his office and showed it to his colleagues who were all amazed. I also told my favorite high school English teacher in China that if he needed any books, please let me know, that I might help him better than anyone else. In my mind OCLC Online Union Catalog is truly an international bibliographic database.

Because of OCLC, I became interested in cataloging. So I decided to work as a cataloger before I graduated. That is what I have been doing since my graduation from the library school in December 1994. I am really proud of my profession and happy that I live in this exciting world and time. OCLC makes my life, both professional and personal, richer and more interesting. Every time I log on to OCLC, I feel like entering a wonderland and embarking on a library journey. One never knows what to expect, and that's exciting!

———————————— *ql* ————————————

## Susan A. Tennis
Urban Institute
Burke, VA

(Part 1)

> Original information highway
> Connection to libraries around the country and the world
>     for the (stop words)
> Literary access
>     of the (stop word)
> Community, to which we all belong.

(Part 2)

When I first met OCLC, I was very daunted. Computers were not user-friendly and I was just a little wet behind the ears. In 1985, my first experience with OCLC was sitting at a terminal at a reference desk and trying to figure out how to sign on. After thirty minutes, I finally did (with the help of a reference librarian). Thirty minutes later, I was still trying to figure out the commands...was that display? or F4 or scan? or Shift + F9 or...

As my exposure to OCLC changed from student to library technician, it too has changed.

Just last January, I sat down to my first session of FirstSearch, and within thirty minutes had accessed several hundred journals to order an article needed for a law firm. This January, I also had the pleasure of learning how to catalog new materials and re-catalog old materials for a recon project. I found that OCLC has become a less intimidating conduit to materials.

OCLC is a helper and teacher in this rapidly growing technology. At times, this technology as a whole seems to threaten to overwhelm us with the information possibilities. Yet the original vision of OCLC has become a reality. And as I become more comfortable with OCLC, I find I become more comfortable with the Library of Today. Tomorrow is another day...

———————————— *ql* ————————————

## Cid Tenpas
Riverside Community College District
Riverside, CA

CONNECTIVITY...

The warm, clean desert air rushes over us as we travel the freeway in our rented convertible. Our faces and arms have been slathered with sunscreen. We're wearing wide-brimmed hats and sunglasses. We're on our way to Carlsbad Caverns in New Mexico.

My traveling companions are Ben, my teenage son, and his sister, Hannah, a pre-teen. It is Spring vacation and school is out. Papa, unable to escape from the work world, has been left behind. But this road trip could not be denied. With no small amount of nostalgia, I know that the time is soon approaching when family outings, such as this, will become rare. The differences between our generations are starting to appear. Mom isn't quite so funny, not quite so cool, anymore. We don't share opinions, likes and dislikes, quite as much, as before.

As we travel, we listen to the radio. We share some of the same tastes in music. We all like classical, we all disdain country/western. Everything else is arguable. A song is playing on the radio. I like it. I turn up the volume. The basic premise of the lyrics is that you can't judge people by their appearance. "How nice," I think, "a song with a decent message." My son, a budding trombone player, is impressed by the awesome trombone solo. My daughter likes the humorous lyrics. For the rest of the song, and for the rest of the trip, we are connecting.

Connectivity—this is what the OCLC Online Union Catalog means to me. As usually happens, when "our song" completed, we received no clue to the name of the performers or the title of the song. No problem. When I returned to work, I made use of FirstSearch, accessing WorldCat (which is, of course, the OCLC Online Union Catalog). I searched for the key words from the main refrain of the song ("judge," "man," and "hair") in the contents field. I found the bibliographic record for the CD entitled "Skafunkrastapunk" by a group named "Skankin' Pickle." I bought that CD, and every time one of my children asks to borrow it from me—our connection is affirmed, once again.

Connectivity—the ability to access the world's largest bibliographic database using a multitude of methods—the World Wide Web, the Internet, direct line, etc.

Connectivity—the ability to find information on just about any subject. How did I find out whether or not Carlsbad Caverns would be of interest to all three of us? An easy search of WorldCat produced more than enough connections to materials on that subject—as well as telling me where those items were located.

The OCLC Online Union Catalog connects people to information. This information connects people to other people, or to society, or to their own inner selves. It's all about connectivity.

**Ian S. Thomas**
University of Georgia Science Library
Athens, GA

OCLC: A vital fixture in the Information Age...

We are living in the Information Age. Every day, humans are bombarded with countless bits and bytes of data from a vast array of sources. The content, medium, and sheer volume of this data flow is both overwhelming and bewildering. It shouldn't be. Most of this data is of only limited use to society at large or is used only by an extremely small segment of society—the best example of this being a web page devoted entirely to providing the world with a new light bulb joke every

10 seconds. The challenge for both organizations on the cutting edge of the information revolution and the users being sliced-and-diced by this self-same edge, is to create a way of cutting through this information "static." Only then can we effectively utilize the data resources currently at our disposal. OCLC is an industry leader in this regard.

The best example of OCLC's prominence in this area is its contribution to the Galileo project. The Galileo project is an ambitious program designed to organize two of the "noisiest" parts of the information field: periodicals and the many databases designed to catalog them. When the University System of Georgia decided to create a research resource on the World Wide Web, it wanted a database that was both extensive in scope and user-friendly. Only then would the stated goal of providing the general population of the University System with easy access to relevant bibliographic information be met. OCLC, with its FirstSearch databases, helped Georgia reach and even exceed this goal. Now not only do students, staff and faculty have easy access to data sources, but there are several databases which have the full article text included in the citation! If the article text isn't in the database and that particular journal isn't held by the patron's library, they have the option of ordering fax copies of these articles directly from the computer to a fax machine of their choice. Billing is also handled online via account numbers or by credit card. This is a major advance in the interlibrary loan process.

Not only did OCLC help begin the Information Age by its creation of the most extensive online database of books, serials and other publications, but it continues to transform the information field by projects such as Galileo. OCLC is making knowledge more accessible to the public by speeding up and simplifying the process by which this information is retrieved; therefore it continues to be an integral part of our modern, information-driven society.

## Thomas A. Thompson
University of Dayton
Dayton, OH

Before the advent of the OCLC Online Union Catalog, knowing who had what (that is, which libraries had specific titles) was largely dependent on intuition and individual contacts. When the Marian Library of the University of Dayton was inaugurated in October 1943, a nationally prominent librarian, Colman F. Farrell (a founder of the Catholic Library Association) suggested that the new library establish "a union catalog of Marian literature to be found in all the libraries of North America." The project's purpose was to be able to "tell inquirers the library nearest to them which contains the work they are seeking." (Remember these were the days before interlibrary loan.)

The suggestion was accepted, and the part-time director of the library, along with many volunteers, worked on the union catalog for the next five years. The library's newsletters and publications described the development of the project. First, letters were sent to book publishers and leading libraries across the country asking for lists of their Marian works. Harvard, Notre Dame and Catholic University were among those responding to this request. In April 1945, the project's director announced that "a milestone" in the library's history had been reached with the publication of the first booklist of 2,600 titles. (A supplement issued in December of that year increased the number to 4,421.)

Using these lists in which each book was given a number, volunteers were to check the books available at local libraries. College students and women religious enthusiastically examined the holdings of their local libraries. (The School Sisters of Notre Dame under the leadership of Sister M. Gerard Majella, SSND, sent in record cards for 116 different libraries in Illinois, Indiana, Michigan and Wisconsin.) Over 1,100 libraries were examined, and the library holdings card, containing the number of the title from the Marian Library booklist, were returned to the project director. The next step was to add the holding library's code name to the book's author card.

In 1949, a second booklist was published, this one containing 10,539 titles. Some were surprised that so many books had been discovered. This second booklist was not intended as bibliography in itself (or the end of the project) but a tool "to check other libraries and to discover new titles with a minimum of effort." However, the effort to examine the holdings of new libraries from the expanded booklist and to update the information of the 1,100 libraries which had already been investigated proved too much for a volunteer staff. With the change of the project's director, the project was discontinued.

The Marian Library's union catalog of Marian literature in the 1940s was a response to a great need of establishing a complete bibliography on a specific subject and of letting people know where books could be found. The individuals involved brought much energy and dedication to the project, but, without an automated database and a method for updating the information, the project proved impossible to maintain. So I am grateful for the OCLC Online Union Catalog, which is a current and ever-expanding resource for compiling bibliographies and for making interlibrary loan an everyday possibility.

**Teresa Thurman**
Southwestern College
Winfield, KS

Leveling the playing field...

What happens when you are a librarian at a small college with a limited science reference collection and the science faculty assigns students in-depth research papers? Energetic and anxious, the students trickle in one by one and ask for information pertaining to Euglenidae, Heteroptera fossils, or microbial biomass lipids. Since our library does not have the vast resources of a university, I guide them to the OCLC Online Union Catalog, where they can find the information they are seeking. Students are then pleased and reassured to realize that they can find data on their respective topics.

Not only do they find the materials they need, they can also check to see where these resources are located. If they need the materials immediately, they can usually drive to a large city fifty miles away and retrieve the resources. Another option offered by our library, and more commonly used, is interlibrary loan. Our interlibrary loan librarian also uses the OCLC Online Union Catalog to find the requested materials.

"The playing field is leveled," stated one of the chemistry professors the other day in the library, as she searched the OCLC Catalog for data. She said that in the past, she would have to drive for at least an hour and spend most of the day searching and retrieving the needed information. She said this trip was necessary in order to obtain the resources she needed for most of the upper level chemistry classes, especially biochemistry and molecular biology. However, this is no longer the case. She can now, with one-stop searching in our library, retrieve the materials she needs for classes.

Consequently, what the OCLC Online Union Catalog means to me is that our students and faculty are successful in finding and obtaining the materials they need easily and conveniently, no matter how scientific or unique the resources are that they are requesting. Most important of all is the leveling of equal access to materials. No longer do libraries have to be humongous in order to satisfy all the requests of the patrons. The smaller libraries are now able to participate and be successful players on the OCLC Online Union Catalog field.

——————————— ⚹ ———————————

**Roger Tol**
Royal Institute of Linguistics & Anthropology
Leiden, The Netherlands

OCLC
or
**not to be**

——————————— ⚹ ———————————

**Anne C. Tomlin**
Auburn Memorial Hospital
Auburn, NY

From its staggeringly successful growth from small academic library consortium to its development into the world's foremost bibliographic database, the OCLC Online Union Catalog daily affects the work librarians do. So, what does the OCLC Online Union Catalog mean to me? It means:

**Sharing.** Gone are the days when a single library or small regional collection of books and magazines was enough to satisfy the demands of patrons. Gone also are the days of thumbing through paper union lists or scrolling through microforms hunting for a suitable lender. And, happily, gone are the days of shrugging regrets at being unable to fill a request. With thousands of member libraries around the world and millions of holdings in all formats—book, journal, audiovisual, microform, software—using OCLC means never having to say, "I'm sorry."

**Efficiency.** The OCLC Online Union Catalog may not be faster than a speeding bullet, but it's super for quick confirmations of holdings, lender identification and interlibrary loan policies. It offers maximum results for minimal effort.

**Reliability.** When you search the OCLC Online Union Catalog, you can be assured of finding accurate, authoritative information. I use it with confidence to verify authors, titles, publishers, editions, and other bibliographic data that may be difficult to find elsewhere.

**Value.** The low cost of accessing the OCLC Online Union Catalog is a definite plus in these lean-and-mean days of bottom line budgeting. Time truly is money, and with so many libraries understaffed, the OCLC Online Union Catalog makes it easier for those of us who wear more hats than the many-headed Hydra to find what we need quickly and efficiently.

**Immediacy.** Whatever your schedule, the OCLC Online Union Catalog is there, ready when you are, no muss, no fuss, no frustrating downtime. Its holdings are current, and because it's online, your interlibrary loan requests are routed instantaneously. There's no more waiting for snail mail or telephone requests.

**Courtesy.** The OCLC Online Union Catalog offers unparalleled service in its customer support personnel providing librarians around the world with prompt, knowledgeable assistance. If technology is the soul of the system, these folks are its heart.

**Ease of Use.** Even the computer-phobic among us can use the OCLC Online Union Catalog with a minimum of anxiety. The users' manual is clear, revised as needed, and devoid of unnecessary techno-babble. And they're working hard to add features which will make using the OCLC Online Union Catalog even easier, while expanding its capabilities further.

So, what does using OCLC's Online Union Catalog mean to me? It means **service**, a dependable, cost-effective way of broadening an individual library's resources far beyond its own collection and offering its users what they need, when they need it. And isn't that what we're here for?

## David M. Turkalo
Suffolk University Law School Library
Boston, MA

The quietly authoritative glow of an OCLC terminal is the hallmark of a new world to professional librarians, library users, and bibliophiles in general. Over its 25 year history, the OCLC Online Union Catalog, along with its various subsystems, has unified mankind's diverse knowledge and its sometimes chaotic delivery. The Online Catalog of OCLC has pushed the realms of availability beyond the mere scope of one's current geographic moorings. This is a boon to scholarship and even just "passing interest" in the world's accumulated knowledge. Subsequent refinements over the past 25 years have made the Online Union Catalog just all the more useful. Obviously this is the greatest impact for reference librarians and their patrons: the ability to pinpoint the location (and even just the existence) of desired materials in all types and formats. But what of those who toil in the "back rooms" of librarianship, the technical services librarians? For cataloging librarians, the Online Union Catalog delivers the hard cataloging data that so many of us need to construct with ease the accurate records that appear in our OPACs or on our cards. It allows acquisitions librarians to investigate publishing histories, analyze subjects, and to see the geographic disbursement (or lack thereof) of a title. When all is said and done, the OCLC Online Union Catalog is the cyber-glue holding together today's and the future's bibliographic universe.

## Winnie Tyler
University of Central Florida
Orlando, FL

"Our OCLC computer finds publications all over the United States and beyond. We can order a copy of that article for you."

"Since you need that book so quickly, let me search OCLC and see if it's available somewhere else in town. …Yes, you can pick it up at the public library."

"I'm calling to let you know that the thesis you ordered is in, in the form of microfilm. Yes, it came from England. You can pick it up in our office."

These and similar words can be heard all day in our college interlibrary loan office, where we search requests for books and articles in the OCLC Online Union Catalog, then order them by means of the OCLC interlibrary loan subsystem. Undergraduates, graduate students and professors tell us what they need for their research, and we are almost always able to locate the materials for them. They leave our office happy and hopeful.

Often our patrons talk to us with enthusiasm about their projects and come back to say, "Thank you, we couldn't have done it without you," when they graduate, publish a research paper, or find a job in their field. When I think about the amazing vision of the founders of the OCLC Online Union Catalog and the patient efforts of thousands of library workers who have done retrospective conversion of their library collections, I wish all these people could share in hearing the thanks.

In our interlibrary loan office alone, one of thousands using OCLC, the following were a few of the exciting projects pursued recently:

A graduate student in biology ordered books and articles on polar bears. He was helping plan the opening of the new arctic exhibit at Sea World of Florida.

A civil engineering professor ordered publications on the tensile strength of plastic. He was working on a plan to reinforce bridge supports with plastic jackets, thus preventing corrosion in sea air or beneath salted roads.

An art student ordered books to help her learn the best techniques for firing a salt kiln, and she succeeded in producing beautiful pottery.

A nursing student ordered articles on tracheostomies, and her research has enabled many children to return to normal breathing capabilities.

Lives are saved and the quality of life enhanced. The OCLC Online Union Catalog is a product of generosity and willingness to share on the part of all its members. These are contagious qualities. Researchers to whom information is freely and willingly given will continue to build on what they have received and share their achievements.

The OCLC Online Union Catalog is a treasure map ready to point the way to what is important to each traveler. Our role is to be skilled and generous guides. Who could ask for a more useful and exciting job?

## Dele C. Ukwu
Long Beach City College
Long Beach, CA

OCLC is not the only bibliographic database available. Ever wonder why more libraries choose it? I began using the OCLC Online Union Catalog in 1988 as a paraprofessional. Since then, I have used OCLC as a student while in library school, as a reference librarian, and I guess, as a full-time cataloger, I now "surf" OCLC on a daily basis.

Probably no one comprehends better than a cataloger OCLC's magnificent interface which facilitates information access and retrieval. As a student, one of my assignments was to visit a library to conduct a case study. The library I visited performed original cataloging, because the catalogers did not have access to OCLC. Imagine performing original cataloging for thousands of items when OCLC has full records already available for most of them! Perhaps the library had limited funds, but had the administrators analyzed the enormous cost of original cataloging, presumably, they would have realized the advantages of using OCLC in terms of efficiency, quality of cataloging, and reduced labor costs.

OCLC is an innovative leader in modern technology. The OCLC Online Union Catalog is continuously updated to reflect changes in technology. PRISM's enhanced searching features offers catalogers flexible access to the database. Since OCLC offers high "hit rates," it thus facilitates cataloging by maximizing workflow and increasing productivity. Who wouldn't agree that the "sca" search is the best thing invented since sliced bread?

OCLC's goal of providing expedient access to information has resulted in the implementation of easy-to-search reference systems, such as EPIC and FirstSearch, for librarians and end users. In achieving all this, OCLC has never lost sight of its primary objective: offering users leading-edge technologies to access information at competitive prices.

OCLC has an outstanding staff of professionals, one that all companies should strive to emulate. The customer-service representatives are courteous and knowledgeable about their products. Their response time is wonderful. Never have I encountered an OCLC-related problem, which the staff was unable to resolve. From configuring function keys to answering questions about products or workshops, the representatives stay on the line with me and politely answer my questions, even if it is for the millionth time. OCLC staff members never make me feel "dumb" for not knowing the answer. To the best of my knowledge, OCLC has never introduced a new product or software into the marketplace without first fully testing its reliability and showing customers how to use it. Over the years, the integrity of the products and services, as well as the extensive training programs, have earned OCLC a broad base of loyal subscribers.

A library without OCLC truly exists in isolation. Through OCLC, libraries borrow and lend materials to each other, thereby expanding a library's resources.

OCLC unites catalogers from various institutions with different backgrounds and experience by allowing all of us to input or upgrade records to one common source. In doing so, we are not only sharing and exchanging knowledge and ideas; we are also constantly learning.

———————————— ⚕ ————————————

## Grace Veach
Decatur Public Library
Decatur, IL

Hi! My name is Vincent and I'm ten months old. I'm writing to tell you what OCLC means to me. When my Mommy first brought me a Spot book home from the library, I was too little to know what it was, but pretty soon Spot got to be my favorite little dog. Before long, there were no Spot books at my Mommy's library that I hadn't read. I am hoping that the library will get all the Spot books, so I got my Mommy to look on OCLC. She could find on OCLC every Spot book that had ever been published. She gave the list to the children's librarian, and I hope she will buy them all!

Another book I really like is *I Am a Bunny*. Mommy can use OCLC to find out what other libraries have it. Then when I go on a trip with my parents and I need to read *I Am a Bunny*, I can tell them the nearest library to visit so I can see it. Instead of visiting the other libraries, sometimes Mommy can just ask the OCLC libraries to send us a book. If I want to read *I Am a Bunny* in Swedish, they will send it to me. OCLC has tapes and records and movies too, so whatever I want to see or hear, Mommy will get for me. It makes her happy because I can try everything out to see if I like it before she has to go out and buy it for me.

I can use OCLC to find out all kinds of things. If I need to do research on animal noises or find the music to "The Wheels on the Bus," I can use FirstSearch and find books and articles on anything I need to know. (Of course, Mommy has to type for me.)

My Mommy uses OCLC to help her in her work. She tells me bedtime stories about how it was before she had OCLC...

"Once upon a time, long, long ago, Mommy was a cataloger without OCLC. She had to work with a terrible monster called NUC. NUC was huge and segmented (like a giant worm). Every day she would come to work terrified of her meeting with NUC. And when she gathered up her courage, she would look in book after book, checking editions and laboriously copying cards. Even though she was a very young cataloger, she would go home tired every day from carrying heavy volumes to and fro..."

Now my Mommy comes home from work with enough energy to play hide-and-seek with me, because OCLC makes her job so much easier. She says that OCLC is always coming up with improvements to make her job better and faster. She especially loves that CAT ME thing because it saves money and time.

I saved my most favorite thing about OCLC for last. If I hold down the buttons just right, I can almost always get it to beep for me!

———————————— ⚕ ————————————

**Kathleen M. Vera**
Capital Library Cooperative
Mason, MI

ACCESS, that's what the OCLC Online Union Catalog means to me. In 1981 when my institution first became an OCLC user, the INTERLIBRARY LOAN SUBSYSTEM enabled me to do my first E-MAIL ever. It opened up doors to libraries outside the cooperative. It also opened up our doors to libraries throughout the state and across the nation.

The access provided patrons by the interlibrary loan subsystem was expanded when OCLC was used to provide the mechanism by which a regional UNION LIST OF SERIALS off-line product was created. With that union list, multi-type library resource sharing in my own local area became viable. Neighboring libraries with no access to OCLC now had access to area magazine holdings. I had access to their holdings; they had access to mine. From these new regional ties evolved a need for referral centers. OCLC had a way to address that need. Once my institution was designated as an OCLC REFERRAL LIBRARY, I could provide my non-OCLC neighbors with access to OCLC as well.

OCLC was also my first experience with DATABASE SEARCHING. When I first began to search the OCLC Online Union Catalog, it seemed to me like an amazing reference tool—Books in Print, Forthcoming Books and Cumulated Books Index all in one tool. Using the OCLC Online Union Catalog was my first step into an electronic library world—a world without walls, a reference book without pages. With FIRSTSEARCH, OCLC provided the means to expand that electronic library.

When I gained access to FirstSearch, my patrons gained access to many electronic reference books—affordable access to an ever growing number of reference databases. In this age of evolving technology, patrons have come to expect the bibliographic access that those databases provide. As a librarian I appreciate only having to learn one set of simple searching strategies to access that bibliographic information in their behalf.

What access will be next? It is only a question of time before something that OCLC is offering will be something that I will need to provide the service cooperative members expect and need. Perhaps it will be Passport for Windows. Perhaps it will be a new workstation. Perhaps it will be something connected with the Internet. OCLC IS ALWAYS EXPANDING MY HORIZONS.

So . . . . what does OCLC mean to me?

Access to bibliographic data on books, articles, magazines, recordings, videos, etc.

Access to holdings information on all those items.

E-mail to send and receive requests for those items.

Access to local magazine holdings by way of a paper union list product that has become a valuable reference tool.

Access that I can provide to non-OCLC libraries.

Access to reference databases.

Future access to whatever will be needed to provide the libraries and patrons I serve with the materials and information they need.

Indeed . . . . ACCESS, ACCESS, ACCESS and more ACCESS, that is what the OCLC Online Union Catalog means to me.

## Nancy Fitz-Gerald Viens
University of North Texas
Denton, TX

OCLC Online Union Catalog means magical access to the Information Highway where I am the wizard—I wield the wand in the dull land of facts, creating wondrous order out of intellectual chaos, sifting salient solutions into verbal alchemy, sparkling gold from dross, all with the touch of my enchanted fingers. The OCLC Online Union Catalog means easy availability of information with simple commands that are user-friendly, making my job a bit more pleasant. "Look," I tell our patrons, "Let's use OCLC. It is the most comprehensive program out there. OCLC makes Reference work a snap, and saves you so much time." The Online Catalog opens doors to a whole wide world of libraries, making information accessible that would have been impossible twenty years ago. Can you imagine what you would have had to go through to find out all the facts that are right at the end of your fingertips? Expensive phone calls, letters, maybe even trips to another university library. But presto: here it is, right in front of your eyes. OCLC is truly a magical program, and never ceases to amaze me. I remember what research was like not that many years ago, when you had to get everything out of journals and encyclopedias, and cart multitudinous pads of paper and pencils around, in order to find out what you want. Now, voila! Into the spellbound forest of the Online Catalog you travel where miraculous things happen and all the libraries you could ever use stand with doors wide open waiting for you to walk through them into their hallowed halls.

In a time of ever-increasing frustrations, where burgeoning mechanization often bogs down in clumsy, time-consuming electronic mazes, we maneuver through the OCLC program with the ease and agility of a pro basketball player. (Have you ever tried to place a phone call to a large organization and had to wade through fifteen or more recorded announcements before you ever got to a real, live body, who might or might not be able to answer your question?) So when a distraught student or professor stands before you, hat in hand, with a desperate look on his or her face, begging for help on a subject, you now have this Arthurian sword ready to swing. "Do not despair!" you say as you head for the terminal. "Help is on the way! There is no reference too vague or moat too deep to leap. OCLC to the rescue. Give me your subject matter, and I can show you how to do this for yourself." And you hand the magic over and go back to your desk, another patron saved, another good deed done.

**Dawn Vogler**
University of Houston at Clear Lake
Houston, TX

OCLC generations: past and future...

The year 1971 was a very good year for me. It happens to be the year that I was born. Just as 1971 is remembered as a momentous year for my mother, it is also a well-loved year for librarians around the globe. In 1971 the OCLC Online Union Catalog progressed from concept to reality. I have been alive for a quarter of a century and OCLC will be reaching this milestone in the coming months. Perhaps OCLC has managed to revolutionize library services more than me in 25 years, but I have only recently become a library associate. I sit now, perched on the precipice of knowledge, about to become a part of the world known to so many librarians as OCLC. I will join the ranks of interlibrary loan personnel that borrow, search and loan materials of all sizes, colors and shapes.

My companion on my journey into the depths of library catalogs throughout the world is a veteran reference librarian. I tell her that I am as old as the OCLC Online Union Catalog and she snickers. She remembers when ILL was a minuscule part of library services. Before OCLC, even large libraries had only one or two employees working on ILL. Could it be that I owe OCLC a bit of thanks for my new job? My aged blue-haired teacher snaps me back to attention as she begins to explain the old way of obtaining materials. She leads me to a section of our library that bears the weight of the NUC. These huge green volumes, the *National Union Catalog*, are the relics of past ILL practices. I try to imagine these massive texts housed in a corner of our already burgeoning ILL office, being searched on a daily basis. My guide tells me that an ILL citation had to contain the exact year of publication and the author's correctly spelled name in order to find who owned the book! That is enough to make even an amateur ILL technician cringe, knowing that so many requests lack such essential bits of information. After the legwork of searching the monolithic NUC was complete, the trusty U.S. mail system took over. Requests and denials were mailed back and forth to various (sometimes numerous) libraries, card catalogs were searched and all the while, days passed. I gazed in astonishment at my battleworn co-worker as thoughts of life without computers flashed before my eyes! OCLC turned a potential 8-week ILL process into a matter of a week's time.

I eventually learned OCLC's interlibrary loan passwords, codes and symbols. I mastered the use of F11 and only rarely use my return key in error. All types of materials appear on the black and white screen, some available in exotic locales. As I log out of OCLC, the day's loans having been requested, I think about the coming of OCLC: The Next Generation and I contemplate "the olden days." I am the next generation in librarians that will be looking to OCLC to make as many advancements in library technology as it has offered over the past 25 years. I now look forward to using speedy document delivery systems and the Internet, just as my mature mentor probably looked forward to getting rid of the cumbersome card catalog some 25 years ago. What does OCLC mean to me? OCLC means a future full of innovative change and greater efficiency in accessing materials from around the world. I have grown and changed in my 25 years, probably as much as OCLC has managed to reinvent itself and adapt to evolving needs and circumstances. I can only hope to be as influential in my sphere as OCLC has been in its many areas of library technology.

## Elaine Wagner
Emory University
Atlanta, GA

In 1975, I—a library paraprofessional—asked a colleague, "What is OCLC?" Now, twenty years later, as a professional reference librarian, my question would be, "How could I provide reference service without OCLC?"

OCLC's bibliographic database, the authority file, FirstSearch, and the OCLC-created serials table of contents databases, ArticleFirst and ContentsFirst, provide access to essential information and enable reference librarians to answer many reference questions without leaving the reference desk.

I log on to the bibliographic database daily in my dual role as reference librarian and materials selector for the sciences, and the public access version is available to scholars from remote locations within the university. The authority file, although designed to facilitate cataloging, is also an excellent reference tool. Lawrence Olszewski's article, "Madonna, Brahms, and President Clinton: Reference Use of the OCLC Authority File" in *RQ*. v. 33 (Spring '94) pp. 395-403, gives some great examples of authority file use. My most recent use of the file gave me the former name and latitude and longitude of Ulan Bator.

The FirstSearch reference databases are easy to use; Boolean search capability, adjacency operators, and limit search offer search flexibility; and the online help screens are comprehensive and user-friendly. I recently located papers from the "Chocolate in Perspective" symposium in the proceedings database after failing to locate the conference in two print sources. In INSPEC, we found an elusive article on pre-Columbian astronomers (after a word list search indicated that the term "precolumbian" should be used).

The serials table of contents databases, ArticleFirst and ContentsFirst, provide very current information to users on subjects such as current book and film reviews. ContentsFirst makes tables of contents of journals available before the library has received the journal issue.

The OCLC Online Union Catalog, complemented by the SOLINET Successful Searcher workshops, help screens, and the Searching the Online Union Catalog reference card, has become one of the most valuable resources available to reference librarians.

**John Walker**
Presbyterian Church
Montreat, NC

While daunted at first by the weighty title imposed on this essay, I then remembered a reply of Colonel Potter to Frank Burns and Margaret Hoolihan in an episode of the television series "M*A*S*H." Burns and Hoolihan have just encountered a cool reception to another of their numerous complaints about the unmilitary conduct of Pierce and Hawkeye, and accuse Potter with: "Colonel, you're not taking this seriously!" To which the unflappable and acerbic Colonel replies: "No I'm not, why are *you*?"

With this thought in mind, I will "join in the fun,"as your instructions dictate, and touch on the lighter side of life with Deep File. In my twenty years of working with the world's premier bibliographic database, I remember a lot of fun. It seems like only yesterday that I received my orientation by watching a colleague do four-letter word title searches (and hit on record album analytics) during our initial training session at an unnamed university library. Later, one of our amusements during hours of copy cataloging was "OCLC Poker," in which the digits of your current OCLC Online Union Catalog record control number were bet against those of your coworker/opponent, as we all cruised together toward the ultimate (?) 99,999,999. It's been a great twenty-five years, guys. It's been stimulating, it's been the best thing that's happened to the library community, and it's also been great fun! Keep up the good work.

**Laura Walth**
Public Library of Des Moines
Des Moines, IA

OCLC: Past, present, and future...

Just five years after OCLC Online Union Catalog came into existence, my husband Donald Walth completed his thesis at Pratt Institute on fiber optic networking through libraries nationwide. It took about 19 years for his idea to become a reality. Since then, OCLC has become an international system. It provides libraries with quick and accurate access to information we now take for granted.

There are about 15,000 libraries participating in the OCLC network. Many of the smaller libraries benefit from it even though they may not have the system in their library. In our area, they contract with the central regional library, which submits the request to the Public Library of Des Moines, which uses OCLC to process the interlibrary loan requests.

FirstSearch is an extremely useful tool from OCLC to locate materials nationwide. We use it in the reference department for locating sources requested for ILL (Interlibrary Loan). It provides an accession number that saves our librarians time spent writing all the details on a form. There have been many times when we have been able to locate books through FirstSearch that we could not have found any other way. This is especially true when the patrons are not sure of the exact title or spelling of an author's name.

Although I use OCLC mainly for FirstSearch requests, I spoke with other staff members who use OCLC at the Public Library of Des Moines, and they all agree it is a vital part of our system. Nancy Clayton, Senior Clerk in Support Services, uses OCLC for authority work to verify how authors and series are entered in the OCLC records. She feels it will be to our advantage when our library has a workstation that will access both OCLC and our local network. Jane Horn, Senior Clerk for Book Selection, uses OCLC to verify official titles of books before placing the orders. Margaret Clason, Senior Clerk in Information Services, is impressed with how much time OCLC saves on patrons' interlibrary loan requests. She does not need to type time-consuming forms. The requests do not have to go through the mail; they are done instantaneously. When she enters a request, it automatically checks five libraries. If one library is unable to fulfill the request, it checks the next library on the list. Deborah Sulzbach, Librarian in Technical Services, said OCLC saves money and time from duplicating information when she is cataloging the books. She said, "I don't know what we would do without it!" Elaine Wedeking, substitute Librarian, remembers the "old days" when the OCLC system was frequently down, and how remarkably well it works now. She is impressed with the relatively high level of cataloging on OCLC.

Just imagine what life may be like 25 years from now, when OCLC may be accessed through homes. Libraries could be able to provide the information for the general public through home televisions. It will be interesting to see what the future brings.

———————————— *∥* ————————————

### Rong Wang
Historical Society of Pennsylvania
Philadelphia, PA

OCLC is a bridge:
    seven formats integrating;
OCLC is a bridge:
    four thousand years of records spanning;
OCLC is a bridge:
    three hundred seventy languages speaking;
OCLC is a bridge:
    sixty-three countries connecting;
OCLC is a bridge:
    five hundred sixty million location listing;
OCLC is a bridge:
    thirty-five million records containing;
OCLC is a bridge:
    global resources sharing;
OCLC is a bridge:
    info-highway traveling.
OCLC is a super vehicle,
    the super info-highway accessing;
OCLC is a historian,
    four thousand years of records chronicling;

OCLC is an airplane,
    sixty-three countries flying;
OCLC is a linguist,
    three hundred seventy languages speaking;
OCLC is a bridge,
    five hundred sixty million location listings;
OCLC is an ambassador,
    thirty-five million records sharing;
OCLC is a museum,
    multi-cultures preserving;
OCLC is a rainbow,
    libraries, patrons, & global resources connecting.

<pre>
                            OCLC
                 Arabic    Indonesian    German
          Chinese    Japanese    Vietnamese    Portuguese
          Swedish    French    Hebrew    Dutch    English
          Hungarian              Cyrillic              Norwegian
          Spanish                                      Turkish
          Ukraine                                      Bulgarian
   Thai    Polish                                         Finnish
Urdu
   Czech    Russian                                     Romanian
Latin
   Hindi    Danish                                      Yiddish
Korean
   Roman   Italian                                      Persian
Greek
</pre>

———————————— 𝒲 ————————————

## Stephen G. Washko
Immaculata College
Wayne, PA

The existence and widespread use of the OCLC Online Union Catalog means that many people, in many different roles, have made and will continue to make sacrifices to help others succeed.

My father was a great advocate of sacrifice. While I was growing up he gently but firmly taught me to replace my self-centeredness with caring more about others than about oneself. He would have fit in well with the people who maintain, improve, and use the OCLC Online Union Catalog. Interlibrary loan librarians come in on their own time to use the PRISM ILL module to catch up on patron requests. Researchers travel great distances to expedite information retrieval after using WorldCat to discover that a particular library is the only one in the area which subscribes to a needed journal. Serials librarians tirelessly create and update LDR after LDR using the Union List module so that those researchers have up-to-date holdings data. Systems librarians study library automation at home so they can better maintain and upgrade the hardware and software needed to access the

Union Catalog. Programmers work overtime to perfect the latest release of Union Catalog software. Catalogers painstakingly pay attention to detail to create the best possible records to add to the database. Reference librarians stay after the end of a shift to ensure that the chiaroscuro of a student's mind consists of more and more light by translating information gleaned from the Union Catalog into a form the student can understand.

Like these people, my father was constantly sacrificing to help others learn. Sometimes he would only get an hour of sleep because he was helping my sister and me with difficult homework. He used the local libraries so skillfully to help us with our research projects that other parents in the neighborhood began asking him to help with their children's projects, too, which he did.

In a few moments of uncanny lucidity after cancer ravaged his mind so much it was all he could do to understand how to eat and drink, he shared with an oncology nurse his philosophy of life. "You live your life for your kids," he instructed her; "that's what it's all about." Hearing those words with her, I wondered whether I was ready to pick up the flag once carried by my fallen friend. At Dad's funeral, his brother said that Dad was probably wandering up and down the aisles of Heaven's library as we spoke. If that is true, possibly he is using an Online Union Catalog even bigger than OCLC's to find the knowledge he is seeking. Undoubtedly, as new patrons enter the library, he is sacrificing much to help them succeed. Even if I cannot carry the flag perfectly all the time, I am encouraged knowing that, because the myriad of aforementioned people associated with the OCLC Online Union Catalog share my father's ideals, those he left behind have an excellent chance of succeeding too.

—————————— ❧ ——————————

## Elaine Wassink
Dordt College
Sioux Center, IA

OCLC is like my mother...

OCLC is like my mother and I am proud to be in her family. She was created by her Maker with a plan for inherent growth and service. She has faced some hurdles, but overcome them, to become a very influential force for many. I feel secure knowing she is a stabilizing part of my past, my present, and my future. She is one grand lady and I love her!

When my mother married my father, she took all of him: heart, soul, mind, and strength. And, as is normal, she took his name. OCLC, in its early stages, was "married" to the Library of Congress. "She" took "his" heart, the record of the United States history and government. She accepted his soul, the spirit of unity. She communicated with his mind, accessing his knowledge by means of his classification schedules and subject headings. She loved his strength, the size of his record base and his pure standards. OCLC took his name "LC" as part of her own.

In building a home for ten growing children, my parents worked long and hard. They built a bigger house. They maintained financial records for the IRS, and obeyed government's laws. My mother was led by love to train her children, and nourish them well. She often worked on school and church committee projects. She developed her own moral code: to serve others before herself. Similarly, OCLC and LC, worked to establish a home database: accessible, useful, and large enough for their growing client-family. They maintained the records under the AACR2 rules and the MARC format. Loving the work, the goals, and the members has been OCLC's driving motive. She has worked in committees for the good of the whole resource sharing community. She has established a strong code of her own in the Bibliographic Format and Standards. She is a true client server.

While my parents began their life together as 2 people, their direct family will become 58 in number next month. OCLC began with 2 million records: her database is now approaching the 35 million mark. I think this proves the success of both marriages.

OCLC, like my mother, is full of knowledge gained from experiences with a variety of people, places, media and music. Both have read, studied, listened, experimented, and traveled to acquire and catalog treasures for her memory files and display. Both are willing to share this wealth of knowledge with anyone who knows how to ask. Both accept new members who marry into the family, even international ones, adapting well to the expansion, and appreciating the new language and color of this addition.

Both OCLC and my mother are user friendly. Though they each have many family members, they have a "dedicated line" to each, and greet each one by name. Both send letters regularly—letters filled with news of other family members, their concerns and accomplishments. These letters also serve to inform family members about changes she is planning. She is not afraid to update her displays or methods, keeping current on the latest equipment for kitchen or computer.

Mother appreciates the help and input of the children she has trained. OCLC is getting help from her old and new trainees, MARC, ANSI, EDI, and GUI. Both give a monthly allowance or work on the home base. Both set time guidelines for a project, but they allow me to "let it soak" for awhile in the save file. But if I forget, or delay too long, they throw it out and say, "I guess you will have to forget it or start over." That makes me annoyed and quite frustrated. But I'm learning!

My wish for OCLC, and for my mother, is for "a long and happy life." I will need both of them for a long time yet and I want our relationship to be enjoyable. Like a typical daughter, I don't think I've thanked her enough or praised her often enough for all she means to me.

———————————— ⚜ ————————————

**Katherine C. Watson**
University of Houston Libraries
Houston, TX

Every day, we use many tools to keep our lives running smoothly, to learn with, and to make our jobs easier to do. As a request searcher for my university library's interlibrary loan office, I use many tools to search and locate materials for our patrons. One of the most used tools in my workday is the OCLC Online Union Catalog. It not only helps me do my job better, but also helps many people find the knowledge and information to fulfill their education and enhance their own work. This OCLC database makes searching easier, helps find more complete information about needed materials, and also provides faster retrieval from other libraries.

For me, in my job, I need to find my patrons' materials easily and quickly. The OCLC Bibliographic Database provides a strong resource for locating material. As OCLC has grown over the years, so have the ways for material information to be retrieved. With the advent of PRISM, I can find materials by using key words in author, title, subject and publisher formats. This is very useful when our patrons do not have complete information to find their materials. Using the scan titles mode, I can type whole titles and words which helps, because it gives me more choice in locating materials that don't come up using other search strategies. By using the database, I can find materials that have sometimes seemed impossible to find. I have often said to my coworkers that if the material has been cataloged into the OCLC database, it can be found. The OCLC catalog makes finding things a possibility.

The OCLC database also helps me to find more complete records to locate requested materials. Complete bibliographic records insure finding more available locations where we can get the material from other places. Complete records help me find alternative sources of information for finding requested materials. Although these records help me find other records that give more locations where we can retrieve materials, some records do not have enough holders for that material. By having good records and complete information, requested material can be retrieved more easily and quickly.

Besides helping to locate materials and finding complete information, the OCLC Catalog insures that our patrons will be able to get their requests filled quickly. In our time, when everything we want needs to be retrieved in less time, having a good, reliable resource to use keeps that a possibility.

Many of the patrons at my university need the materials for completing projects or for completing studies for classes in a speedy manner. Most of our patrons have short deadlines and few resources to complete their projects. Having the OCLC database at our fingertips makes our job in filling the patrons' requests easy because we can find more information and locations for material faster than if the patron called or wrote every location where the materials might be. This insures that patrons complete their projects and our office provides much-needed information and materials.

In short, the OCLC Online Union Catalog helps our office and other university libraries provide better service and more materials to patrons. For me, the Catalog is a valuable resource to help my patrons find and use information to help them in their studies, enhance their lives, and make more knowledge in our world. The ease in searching, the complete information that I can find out about requested material, and the speed that we can use and retrieve that material from other places makes knowledge more accessible and useable in our changing world.

**Janet Cooper Weiss**
Rider University
Lawrenceville, NJ

The OCLC Online Union Catalog was our lifeline...

The online catalog (CLSI) was dying in stages. There were plans to replace it with Notis Horizon. We were forced to re-evaluate our situation when Notis folded into Dynix and Dynix folded into Ameritech in the Spring of 1994. In the Summer of 1994, we looked at the alternate products available to us. A decision was made to purchase the Voyager system from a small company called Marcorp (now Endeavor). The money was there; unfortunately, the system was not.

In Fall 1994, the system was becoming increasingly fragile and the cataloging, circulation, and acquisitions modules were taken off-line in an attempt to preserve access to the public catalog. Then, with a dramatic flair, in January, 1995, the controller smoked, whined, and finally died. Unfortunately, Voyager was not ready to go as promised and as we headed into the Spring Semester, we had NO CATALOG!!!

The OCLC Online Union Catalog was our only link to our holdings. A workstation was brought to the Reference Desk and *voilà*, we had access. Granted, it was cumbersome to help students and faculty one by one and there was no way to know what was actually on the shelf, but it was our lifeline.

**Christopher Wells**
Brandeis University
Waltham, MA

As a member of the library staff at my university, there is no resource I enjoy introducing patrons to more than OCLC. Researchers who have used this online catalog for years (some since its creation in 1971) can come to take it for granted, but new users are always amazed. I tell them that the catalog contains more than 35 million records and they are sometimes impressed, but we're used to big numbers these days, so sometimes they are not. Then I tell them that the Catalog contains holdings information for libraries in 63 countries, and sometimes that's enough. Then I tell them that the dates of the materials covered range over 4,000 years of recorded knowledge, and that the catalog includes materials in 370 languages, and that they can find not only books and serials, but also audiovisual materials, maps, archives and manuscripts, sound recordings, musical scores and computer files. By now most patrons are impressed. Then I let them know that OCLC makes it possible for many of these resources to be delivered to our library through interlibrary loan; at this point, they are more than impressed—they're excited. It's a wonderful feeling to be able to let people in on this secret: the world that they've been told is coming through the information superhighway is already here, and open to them. It's as if I've given them something precious they couldn't get anywhere else, and in a way, I have, because there is no other resource that does so much to draw the overwhelming world of contemporary information resources together.

What is even more rewarding, though, is using OCLC to help those with a specific need get what they're looking for. For example, I had to tell one student that our libraries don't have a lot of popular fiction—like many institutions, we've had to pick and choose our holdings carefully, due to budget cutbacks. She would have been disappointed, since she was very interested in pursuing her research into what we as a people enjoy reading. Fortunately, I was able to show her OCLC, and together we discovered that it had records for every single one of the books on her lengthy list, and that she'd be able to order them all through interlibrary loan. She was ecstatic, and I was equally delighted, not only to have had the chance to assist some promising research, but also to have opened up for this student a resource that she could return to throughout her life.

There aren't many university libraries today that don't make regular use of OCLC, and it's easy to take it for granted. For experienced researchers, the proud announcement that our libraries offer access to OCLC may be analogous to announcing that our libraries have walls. But walls don't grow, and at an additional two million records a year, OCLC promises to grow as fast as research can explore it. Our library is a special place, but it would be less so without OCLC.

## Alma Williams

Parkview Episcopal Medical Center
Pueblo, CO

OCLC means a lot of things to me by helping me at my job as library coordinator in a small medical library.

First, I know that my patrons think I can get almost any book for them. They don't really understand the process but that doesn't matter to them as long as I can do that. I really don't know how I would satisfy their requests for interlibrary loans without it. I like the fact that I don't have to browse through the catalogs in many different libraries to see what they have. With OCLC, I can find easily what libraries have whether they are in my area or not, and can request them right at the time I find them.

Second, even though we do use Docline for a lot of our article requests, some pertain to the administrative side or business and they aren't found in the medical libraries. I use OCLC to request this type of article and most of the time I can get what I need.

Third, I use OCLC to catalog my books. I can get books one day and the next I can have it cataloged with the labels all printed and ready to put on the books so that they can be shelved, instead of being held someplace until a service does it and sends the labels to me. The cards for our card catalog are here in a few days.

Another thing that I enjoy is having a patron ask what books by a certain author are available and I can quickly search by that writer and print the book titles out for them.

One of the things that has really frustrated me in recent years was the fact that our public library isn't using OCLC anymore, so I have to go into their online system to see what they have. Most of the time, I just go ahead and search for the book through the display holdings and request the book that way, saving time and effort of going to get it from our own library.

I have been using OCLC to help me for all thirteen years I have worked at Parkview Episcopal Medical Center, and I hear many of the patrons saying that if you want to look at a book in anticipation to buying it, Alma can probably get it so you can decide if it is what you really want.

I am happy that I have this opportunity to show how I use OCLC and what it means to me.

## Andrea L. Williams
Midwestern State University
Wichita Falls, TX

OCLC means a lot to me now, but back when I was in library school I ran from the very word. Cataloging was not a happy experience. I left hoping that, when I got my first job in the real world, I would not be forced to enter the dark world of technical services. I thought to myself, "What do AACR2, OCLC, and other references to alphabet soup have to do to the real world of helping people find and make use of information sources that fit their needs?" Reality struck in my first job. I became a curriculum materials librarian. The library had a sizeable collection of textbooks that were entered into an automated system in a "casual" fashion. We did not look for OCLC records, but created our own as quickly (and "dirty") as we could. Subject headings were nonexistent. There was no description of the items, nor was there any notion of how many copies existed for the public. Our user population, which consisted primarily of education department students, other college students, and an occasional stray outsider, always had to ask to determine whether we had a title. Then we still needed to check the shelf to see if copies were still available. The longer I worked with these curriculum materials, the more I felt we had a mother lode of useful "stuff" for a variety of users if only the public knew they existed.

Fortunately, this state of affairs changed when the automated catalog system was about to change. All givens were up for grabs. I pleaded that we start requiring OCLC-based records, even for lowly textbooks. Other librarians felt (alas) that changing policy was too much work for too little (and humble) a collection. My "wisdom" or naive stubborness prevailed. The cataloger at that time said he had more than enough on his work plate to do. Nevertheless, he would take time to instruct me. I began hunting for acceptable records. I learned to modify records so that they reflected the precise records we had. I learned to add detailed notes to describe materials. I began adding additional subject headings when I felt it would help library users. Now this Eden has existed for approximately three years. I feel that the OCLC staples, such as subject headings and detailed notes have created greater satisfaction among all library users. I am much like a former drunkard turned teetotaler. I am a firm believer in libraries making use of OCLC. I hope others can either begin a relationship with OCLC or strengthen the ties that already exist.

## Sheila Wilson
Northeast Louisiana University
Monroe, LA

"The Online Union Catalog Banner"
(Sung to the tune of "The Star Spangled Banner")

O-oh say can you see
The-ee O C L C?
Where we all have a chance
To search titles and authors.
Though the terminals blink,
And our ey-eyes get weak,
It is aa-all worthwhile
To provi-ide our patrons.
To the research they cleave,
To solve all human needs,
And to make our profession
The-e one that will please
Our peers and our consciences
Know wha-at we-ee do-oo.
Will make our lives be-etter,
And our chi-ildren's too.
Oh say does tha-at O C L C ye-et wa-ave
O'er the la-and of the free
And the home of the brave.

———————————— ⑆ ————————————

## R. Conrad Winke
Northwestern University
Evanston, IL

As a catalog librarian at a large research library and a library science educator, the OCLC Online Union Catalog naturally means many things to me. It is first and foremost a tool from which I can retrieve copy for works which pass across my desk that are in need of processing. In this capacity, the database is a time saving device, allowing me to utilize the intellectual efforts of colleagues elsewhere and consequently speed up my own work. I am routinely awed by the sheer depth and breadth of the catalog, where I find records for the most seemingly obscure works. Conversely, the catalog is also a source of professional satisfaction, for I know that my original contributions will allow people to do their jobs more efficiently at countless institutions elsewhere. For me, this reciprocity is emblematic of the feature of librarianship which has always made me proud of my chosen profession, and that is sharing. The catalog permits the sharing of institutional workloads, the sharing of institutional resources, and most importantly, the sharing of human knowledge.

The catalog is also, without rival, the world's largest information "department store," a real boon for doing research, both professional and personal. It is always fun to wow the uninitiated with the sheer vastness of the database and the speed at which it produces results.

However, on its deepest level, what the Online Union Catalog really means to me is immortality and a sense of leaving something positive behind after I am gone. As societal advancement is made possible only by using the knowledge of others in new and innovative ways, it is imperative that members of our society have access to this knowledge so that we can move ahead. The catalog allows researchers at all levels to do just that. By working on the enlargement and improvement of the catalog, I know that I am contributing daily to the organization of human learning, and subsequently enabling others to locate needed information as efficiently as possible. Just as we today continue to use the catalog records created by our professional forebears, I feel safe in assuming that librarians and scholars of future generations will continue to use my catalog records, and thereby my intellectual contributions, in conducting their work. I know that I will never affect the course of history in the manner of Cleopatra or Thomas Jefferson or Shakespeare, but I believe that, in contributing records to the catalog, I am leaving behind some small intellectual contribution for future generations and contributing in some small way to the betterment of our civilization. This is how I shall leave my mark, albeit only a small scratch, of my time here and live on in perpetuity.

———————————— ⅋ ————————————

## Beverly Wise
Midland County Public Library
Midland, TX

In 1956—forty years ago now—as a graduate student at the School of Library Science at the University of Texas, I typed sample sets of catalog cards on a typewriter that had no correction ribbon.

This past week—March 1996—I logged on to the OCLC Online Union Catalog and, in less than an hour, downloaded and edited 55 bibliographic records while working on our library's retrospective conversion project. In the 1950s I could have typed no more than two or three card sets in that same amount of time, and I certainly would not have had time to format the information to put on those cards.

The public library where I am head of technical services is located in west Texas, six hours driving time from Dallas-Fort Worth to the east or El Paso to the west. In this barren landscape of mesquite, sand, tumbleweeds and pump jacks, it might seem that we would be somewhat out of touch with the rest of the world.

Yet one morning recently when I typed in the search key "lan,of,th,l," the following list of titles instantly appeared on my monitor screen: "Land of the little angel—a history of Angelina County, Texas," "The land of the lamas: notes of a journey through China," "The language of the law" and "Ao te a roa=The land of the long white cloud." Here before me was a window to the world—the history of a small county in Texas, a Tibetan travelogue, a treatise on the law and a book of poetry from New Zealand.

Another time I sat mesmerized looking at the words, "Hsi fang che hsüeh shih chi ch'i yü ts'ung ku tai tao hsien tai ti cheng chih, she hui ch'ing k'uang ti lien hsi," one of a list of titles retrieved by the search key I had just entered, the Chinese translation of Bertrand Russell's "The History of Western Philosophy." My curiosity was aroused. I had to look at the full record. It had been created and added to the OCLC Online Union Catalog by an OCLC member library—the University of Washington in Seattle.

Our library will probably never acquire materials in Chinese, yet I feel a sense of kinship with the unknown cataloger in Washington who created this bibliographic record. As I cataloged U.S. Bureau of Mines bulletins from the early 1900s a few months ago, I couldn't help but wonder how many other libraries would ever make use of those records. I could only hope that somewhere, some cataloger or ILL librarian searching the OCLC Catalog would be grateful to find them.

So what does the OCLC Online Union Catalog mean to me? It means speed and efficiency undreamed of when I began my library career, unbelievable breadth of coverage and—most of all—a shared sense of pride that comes from knowing that I have had a very small part myself in helping to create it.

———————————— ℐ ————————————

## Timothy R. Wiseman
Kemp Public Library
Wichita Falls, TX

On August 26, 1996, OCLC and its community of librarians, regional networks, and international distributors will be celebrating its silver anniversary of providing access and facilitating library and information center cooperation. The OCLC Online Union Catalog is much more than a bibliographic database for copying and contributing MARC records. Whether it be a librarian, library patron, student, or faculty member, the OCLC Online Union Catalog means access to a wealth of information—some 4,000 years of recorded knowledge in 370 languages.

Library patrons and students can have access to these materials through library OPACs or through the FirstSearch database. Without the OCLC Online Union Catalog, the FirstSearch database would not be a reality. In addition, the MARC records would appear to library patrons as "gobbledygook" and make no sense whatsoever. FirstSearch organizes the information in a system with an easy-to-use interface. Patrons and students can then take the information obtained from the FirstSearch database and get the material through interlibrary loan, document delivery, or a visit to the institution holding the item if it is practical. Librarians benefit from the FirstSearch database because library users can take the information to the librarian, eliminating time in the searching process as there is a link between the PRISM interlibrary loan database and FirstSearch. The OCLC Online Union Catalog also allows libraries and patrons to greatly benefit by allowing shrinking collection development budgets to be spread further by allowing access to infrequently requested items through interlibrary loan.

Faculty members can have access to very rare or hard-to-find materials through the OCLC Online Union Catalog. While it is likely that they would find OCLC difficult to use, they can use one of the many FirstSearch databases dedicated to academic research and even find about the availability of the item—all with a few keystrokes!

It would be difficult to think of another place where one can have access to the wealth of information that is in the OCLC Online Union Catalog. Materials in all formats and multiple languages are available at some 560 million locations, and can be located and used by using the OCLC Online Union Catalog without having to leave the library to have access! OCLC continues to show great potential as approximately two million items are added each year. It's no wonder that libraries have found the OCLC Online Union Catalog eliminates duplication of effort by allowing the sharing of MARC records, allowing materials to be made available to patrons much faster, and providing scholars and researchers access to some of the world's most valuable information. While it can be argued that this information can be found in other locations on the information superhighway, it would be difficult—if not impossible—to find any other location where such a wealth of information is available in such a well-organized and uniform format. There is no doubt that the OCLC Online Union Catalog will be celebrating its golden anniversary on August 26, 2021.

**Carolyn Wolf**
Northwood University
Midland, MI

What does OCLC mean to me?

It means not pulling countless card sets for a reclassification project. It means not hearing the whine of the electric eraser reduce the cards to gossamer quality, if lucky, or, to Swiss cheese quality, if concentration is lost. It means not typing new call numbers on those thousands of cards and then going back to the drawers, round and round, refiling, refiling, refiling.

What does OCLC mean to me?

It means not searching through bound volumes for LC copy. It means not spending time on original cataloging when another librarian somewhere out there is doing or is about to do the same item. Our time is wasted in tandem, is spent in isolation, and our original work is used by few.

What does OCLC mean to me?

It means that I an still doing technical services work; it means that having done such work in the sixties, the seventies, the eighties, the nineties, I can still enjoy my job. Without OCLC, I would have left such work a decade or so ago.

What does OCLC mean to me?

It means that I work in a global library. It means that my work may have value to someone far away in distance and to someone far away in time.

What does OCLC mean to me?

It is a sea change in my working world. To make Dilbert's and my boss happy, I can easily call it the most monumental paradigm shift of the 20th century library world. Being involved, in a very small way, in moving from islands of libraries to a unified library database, has been an honor. What has been special about OCLC is that it has allowed thousands of small contributors, just like me, to build a global library without walls.

### Christy J. Wrenn
Magale Library, Centenary College of Louisiana
Shreveport, LA

"No sir. I do not want to be a cataloger..."

These were the very words that I stated at the end of a job interview in 1982. Cataloging had not been my favorite class in graduate school. Young adult literature and Interlibrary Loans topped my list and every librarian always gets her first choice job with an MLS degree.

The interviewing library director had known me for about seven years. The statement that rolled off his tongue after my job rejection was, "Oh, but yes you do. Cataloging has changed since library school. It is much easier with our OCLC computer system." A second rejection panic hit, because I had NEVER touched a computer.

Using the praises of OCLC, the library director talked me into my first Head of Cataloging job. In 1982, OCLC became a milestone in my life. At the time of this interview, I did not realize that OCLC would become a daily function of my library work, plus a technological bridge in my library knowledge.

As Head of Cataloging, and using OCLC to process 4,500 books per year, for 9-1/2 years, greatly helped me fracture my phobia with computers. I began to enjoy the problem calls and the helpful voices connected to the OCLC Contact Desk. The more I worked externally and internally with my computer, the more I felt the comfort that would speed me to a promotion to Technical Services Coordinator. During that first year I worked with OCLC in the field of Interlibrary Loans, advisor to the new cataloger and an added adventure of troubleshooting all the PC in the library.

After almost 14 years, and because of my acquaintance with OCLC, I am speeding into the 21st Century at work on a second master's degree in Computer Systems Technology. Thanks to you OCLC, and Thanks to all of the people behind these four letters.

### Gail Wright
River Bend Library System and Illinois State Library
Tampico, IL

The OCLC—with its more than 35 million records and over 560 million location listings—provides many global journeys and explorations that touch many lives daily, including my own. The most important is the fact that it fits into the many roles I play during my week.

Information gathering is at my fingertips to fit the many roles I perform. As a media specialist, being of service to our students is very important. Accessing sources of information helps to serve our students. It assists me in finding and obtaining materials for students. It speeds up the acquisition process by the time saved using LC MARC records. The availability of global resources and the LC MARC cataloging records assists me in serving students. OCLC Online Union Catalog means time savings and information access to me.

As a student, I can find information for my classes. As a library user, I can find information on topics of interest to me. As a lifelong learner, I can continue to find information to help me grow in my current career area and new areas. Because of the 35 million records that have accumulated over the last 25 years, I can access information which would not be available in the rural area I teach. The OCLC Catalog has provided a network of information to this rural community that has only a volunteer, donation-based public library. The school districts' connection through our library system and state library extends the reach and availability of the outside world to our students and community residents in this rural area through online catalogs. It has brought the world to us. The information and materials are an order form away at our library.

As a faculty member, it provides necessary information to share to increase instructional effectiveness. The information accessed touches several hundred lives in my school, and has a profound affect on my life as well. It is the end product of each user that is affected by having these 33 million records available. Look at all of the people who end up being served by integrating individual purposes and needs, individual capacity and results into learning by doing, self-development, and the many other uses of the material found in the OCLC Catalog. It provides for the knowledge worker in our modern society of lifelong learners an integrated network of resources that sees our global community as a resource for learning.

To be a successful teacher and learner, I need access to information. The OCLC Online Union Catalog is a lifeline to global resources to explore while taking our learning journey outside our community. In the world today, learning is everybody's business and the OCLC Catalog provides the best available on the information highway.

## Xiaohong Xiao
University of Arizona
Tucson, AZ

I still remember the first time I heard about the OCLC Online Union Catalog. It was at my first class in the library school three years ago. The professor was so enthusiastic about the development of OCLC, and he excited much interest among the students. But I was totally strange to it and felt embarrassed when the professor mentioned that the OCLC was developing an advanced CJK database, since, as the only Chinese student in the class, I had nothing to say because I did not even have a sense of what OCLC was about.

After that class, I continued to use FirstSearch and the CJK database very often due to my course assignments and duties as a student assistant in the Oriental collection, and soon I became quite familiar with it. I even became crazy about OCLC, not only because it revolutionizes information resource accessing and sharing with more than 35 million records spanning through 4,000 years of recorded knowledge in 370 languages, but also because it is user-friendly with clear instructions, help files, easy file transformation and daily updating. I enjoy consulting OCLC whenever an opportunity arises for me to use a bibliographic tool, and I enthusiastically recommend other Chinese students to use and experience this wonderful mobile library.

Recently, Chinese students and scholars began building an electronic collection on the Chinese Cultural Revolution through the Internet, to commemorate the 30th anniversary of the movement which resulted in disaster for the Chinese. This electronic collection will enable people to study the history of the Chinese Cultural Revolution so that it will never be forgotten. Therefore I entered FirstSearch to locate information on this special subject to contribute to the collection, then I found 232 entries.

The search results covered assorted sources dated between 1966 and 1996, and included books, articles, manuscripts, and cassettes in languages of Chinese, English, French, and others. I was surprised that there are Mao Tse-Dung's works, Red Guard publications, glossary of Chinese communist terms and phrases used during the cultural revolution, as well as even cultural relics excavated during that period, besides the broad coverage in literature and research works. What a great contribution to the special collection on the Chinese Cultural Revolution! At least, to me, this bibliography is an valuable treasure. I cannot imagine not having the OCLC Online Union Catalog to help me find what I need.

For me, the OCLC Online Union Catalog is not only the place where you can access information and obtain satisfactory results wherever and whenever you need them, but it also represents a cultural shock, since ancient Chinese characters can appear on the computer screen under the systematic control that requires advanced technology the same technology that has harmful potential when it is used to develop killing weapons. For me, the OCLC also means that it allows for intellectual and information freedom, in which cultural and political bias do not exist, but which fosters love and knowledge of different cultures.

**Alida Young**
Amherst College
Amherst, MA

Sleuthing it out...

As Hercule Poirot, detective extraordinaire of Agatha Christie's mystery stories, would put it, everything depends on the proper workings of the "little grey cells." As a mystery buff and user of OCLC, the OCLC bibliographic database represents to me a link between the world of literary mysteries—the kind written by Agatha Christie, P. D. James, Sue Grafton—and the more literal mysteries a librarian encounters every day working with the printed word. Like Poirot's "little grey cells," the individuated OCLC circuits or cells, each with its own address and carrying its highly specific codified information, are the keys to accurate and authoritative bibliographic documentation.

OCLC enables one to be a detective, to solve a mystery. Frequently, the librarian researcher may have bits and pieces of information about a particular monograph or journal, but there is a missing link, and therefore the literary identity of the work eludes one. Depending on the librarian detective's skill in selecting search mechanisms, in assembling an effective search formula, the correct OCLC record will be found and the work's true bibliographic profile uncovered.

Sometimes, one discovers that the same document has been given duplicate records, one more accurate or complete than the other—perhaps because of the date it was entered, or because a cataloger was unaware of an existing record. Perhaps a 490 or 440 field was overlooked, and the title was identified as a lone monograph before there was investigation to discover whether it might be part of a series. Perhaps clues in field 300 were too deeply hidden and a multiple volume set was considered complete, when in fact its volumes were still on the loose. Or, perhaps a fixed field was unclear and, whereas one was in hot pursuit of a "French connection," the tome in question was actually published in Canada. If the librarian detective is not careful, these "red herrings" can lead off on a trail that eventually runs cold. If only that original cataloger had been more observant, had gotten the facts straight and been a more reliable witness! But, reassuringly, the OCLC cells will not let you down. By shifting strategy and calling up another record—one hopes this time it is a DLC record—the librarian detective sheds new light on the case and is once again on the right track.

Even with the mystery solved, OCLC is not without its mystique. The way OCLC can, with a few key strokes, scan the "cataloging soup" and in seconds span four millennia of recorded knowledge in 370 languages, is every time again breathtaking—truly mysterious. While so much in cyberspace is being challenged as to its utility and worth, OCLC is indisputably a database *par excellence*, a powerful research tool delivering speed and accuracy unimaginable before.

Always quick to point out that his "little grey cells"—the seat of his cognitive processes—deserve proper respect, Hercule Poirot would be the first to insist that OCLC be given its due. I can hear him saying to Hastings, his faithful assistant, "Do not give me the shilly-shally, my dear Hastings. OCLC, c'est magnifique, n'est-ce pas?"

## Elizabeth Young
State University of New York–Oswego
Phoenix, NY

Outstanding. Celebrated. Loyal. Creative.

These are just four qualities that come to mind when I consider what OCLC means to me. Even before I became a catalog librarian, OCLC has played an early and important role in my professional career. While still in Library School at Syracuse University, I used OCLC in an academic library for Interlibrary Loan (mainly to decipher library holdings), the music department, (for K. numbers especially!), and technical services as a catalog assistant, where I became most intimate with this friendly database. Since receiving my MLS, I became even more aware of OCLC's applications as the coordinator of a Retrospective Conversion project, and—single-handedly cataloging our local church library. The services OCLC provides have always been outstanding. This became very clear to me shortly after being laid off from my temporary cataloging position and still expected to maintain our church library, plus—catalog the private collection of one of the village residents! Luckily, I still had access to OCLC, albeit on a much reduced level. I depended on OCLC (and still do) for its authority, its exactness in cataloging, and even the flexibility it allows one for original cataloging. I have always looked to OCLC (esp: DLC=DLC) as the standard for which all other cataloging must compare to. It has made my job much easier, even throughout all the changes and enhancements it has gone through—as OCLC grows, I feel I have also grown, professionally as well.

More recently, I have been re-introduced to OCLC, as I have accepted a position at another academic library—one in the SUNY system. My fondness for OCLC has not wavered, even after a couple of years being away from it. Its quality is still at the level I had been used to and was comparable to "returning home," being able once again to access this system on a daily basis. I am still discovering how many "treasure troves" of excitement there are, such as FirstSearch and FirstSearch2, but my main focus is on cataloging and Authority File searching and verifying. In general, OCLC means a great deal to me: security, a sense of authority, and again, the flexibility to create at a cataloger's level—any item that may come across one's path! I have been a "user" for 17 years. Here are fond wishes for many, many more—for all of us—on your 25th anniversary.

## Linda Young
Cambria County Library
Johnstown, PA

If someone had told me twenty-five years ago that I could visit libraries all around the world I would have questioned his sanity. If someone were to tell me the same thing today I would react differently because I have been to libraries beyond counting and I will visit even more in the future. No, I haven't set foot in most of those libraries but I have accessed their collections, have shared information with them, and have even held their books in my hands. Like many others I have benefited from the worldwide resources available through OCLC.

As a cataloger I constantly use OCLC. Quite a few years ago I worked in a library which hadn't yet joined OCLC. In order to process new materials I consulted a variety of sources: DDC, Sears, CIP, AACR, the catalog of a larger library in a neighboring town, the brains of friends and family members, even a chart at which I threw darts, though I only used the dart technique once. Now I sit down and access the expertise of catalogers everywhere as I export records for my library's computer catalog, check out suggested Dewey numbers, and find subject headings for hard-to-classify items. With particularly difficult materials I might check the symbol of the library which created the record since, even though I might not know the person who did the work, there are some symbols which I greet like old friends whose opinions I respect. On rare occasions I have something which nobody else has cataloged so I create an original record and attach my own symbol. And I confess that sometimes I go back later to see what libraries have added their symbol to *my* record. When I compare the OCLC database to the sources I once used I can only shake my head in wonder.

As a patron I value OCLC for a different reason. I read quite a lot and in the past got frustrated if I heard about an intriguing book, or read an interesting review, or had a friend recommend a must-read title, only to check my library's catalog and discover it wasn't there. Now I simply fill out a form and sit back while the interlibrary loan librarian works magic and places a desired book in my hands. I have read books from libraries nearby and from far distant libraries and I constantly marvel at the resource which supports my reading habit.

When I first learned to read I thought the family library would be big enough. It wasn't.

When I went to school I thought the classroom library would be big enough. It wasn't.

When I applied for a library card I thought the public library would be big enough. It wasn't.

Now I have a world-sized library which is big enough. I think.

## Beverly J. Zagar
Hartford Public Library District
Hartford, IL

"Could you please try to borrow these books and/or magazine articles for my research?" (Patron is working on her Master's in Greek art.) "Would you see if there is an autobiography on James Clarence Mangan?" (Patron is searching for her husband's Irish ancestors.) "Could you please?" OH, DO WE PLEASE!

From a small town library's point of view, the OCLC Online Union Catalog is another "Golden Door." This is what it means to me when I am asked to search for items for our library patrons. The only word I can use to describe it is JOY. Well, BIG might be another word. The big selections to choose from in the catalog bring a joyfulness to my mind. It's very rewarding to be able to find the things our patrons are searching for and to see their happy expressions when they come to the library for the items we have reserved for them.

## Zhu Zhanbei
China Europe International Business School
Shanghai, P.R. China

There have been three most exciting changes for me since the library of CEIBS (China Europe International Business School, newly established in November, 1994) became the first member of OCLC in the P. R. China in October 1995.

First, the OCLC Online Union Catalog is a magic wand which allowed our library to be connected within a couple of days. Over 96% of our present holding books have been catalogued from it, and this data was transferred to the library automation system. Therefore, through OCLC, we implemented a computer management system for our reading room in just one month.

Second, it provides an ocean of information from which a small library can get almost anything it needs. In addition to helping with handling ordinary interlibrary loans, I have also succeeded in retrieving several documents which were considered impossible to get by several Shanghai regional libraries in the past few years. This has given our library a great reputation in the field of information retrieval in China. When people have trouble getting the information, they say, "Oh, perhaps CEIBS can help us. They have the OCLC Online Union Catalog."

Third, it provides an excellent compass by which an academic library can develop its collection efficiently and effectively. A good example was when we wanted to order some books about applying for jobs. I simply searched the records according to the subject headings of the Library of Congress, such as interview strategy and cover letters. To make sure that I was getting new information, I limited the search to post-1991 publications. Then we studied the results to see which records had the most holdings and would be good candidates to source from. Finally, I printed this record to get the information necessary for us to contact the bookseller.

Our library has only three staff members, but we serve over 300 readers. Our work covers all the steps from acquisition and cataloging to issuing and reference. Only with the help of the OCLC Online Union Catalog can we run the whole library. So I would like to say now that I could not continue to perform my work at its current level without the OCLC Online Union Catalog.

## Sangliang Zhi
Anhui University
Hefei, Anhui, China

"The OCLC (Ohio College Library Center) is the largest computerized library system in contemporary world," I told my students who major in the information management science department, and also told it to the students who listen to the lecture, "Information Adopting and Using." These students are from all of the various departments of our university who would like to select it as optional subjects.

I said, "The OCLC computer online system initially was for 54 Ohio colleges. Today, OCLC serves more than 23,000 libraries of all types in 63 countries and territories. It is an international library network.

"How many libraries?"

"Teacher Sang, OCLC serves for our library's patrons, too?"

(My students are excited and have many questions.)

"Listen careful! Quiet please!"

I open a sheet from OCLC Asia Pacific services. I read, "154 libraries in Asia Pacific join OCLC in 1995." "The institutions in the Asia Pacific region that began using OCLC products and services in 1995 are in 11 countries. Among the new users are 14 institutions in Australia, one in China, three in Hong Kong, four in India, 72 in Japan, 29 in Korea, four in Malaysia, eight in New Zealand, one in Singapore, 15 in Taiwan, and three in Thailand."

"One in China, four in India, 29 in Korea, 15 in Taiwan, it is true?" one student asked.

"Listen careful, no voice!"

"The OCLC provides information services as below: FirstSearch service, document ordering, interlibrary lending, online ASCII full text, online cataloging and resource sharing system (PRISM), online reference system for reference librarians (EPIC), OCLC Electronic Journals Online service, providing electronic access to full-text journals, and the service about Information Dimensions. The OCLC contains more than 35 million records and more than 560 million location listings. The information in this catalog spans 4,000 years of recorded knowledge in 370 languages."

"Teacher, the OCLC contains Chinese records?"

"Yes, very much!"

I answered the students first time, and the student smiled.

"If I want to use OCLC, how much money should I pay a time?"

"Cheap, very cheap!" I continued. "You can pay little money to get more information on books, series, audiovisual media, maps, archives, manuscripts, sound recordings, scores and computer files. The OCLC is not for profit. Their mission is to increase availability of library resources to individual library patrons and reduce rate-of-rise of library per-unit costs, all for the fundamental public purpose of furthering ease of access to and use of the ever-expanding body of worldwide science, literary and educational knowledge and information."

"Source sharing, it is a good idea!"

"OCLC is good vehicle for source sharing!"

"Which day will the OCLC service come for us?"

"It is not a long time. The director who works in the information service department of our library said, "Our computers should be connected with OCLC if the CHINAPAC covers our city," I said.

"Sharing the source from OCLC," one student said loudly. Some students applauded. "Cheer!"

Almost all classmates expected the day they can use the OCLC network.

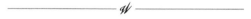

**Zhu Ziwen**
Institute of Medical Biology, Chinese Academy of Medical Sciences
Yunnan, China

In an international seminar on information technologies and information services, which was held on October 20-24,1994, in Shanghai, China, I was fortunate to meet colleagues and friends of OCLC. From then on, I have been receiving OCLC newsletters and other materials from OCLC Asia Pacific Services. I wish to express to you my heartfelt thanks.

Our institute has not made good use of OCLC Online Union Catalog for certain reasons. However, I should like to say what the OCLC Online Union Catalog means to me is enthusiasm, consideration, top quality and disinterestedness. We expect to be a member of OCLC community.

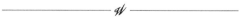

**Thomas R. Zogg**
University of Minnesota
Duluth, MN

As a reference librarian, the OCLC Online Union Catalog has been a cornerstone source for resources and a rapid search for research for two decades. Whether accessing the database in its original name in the 1980s or as FirstSearch WorldCat in the 1990s, its particular qualities have truly passed the test of time to become that cornerstone for this academic reference librarian and for the patrons whom I serve daily.

From its beginning in the mid-1960s, OCLC has had a particular quality of strength. It is the strength of building its database from academia, from its clientele. While not trying to replace venerable union catalogs such as *National Union Catalog Pre-1956 Imprints,* it has depended on its contributors (its database builders) to include classic titles based on their use and significance to academia and the research world. Moreover, its acceptance of variant versions of the same item's record may be viewed as a holistic triumph.

OCLC has had a particular quality of speaking equally to the world of the cataloger and to the world of the reference librarian. While we each utilize and interpret this database for our own purposes, OCLC captured the shared unity of spirit in the profession as it designed its online display and retrieval. There is a nobility to OCLC's three decades of maintaining a user-friendly standard, a standard of reliability that other online vendors may emulate.

Finally, there is the particular quality of being fun for the librarian and for the patron. As an academic reference librarian, I like to teach library research skills as if they are techniques of a treasure hunt. The OCLC Online Union Catalog so often has been the gold at the end of the research rainbow!

# OCLC Headquarters, Divisions and Subsidiaries

## OCLC Headquarters

### OCLC Online Computer Library Center, Inc.
6565 Frantz Road
Dublin, Ohio 43017-3395 USA
+1-614-764-6000
1-800-848-5878 (USA and Canada)
Fax: +1-614-764-6096
E-mail: oclc@oclc.org
http://www.oclc.org/

## OCLC Divisions and Subsidiaries

### OCLC Asia Pacific Services Division
6565 Frantz Road
Dublin, Ohio 43017-3395 USA
+1-614-764-6189 (general information
  and technical support)
Fax: +1-614-764-4331
E-mail: asia_pacific_services@oclc.org
http://www.oclc.org/asia-pacific/

### OCLC Europe
7th Floor, Tricorn House
51-53 Hagley Road
Birmingham B16 8TP
United Kingdom
+44 121 456 4656 (general information
  and technical support)
Fax: +44 121 456 4680
http://www.oclc.org/europe/

### OCLC Latin America and Caribbean Division
6565 Frantz Road
Dublin, Ohio 43017-3395 USA
+1-614-761-5196
+800-848-5878, ext. 5196 (USA and Mexico)
95-800-848-5800 (technical support, Mexico)
Fax: +1-614-718-1026
E-mail: america_latina@oclc.org
http://www.oclc.org/america_latina/

### OCLC Forest Press
85 Watervliet Avenue
Albany, New York 12206-2082 USA
+1-518-489-8549
Fax: +1-518-489-7804
http://www.oclc.org/fp/

### OCLC Pacific
Suite 260
9227 Haven Avenue
Rancho Cucamonga, California 91730
USA
+1-909-941-4220
1-800-854-5753 (USA and Canada)
Fax: +1-909-948-9803
Http://www.oclc.org/pacific/

### OCLC Pacific Portland Office
Suite 17E
111 SW Harrison
Portland, Oregon 97201 USA
+1-503-223-2884
1-800-854-5753 (USA and Canada)
Fax: +1-503-223-6863

### OCLC Pacific Santa Rosa Office
1948 Manzanita Avenue
Santa Rosa, CA 95404
+1-707-539-5427
1-800-854-5733 (USA and Canada)
Fax: +1-707-539-0368

### Preservation Resources
Nine South Commerce Way
Bethlehem, Pennsylvania 18017-8916
USA
+1-610-758-8700
1-800-773-7222 (USA and Canada)
Fax: +1-610-758-9700
http://www.oclc.org/presres/

### Information Dimensions, Inc.
6600 Frantz Road
P.O. Box 8007
Dublin, Ohio 43016-2007 USA
+1-614-761-8083
1-800-328-2648 (USA and Canada)
Fax: +1-614-761-7290
Http://www.idi.oclc.org/

# OCLC-Affiliated U.S. Regional Networks

**AMIGOS Bibliographic Council, Inc.**
Suite 500
12200 Park Central Drive
Dallas, Texas 75251-2104 USA
+1-972-851-8000
1-800-843-8482 (USA)
http://www.amigos.org/amigos/

**Bibliographical Center for Research (BCR)**
14394 East Evans Avenue
Aurora, Colorado 80014-1478 USA
+1-303-751-6277
1-800-397-1552 (USA)
http://www.bcr.org/

**BCR Ames Office**
295 Parks Library
Iowa State University
Ames, Iowa 50011 USA
+1-515-292-1118
1-800-383-1218 (USA)

**CAPCON**
Suite 400
1320 19th Street, N.W.
Washington, D.C. 20036 USA
+1-202-331-5771
1-800-543-4599 (Maryland and Virginia only)
http://www.capcon.net/

**Federal Library and Information
Center Committee (FEDLINK)**
Library of Congress
Washington, D.C. 20540-5110 USA
+1-202-707-4800
http://lcweb.loc.gov/flicc/

**ILLINET/OCLC Services**
Illinois State Library
300 South Second Street
Springfield, Illinois 62701-1796 USA
+1-217-785-1532
http://www.library.sos.state.il.us./isl/oclc/
oclc.html

**Indiana Cooperative Library Services
Authority (INCOLSA)**
6202 Morenci Trail
Indianapolis, Indiana 46268-2536 USA
+1-317-298-6570
1-800-733-1899 (Indiana only)
Http://www.palni.edu/incolsa/

**Michigan Library Consortium (MLC)**
Suite 8
6810 South Cedar Street
Lansing, Michigan 48911 USA
+1-517-694-4242
1-800-530-9019 (USA)
http://www.mlc.lib.mi.us/

**MINITEX Library Information Network**
S-33 Wilson Library
University of Minnesota
309 19th Avenue South
Minneapolis, Minnesota 55455-0414 USA
+1-612-624-4002
1-800-462-5348 (USA)
http://othello.lib.umn.edu/

**Missouri Library Network Corporation
(MLNC)**
10332 Old Olive Street Road
St. Louis, Missouri 63141 USA
+1-314-567-3799
1-800-969-6562 (USA)
http://www.mlnc.com/

**Nebraska Library Commission
(NEBASE)**
The Atrium
1200 N Street
Lincoln, Nebraska 68508-2023 USA
+1-402-471-2045
1-800-307-2665 (Nebraska only)
http://www.nlc.state.ne.us/netserv/nebase/
  nebserv.html

**NELINET, Inc.**
Two Newton Executive Park
Newton, Massachusetts 02162 USA
+1-617-969-0400
1-800-635-4638 (USA)
http://www.nelinet.net/

**OHIONET**
1500 West Lane Avenue
Columbus, Ohio 43221-3975 USA
+1-614-486-2966
1-800-686-8975 (Ohio and West Virginia
only)
http://www.ohionet.org/

**PALINET Headquarters**
Suite 262
3401 Market Street
Philadelphia, Pennsylvania 19104 USA
+1-215-382-7031
1-800-233-3401 (USA)
http://www.palinet.org/

**PALINET Maryland Office**
14231 Catamount Court
Silver Spring, Maryland 20906 USA
1-800-871-1662 (USA)

**PALINET Pittsburgh Office**
103 Yost Boulevard
Pittsburgh, Pennsylvania 15221 USA
+1-412-825-0600
1-800-242-3790 (USA)

**Southeastern Library Network, Inc. (SOLINET)**
Suite 200
1438 West Peachtree Street, N.W.
Atlanta, Georgia 30309-2955 USA
+1-404-892-0943
1-800-999-8558 (USA)
http://www.solinet.net/

**SUNY/OCLC Network**
State University Plaza
Albany, New York 12246 USA
+1-518-443-5444
1-800-342-3353 (USA)
http://sunyoclc.sysadm.suny.edu/

**Wisconsin InterLibrary Services (WILS)**
Room 464
728 State Street
Madison, Wisconsin 53706-1494 USA
+1-608-263-5051
http://milkyway.wils.wisc.edu/

+ Indicates the number requires the addition of an access code when dialed internationally.

# International Distributors
*(in alphabetical order by country name within regions)*

## Asia Pacific Services

D A Information Services
648 Whitehorse Road
Mitcham, Victoria 3132
**Australia**
3 873 4411 (Australia)
+61 3 9210 7777
Fax: +61 3 9210 7788
E-mail: service@dadirect.com.au

Shanghai Union Documentation &
    Information Corporation
Shanghai Jiao Tong University Library
1954 Hua Shan Road
Shanghai 200 030
**China**
+86-21-6431-0310

Akademia Books International (ABI)
Post Box No. 4417
B-6, Skipper Corner
88, Nehru Place
New Delhi 110 019
**India**
+91-11-641-9539
Fax: +91-11-644-8917

Faxon Informatics Pvt. Ltd.
337, III Floor, Karuna Complex
Malleswaram, Bangalore 560 003
**India**
+91-80-367-867
Fax: +91-80-334-4598

Higginbothams Limited
814 Anna Salai
Madras 600 002
**India**
+91-44-831-841
Fax: +91-44-834-590

CV. Sagung Seto
Jalan Pramuka No. 27
P.O. Box 4661
Jakarta 10001
**Indonesia**
+62-21-851-0344
Fax: +62-21-850-6395

ITI (International Transformational
    Information)
609 Jung Woo Building
13-25 Yoido-dong,
Youngdeungpo-gu, Seoul
**Korea**
02-782-7180 (Korea)
+82-2-782-7180
Fax: +82-2-782-7184

Kinokuniya Company Ltd.
38-1 Sakuragaoka 5-chome
Setagaya-ku Tokyo 156
**Japan**
03-3439-0407 (in Japan)
+813-3439-0407
Fax: +813-3439-0497

Kyobo Book Center Company, Ltd.
1, 1-Ka, Chongro,
Chongro-Ku, Seoul
**Korea**
02-739-2710 (Korea)
+82-2-739-2710
Fax: +82-2-735-0030

NOWCOM Company, Ltd.
5F/6F Danwoo Building
852-22 Bangbae-dong, Seocho-Gu
Seoul, 137-060
**Korea**
02-590-3850 (Korea)
+82 2-590-3850
Fax: +82 2-590-3868

OromTech
Daemyung Building, 4th Floor
2-27 Yangjae-Dong
Seocho-Gu, Seoul 137-130
**Korea**
02-576-3721 (Korea)
+82-2-576-3721
Fax: +82-2-577-2915
E-mail: oromtech@chollian.dacom.co.kr

Shinwon Datanet Inc.
2F, Shinwon Building
571-4 Yeonnam-dong
Mapoku, Seoul 121-240
**Korea**
02-326-3535 (Korea)
+82-2-326-3535
Fax: +82-2-326-0219

Pak Book Corporation
Aziz Chambers
21 Queen's Road
Lahore 54000
**Pakistan**
+92-42-636-3222
Fax: +92-42-636-2328

Sang-E-Meel Publications
P.O. Box No. 997
Chowk Urdu Bazar
Lahore 2
**Pakistan**
+92-42-722-0100
Fax: +92-42-724-5101

Info Access & Distribution Pte Ltd.
113 Eunos Avenue 3
#07-03 Gordon Industrial Building
**Singapore** 1440
741-8422 (Singapore)
+65-741-8422
Fax: +65-741-8821

Flysheet Information Services, Inc.
2/F, No. 221
Ming-Sheng East Road, Section 5
Taipei
**Taiwan**
02-718-7668 (Taiwan)
+886-2-766-7668
Fax: +886-2-756-4366
E-mail: info@flysheet.com.tw
http://www.flysheet.com.tw

## OCLC Europe

ITS Czech Republic
Svepomoci 261
156 00 Praha 5
Zbraslav
**Czech Republic**
+42 2 592439

Dansk BiblioteksCenter
Sales Department, Databases
Tempovej 7-11
DK 2750 Ballerup
**Scandinavia**
+45 44 86 77 77
Fax: +45 44 86 78 92
E-mail: dbc@dan.bib.dk
Http://www.dbc.dk

AUROC (Association des Utilisateurs du
        Réseau OCLC en France)
Bibliothèque Interuniversitaire Cujas
2, rue Cujas
75006 Paris
**France**
+33 1 46 33 38 43
Fax: +33 1 46 33 82 61

DOC & Co.
56, rue Dombasle
75015 Paris
**France**
+33 1 48 42 44 46
Fax: +33 1 48 42 44 86
E-mail: 100441.2767@compuserve.com

Fachinformationszentrum Karlsruhe
Postfach 2465
D-76344 Eggenstein-Leopoldshafen
Karlsruhe
**Germany**
+49 7247 808 336
Fax: +49 7247 808 135
E-mail: library@fiz-karlsruhe.de

ITS Hungary
Orlay Utca MF 1 Sz
1114 Budapest
**Hungary**
+36 11 666 996
Fax: +36 11 666 996

Franklins
P.O. Box 111
70800 Gan Yavne
**Israel**
+972 8 8594552
Fax: +972 8 8596797
E-mail: franklin@atcom.co.il

IF srl
V. le Don Minzoni, 39
50129 Firenze
**Italy**
+39 55 5001 357/8
Fax: +39 55 5001 363
E-mail: 100331.2662@compuserve.com

ITS Russia
Moscuoetskija 2a
109240 Moscow
**Russia**
+70 95 298 5090
Fax: +70 95 917 4689

ITS Slovenia
Herbersteinova 14
SI-1000 Ljubljana
**Slovenia**
+38 6611 684 565
Fax: +38 6611 684 565

SABINET
First Floor, Outspan House
P.O. Box 9785
Hennopsmeer 0046
**South Africa**
+27 12 663 4954/9
Fax: +27 12 663 3543
E-mail: sabinet@infol.sabinet.co.za

DOC6, SA
Mallorca, 272
Planta 3a
08037 Barcelona
**Spain**
+34 3 215 4313
Fax: +34 3 488 3621
E-mail: 100141.3062@compuserve.com
[and] doc6@servicom.es

DOC6, SA
Comandante Zorita, 8
28020 Madrid
**Spain**
+34 1 553 5207
Fax: +34 1 534 6112
E-mail: mail@doc6.es

BTJ (Bibliotekstjänst AB)
Database Division
Box 200
S-221 00 Lund
**Sweden**
+46 46 180 000
Fax: +46 46 180 125
E-mail: malmquist_birgitta@mail.btj.se

ITS Turkey
Sanayi Ve Ticaret Anonim Sirketi
Yuksel Cadd. 29/7
Kizilay, Ankara 06420
**Turkey**
+90 312 435 9147
Fax: +90 312 431 8524

CHEST (Combined Higher Education
   Software Team)
University of Bath
Bath BA2 2AY
**United Kingdom**
+44 1225 826282
Fax: +44 1225 826177
E-mail: h.m.franklin@bath.ac.uk

ITS (Information Technology
Supply Ltd.)
Talbot House
204/226 Imperial Drive
Harrow
Middlesex HA2 7HH
**United Kingdom**
+44 181 429 3970
+44 181 429 4455
Fax: +44 181 429 3642
   +44 181 868 2330

SLS (Information Systems) Ltd.
3-4 York Court
Upper York Street
Bristol BS2 8QF
**United Kingdom**
+44 1179 423314
Fax: +44 1179 244367

+ Indicates the number requires the addition of an access code when dialed internationally.